The Book of
BRIDPORT

Town, Harbour & West Bay

RODNEY LEGG

HALSGROVE

First published in Great Britain in 2003.

*This book is dedicated to Tom Perrott
– a friend from Bridport since 1968*

British Library Cataloguing-in-Publication Data.
A CIP record for this title is available from the British Library.

ISBN 1 84114 232 8

HALSGROVE

Halsgrove House
Lower Moor Way
Tiverton, Devon EX16 6SS
Tel: 01884 243242
Fax: 01884 243325
email: sales@halsgrove.com
website: www.halsgrove.com

Frontispiece photograph: *The herring gull has been the symbol of West Bay for centuries.*

Printed and bound by CPI Press, Bath.

Contents

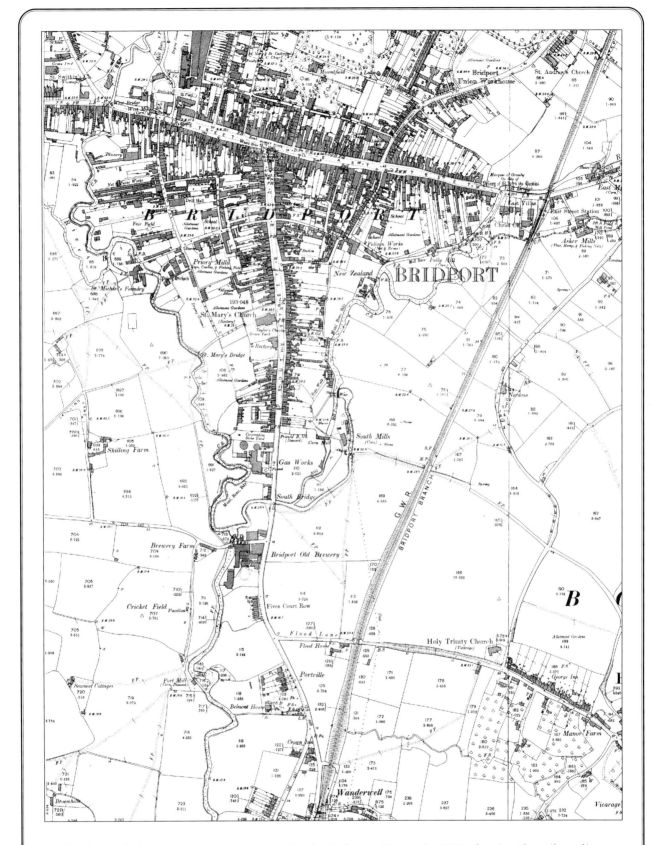

Bridport's T-shape on the map, as recorded by the Ordnance Survey in 1900, showing the railway line from Bridport Station to West Bay (centre right).

Introduction

Knots and nets remain the main theme. The town's name used to bring a shudder to the national spine when to be 'stabbed by a Bridport dagger' was to be hanged. Hemp was the local speciality crop and the town was the national rope-making centre from the time of King John's misadventures in France through to the rigging of the 'wooden walls' of the Royal Navy. Bridport made anti-submarine nets and provided contributions in personnel out of all proportion to its size for fighting the twentieth-century conflicts.

Where Bridport led, Dorchester and Dorset followed, such as with gas lighting which was introduced in the town in 1832. The same retort was keeping the town self-sufficient until June 1958. Voluminous records – interesting and uninteresting, official and private – have been cherry-picked for fascinating anecdotes that bring to life the personal stories of townspeople from the Middle Ages to the world wars. Celebrities through the ages have included King Charles I, on a brief visit, and an even shorter one by a runaway King Charles II, medicine-maker Giles Roberts, highwayman Thomas Boulter, and crime reporter Percy Hoskins. W.E. Forster MP, who was born in Bridport, gave Britain basic schooling by drafting the Elementary Education Act. Playwright Thomas Ridley Sharpe created *Blott on the Landscape* and departed as the Bridport bypass turned fiction into fact beside his own acre and a half of garden. The playwright R.C. Sherriff is remembered for *Journey's End* which for him was Downhouse Farm at Eype, which he gave to the National Trust.

The sea flows in and out of Bridport's history, from the earliest attempts at making an anchorage to J.M.W. Turner's painting of one of its shipwrecks, and the hurricanes of recent memory. The setting is also embraced in terms of its antiquity and scenery. The evolution of the estuary of the River Brit into Bridport Harbour and then West Bay has produced one of the favourite places on the holiday coast. It has also seen the coming and going of a much-loved railway and television soap with 'Harbour Lights'.

Developments have been held in check by a growing portfolio of National Trust and Woodland Trust properties which have preserved key parts of the nearby cliffs and countryside. Bridport remains England in microcosm.

West Cliff, with precipitous beds of banded stone and sand, looking eastwards from West Bay in 1925.

The Grey Mare and her Colts, a Neolithic chambered long barrow, on the downs above Abbotsbury.

Chapter 1
ROMAN PORT, SAXON BURGH & NORMAN TOWN

A natural estuary would tend to be wider and more tidal than the concrete-controlled environment of the modern urban sea front. High tide brought maritime access into wide marshland flood plains. So it was that Bridport came into being beside its River Brit at the bridging point where it ceased to be navigable by boat – as did Radipole on the River Wey, Wareham on the River Frome, and Christchurch at the confluence of the Stour and the Avon.

Traces of human life around Bridport begin within the Bronze Age. Axes from about 1800BC, contemporary with the final stage of Stonehenge, have been found in the vicinity of the golf course where there also appear to have been some burial mounds. A portable rounded stone that originated between the bands of sand in East Cliff, found half a mile inland, is carved with enigmatic cup and ring marks. These are a rarity in southern England but such rock carvings are commonplace on the northern moors. It may be the earliest evidence of cosmopolitan influences arriving on this seaboard. The same may apply to the phallic-shaped sandstone head with a Celtic-style face of Iron-Age date found at Cliff Close, Eype Mouth, and now in the Dorset County Museum at Dorchester.

Vespasian commanded the onslaught of the Second Legion, building a fort on Waddon Hill, and later became Emperor.

The importance of the River Brit to early seafarers was that it offered one of the only havens from the effects of a gale for miles. The opening was much closer to East Cliff before West Bay was created as we know it, when, in 1741, the Brit was re-routed into its present outlet. This historic opening was much wider than the present ship channel between piers which was added to the diverted course in 1824.

It must at times have proved invaluable – literally a life-saver – as Lyme Regis has no natural harbour and the other rivers from Axmouth around to Weymouth, at Charmouth, Seatown and Freshwater, trickle through banks of shingle that become awash with waves. Therefore the Brit estuary would have received visitors, if only to escape the weather or stop for the night, from the dawn of sea travel which became significant for the spread of civilisation with the arrival of Neolithic builders of passage-graves, who travelled the Atlantic seaboard up from the Iberian peninsula after 3500BC. Their megalithic architecture fused with that of local earthen long barrows and evolved into chambered long barrows, such as the Grey Mare and her Colts above Abbotsbury. The great age of prehistoric sea travel saw Celtic tribes from pre-Roman Gaul bringing immigration and commerce to the Dorset coast. The great Iron-Age ports were at Clavel Point on the Corfe Castle side of Poole Harbour and at Hengistbury Head on the peninsula east of Bournemouth.

The changes that took place at West Bay mean that its archaeology is now deep beneath shingle and buildings, but somewhere between the Bridport Arms Hotel and East Cliff stood the timber quay of a Roman military port. It was established a year or two after the Claudian invasion of AD43 when the General Vespasian – later Emperor – commanded the Second Legion (Augusta) in its progress westwards from Chichester against tribal resistance based around the great Wessex hill-forts. At least 20 were stormed, the historian Tacitus tells us, before the area was brought under control. The opposition came from sling-stone firing Durotrigic warriors. Once they had been subdued, conquest turned into taxation, as the thriving settlements and their field systems, across almost the entirety of the downlands of Dorset, Wiltshire and Hampshire, were forced to supply grain to the rulers of the new province of Britannia.

Stormy weather removed the east beach at West Bay in 1835, and before the waves returned the pebbles beachcombers explored the exposed terraces, 'finding Roman coins and many peculiar shells'.

The reason for a Roman base at West Bay was to bring timber and supplies for establishing a Roman

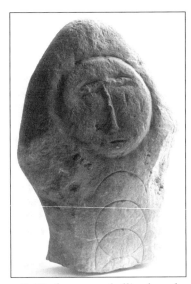

Celtic face on a phallic-shaped stone from Eype, with compass circles.

fort above Stoke Abbott. Similar ports with roads northwards, leading directly inland, were established at Selsey, Fawley, Hamworthy, Radipole and also Axmouth. The last became a frontier station, at the southern end of the Fosse Way, which was the military road across England to Lincoln and the Wash. East of the Axe, mopping up the last concerted Durotrigic resistance – after the capture of Maiden Castle – must have included the storming or surrender of the palisaded multiple ramparts that ring Eggardon Hill and Pilsdon Pen. They overlook the Bridport coast from the north-east and the north-west. Between them are the much slighter traces of the Roman fort that stood on the 635-foot flat-topped ridge of Waddon Hill. I know that large quantities of timber were used in its construction as I was given the job of counting rusty nails during its excavation in 1963.

Post-Roman Bridport was the Bridian of King Alfred's Burghal hidage. This web of fortified burghs restrained and reversed the advance of Viking raiders. An enclosure of 760 hides would have required more than 3,000 feet of earth and timber walling, although the town's two rivers would have acted as a moat on three of the four sides. The exception was in the north where the Town Ditch, beside Rax Lane, formed the inland-facing palisade defences. The eastern line was southwards from West Mill, along St Michael's Lane and Priory Lane and across South Walk to the Chantry where the southern limit ran westwards from the River Brit to the River Asker. The eastern boundary followed South Mill Lane northwards, across Folly Street, into King Street. Here there is an ancient bank behind Prospect Place.

The town's north-eastern gate was at the turn of the River Brit, opposite West Mill, beside the corner with St Michael's Lane. The north-western entrance was at the junction of Barrack Street and East Street. The Chantry, facing South Street, could well be on the site of the town's south gate. Post-Roman towns and monastic establishments tended to distort and divert the combination of prehistoric ridgeways and Roman roads that remained the basis of the nation's transport system until the building of the turnpikes. In Bridport's case it did not have to draw the local main road very far. Although the local course of the Roman road from Dorchester to Exeter is uncertain –

along its descent from Spyway at Askerswell into the Marshwood Vale – it must have passed very close to the northern edge of the town. It would become known as the Great Western Road and pass through the Saxon and Norman town.

Ponchesford Lane, heading towards Watton Cross, indicates a crossing of the River Brit west of St Mary's Parish Church. On the other side a lane serviced hemp fields on fertile and peaty former marshland reclaimed from the River Asker. This was Portmanfield. It derived its name from the 'portman' who guarded the south gate into the town at the Chantry. Saxon usage of the word 'port' was not restricted to the seaside but extended to commercial centres in general. At the heart of bustling Bridport was a Saxon butchers' market in the bulge in South Street on the northern side of St Mary's Church and to the north of the Woodman Inn.

Between the reigns of Athelstan in 925 and Edward the Confessor in 1042, Bridport grew into a community of some 500 people in 120 houses. Coins were minted during the reign of Ethelred II. By the time of the Domesday Survey, in 1086, decline and distress were taking their toll. Power and influence that once centred on Wessex and Winchester had spread to England and London. Bridport was reduced to 100 houses – the rest being in ruins – and the inhabitants pleaded for relief from taxation they were unable to pay.

In Norman times the Shambles of market stalls had moved from central South Street to the great wide street at the T-junction between St Andrew's Chapel and the old George Inn. This became new Bridport in a revival of its fortunes after the old fords were replaced by East Bridge and West Bridge. The axis of a single alignment formed by East Street joining West Street became the town's spinal cord for a millennium. It has its double in Dorchester where High East Street rises into High West Street with an identical T-junction, at Cornhill, into South Street.

The Norman reoccupation of west Dorset by minor gentry followed the fall of Normandy in 1204. King John showed a personal interest in the area, acquiring Powerstock Castle from Robert Newburgh, in

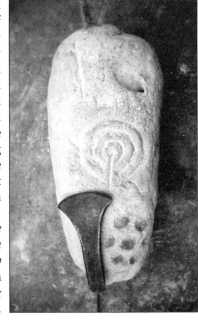

Right: Bronze-Age axe and stone from East Cliff with cup marks (bottom right) and ring marks (centre).

exchange for lands at Fordington, Dorchester, and in Somerset. To this day it is locally known as King John's Castle, with King's Farm to the west, although county historian John Hutchins recorded that 'the common people call it Poorstock Castle and have a tradition that it was a winter palace of King Athelstan.' Henry III 'committed the custody of his manor at Porstock' to his 'dear and faithful Hugh de Nevill' in July 1226. Repairs expenditure of £8 was provided by the King for work at his houses here and at Gillingham, Dorset, and Feckenham, Worcestershire. An additional 4s.6d. was needed 'for a new door to the King's chamber at Porstock' in March 1230. Hugh de Nevill was followed in 1231 by Thomas de Gorges, whose family gave us the 'Gorge' in Shipton Gorge, as Warden of King John's Castle at Powerstock.

The newly knighted Sir Thomas then upset Henry III by making 'a waste and ruin' of Powerstock Forest hunting ground in 1234, by cutting down trees for fuel or timber, although shortly before he died in 1236 he had his right restored 'to take two deer' from these woods that are as wild as ever in the vicinity of former Powerstock Common. His widow, Jane de Nevill, was granted the manor for life. What was probably their thirteenth-century coffin lid was discovered in Powerstock churchyard in 1969 and is now inside the Parish Church.

As with other motte-and-bailey forts with a continuing history, the royal castle at Powerstock had been rebuilt in stone, but by the time that John Hutchins was compiling his history, in the late-eighteenth century, its last walls and vaults were vanishing. Having 'standeth in the memory of man' they were robbed for building stone and reduced to remnants 'curiously carved and jointed'. Apart from a couple of famous exceptions – at Corfe and Sherborne – Dorset's Norman castles are now a much less conspicuous element of the landscape than its Iron-Age hill-forts.

The western power base moved sideways from Powerstock to Chideock in 1379. John de Chideock's modern fortress was a stout square keep with hexagonal towers projecting and rising from each corner. Around it, at the end of Ruins Lane to the north of Main Street, the moat of Chideock Castle has survived as a deep ditch which still occasionally holds a little water. It was designed to withstand a siege by French raiders, but in fact its future and fate lay in the nation's own internecine warfare.

Firstly, having passed to Sir John Arundell, from Lanherne in Cornwall, it became a bastion of western Catholicism and a temporary refuge for persecuted priests, since beatified as martyrs and canonised as saints. The western outpost of the Weld family, more famously from Lulworth Castle, remains at Chideock Manor between the village and North Chideock.

Secondly, it became one of the ruins that Cromwell's men knocked around a bit, being taken by General Sir Thomas Fairfax, commander of the

Designed for sling-stone warfare, the higher inner bank (left) was intended to keep the firing advantage with the defenders' catapults on Eggardon Hill.

East Cliff in 1930, looking south-eastwards along the beach to Freshwater (centre) and Burton Cliff.

Right: *Timeless view of East Cliff, looking north-westwards, showing the beds of harder rock dividing layers of soft sand.*

Below: *The chalk massif above Bridport from Bell Stone (top left) to the Iron-Age ramparts of Eggardon Hill (top right).*

Eggardon Hill and its Iron-Age ramparts seen from the air, in a view looking eastwards with National Trust slopes (right) *overlooking the Bridport countryside.*

forces raised by Parliament in the English Civil War. A substantial shell, looking similar to Nunney Castle in Somerset, stood until 1741 when the site was reduced to earthworks. Eastwards, to the bottom of Quarry Hill, hedges and field names still preserve the imprint of its palisaded deer park.

The ancient curse on lands sequestered or filched from persecuted Roman Catholics is still remembered in these parts. The private devotions of the Arundell family and their chaplains caused no offence to the general population of the Marshwood Vale but caused outrage to the Puritans of Dorchester who provided the juries for the region's assize court in the county town. The excesses perpetrated were horrific; even more so because they were carried out in the name of the law and the Lord.

Father Thomas Pilchard was executed at Dorchester, at Gallows Hill which was at the south end of Icen Way (then called Gaol Lane) on 21 March 1587. For being a member of an outlawed religion he suffered a traitor's death of being dragged from Dorchester Castle on a hurdle, then half-hanged, cut down alive, disembowelled whilst still conscious, and finally cut into four quarters. In the process the executioner had 'plunged the knife into his belly and left it there.' Naked and bleeding he turned to the officers of the court and calmly spoke what were to

be his last words as they provoked the hangman into a frenzy of butchery: 'Mr Sheriff, is this your justice?'

A study of *Chideock and its Martyrs*, published in 1926, investigated the consequences:

All who took part in his death met with a speedy retribution. The executioner and greater part of the jury came to a bad end almost immediately. The Sheriff from being a rich and powerful man died miserably within two years, having fallen into great adversity. The

The chalk escarpment at Eggardon, looking westwards, from above Askerswell.

The Volunteer (left) and the Woodman (right), with just one tree between them, on the east side of South Street.

Right: *The Martyrs' Memorial where the Chideock priests suffered, on former Gallows Hill, at Dorchester.*

Port Mill Cottage in the meadows south of Brewery Farm.

Powerstock village and the site of its castle (top right) *from across the valley in Nettlecombe.*

keeper of the prison fell sick immediately, and confessed to those around him that the devils were striking for him and they would presently have him; but he saw Mr Pilchard standing with a cross betwixt them and him.

Father Thomas was the first of many Chideock martyrs. On 4 July 1594, again at Dorchester's Gallows Hill, Father John Cornelius of the Society of Jesus was executed along with Thomas Bosgrove, John Carey and Patrick Salmon who were servants in the Arundell household. John Cornelius had gained a reputation as an exorcist. After the ritual mutilations his head was fixed to the top of the gallows where it was seen by Miss Arundell who claimed it was encircled by a bright halo. It is said to have been removed because the town started to experience calamities, and the severe visitation of the plague in 1595 was attributed to his execution.

The most duplicitous of the martyrdoms came to Father Hugh Green at the beginning of the Civil War. Obeying a royal proclamation that Catholic priests should leave the realm, he packed his bags at Chideock Castle and made his way to Lyme Regis where he was arrested while boarding a boat for France. He was told that the proclamation had expired the previous day.

He followed his predecessor's one-way trip along the road through Bridport to Dorchester – prison, the law, a Puritan jury, and execution and disembowelling. That took place on 19 August 1642, in slow motion, to provide half an hour of entertainment to a hostile crowd who were tasting their first blood of the war.

Sylvia Creed, from Whitchurch Canonicorum, told me that outbreaks of swine fever and other soil-related ailments in the Marshwood Vale reminded this deeply rural population of 'the Catholic curse on their lost lands'. David Popham – who with poor powers of premonition called it 'the Vale where nobody goes' – gave me a similar story in 1969. He heard about the folk belief when he stopped for cider at the Shave Cross Inn. The quoted incident was that 'only a few years ago a man digging a well died in the clay's oily fumes.' Then the story was told of the young farm worker who electrocuted himself by raising a pipe which touched 400,000-volt cables slung from 160-foot pylons that carry the National Grid from Dorset into Devon.

Chideock Castle, after its Civil War siege and partial destruction – before removal of all the masonry in 1741.

Hemp, now better known as cannabis, was the cash crop in Bridport's countryside.

Fitters finish off a fishing net.

Warping cotton yarn at the works of Bridport Gundry in the 1950s

Chapter 2
HEMP, SAILS, NETS & TWINE

Bridport and hemp for rope-making have been synonymous for at least 900 years. Cordage and sailcloth from West Dorset feature in the Exchequer Rolls for 1211. Then came the first royal endorsement of its products, by King John in 1213, in a letter to the Sheriffs of Dorset and Somerset. This began with the command that 'as they love themselves and their own bodies' they are to buy for his use all the oats they can. The purpose was to provision the King's campaign in France. Money was to come from the Abbeys and elsewhere, on loan if necessary, or by whatever other means they could obtain it. Furthermore, making the military purpose clear, they were ordered 'to be caused to be made at Bridport, night and day, as many ropes for ships, both large and small, and as many cables as they can and twisted yarns for cordage for balistoe'. The balistoe in French, or balister in English, was the Norman cross-bow.

Bridport, or Burporte in contemporary spelling, was controlled and protected by its own statutes. A total of 15 received royal assent, starting with this measure approved by Henry VIII in 1529: 'An Acte for true Makinge of greate cables, halsers, ropes, and all other takeling for Shippes &c, in the Boroughe of Burporte in the Countye of Dorsetshire.'

Males at the head of households were the ropers and wives and daughters the spinners. Intermediate stages between hemp and its products included 'the scutching and hacking of rans and laces'. The situation remained the same for centuries. William Marshall, compiling a two-volume study of *The Rural Economy of the West Country* in 1796, mentions the normal arable crops of inland West Dorset in one sentence and then tells us about the most important cash crop in Dorsetshire:

The arable crops of the interior of the district are chiefly wheat, and oats; no beans! and but little barley

... But what mark the rural management of the environs of Bridport most evidently, is the culture of hemp and flax – to supply the consumption of a manufactory of sailcloth and cordage (from the cable of a man of war, to the finest packing thread), which has long been carried on there, giving employment to the female villagers of the neighbourhood; and, of course, acting as a mutual benefit to agriculture and commerce. A mutual good, however, which can only subsist in a rich-soiled district.

Bridport has benefited from a war dividend from King John's misadventures in France through to the Falklands campaign and no doubt more recently in ways we have yet to learn. The South Atlantic example presented itself to me, literally, as I arrived at John Creed's printing works in Broad Oak hamlet in the summer of 1982. Masses of camouflage netting filled the parking spaces and inside his daughters and other local girls were stitching together the green canvas squares of an emergency consignment that was booked for a Hercules flight from RAF Lyneham. Its onward transit was via Ascension Island and mid-air refuelling for dropping at low level to troops landing in San Carlos Water.

William Hounsell & Co.'s staff at the North Mills works in 1908.

William Stevenson realised the value to Bridport and district of the decade and a half of the Napoleonic Wars. Writing in 1812, in his *General View of the Agriculture of the County of Dorset*, he devotes pages to the techniques of hemp culture, including the following extract:

The culture of hemp in this country is very much increased of late years, as might be expected from the high price it has borne in consequence of the shutting of the ports of northern Europe. The amount of the bounty paid upon hemp, at 3d per stone of 14 pounds, between 1782 and 1792, was £98 7s 6d on the average;

Right: *Multi-shuttle braiding looms for net-making.*

Below: *Polishing machine on the twine-making line.*

Right: *Sliver of spun hemp coming off the drawing frame.*

Softening hemp prior to spinning.

from which it appears that the produce was 7,870 stone weight per annum, and the extent of land annually under this crop was believed to be 170 acres. At the present time, in the opinion of Mr Roberts of Burton, and some others, there are from 400 to 500 acres of hemp grown in the county on average, and about ten times as many acres of flax. According to Mr Conway of Netherbury, hemp is only cultivated in 13 parishes in the county, viz Bridport, Loders, Bradpole, Powerstock, Symondsbury, Chideock, Bothenhampton, West Milton, Walditch, Stoke Abbott, Beaminster, Netherbury and Abbotsbury.

The soil most adapted to the growth of hemp is a rich dark-coloured warm and deep loam. The soils where hemp is grown in this country are deep loams of a reddish colour, and termed fox-mould. They consist of a large proportion of very fine-grained sand, and are of great natural fertility; but scarcely tenacious enough in general to produce a good crop of beans.

Major Travers of Loders, observes that such of the lands in that parish on which hemp is grown, would be worth, if separately let from the farms, not less than £4 an acre. Mr Strong of Powerstock, says hemp will not succeed on hilly ground, though of a good loamy kind. In a trial of this kind, the hemp grew only two or three feet high, though a good crop generally reaches the height of six or seven feet.

The hemp-growers seem to be unanimously of opinion, that hemp cannot be advantageously grown on soils that are not naturally rich enough to make good gardens; and that the notion entertained a few years ago, that it would succeed on any kind of soils newly broken up, is entirely erroneous. Mr Travers observes, that the growth of hemp was not deemed profitable, before the late high prices of that article added an additional stimulus.

Tillage. The land should be ploughed three times, the first time at Candlemas [2 February]; after which it is dunged; the second ploughing is performed about the beginning of May, and is followed by repeated harrowings; the last ploughing takes place near the

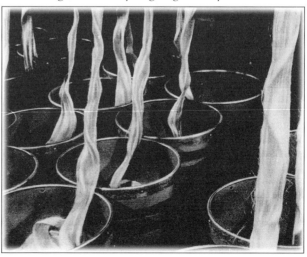

Slivers of spun hemp being drawn out of cans.

Right: *Hemp sliver being sewn to a length of tennis net.*

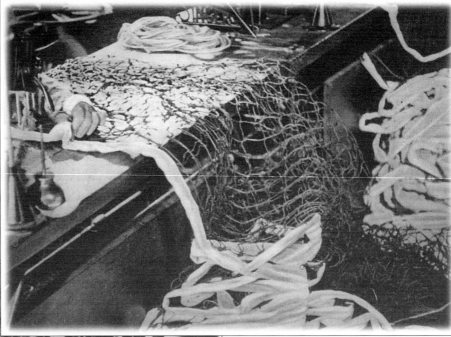

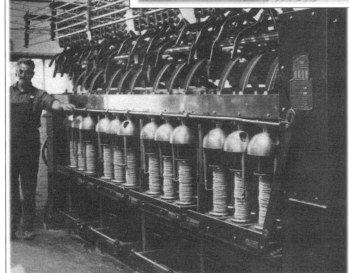

Left: *Heavy-duty twisting frame for twine-making.*

Right: *Hand-operated jumper loom – the precursor of modern netting looms.*

*Van man collecting work from cottage
outworkers in the villages.*

end of May, when the furrows are righted, or pecked
across with hoes, to fill the slacks or hollows between
the furrows, that the seed may not grow in lines, but
come up as suant or regular as possible.

Manure. Should be very liberally applied; an acre
should be dressed with 20 pot-loads of yard-dung, 20
hogsheads of lime, and have a good folding besides,
though the latter may be omitted.

Seed. The common quantity is two bushels per
customary acre, of 134 statute perches. The average
price per bushel is about 10s but sometimes as high as
a guinea.

Sowing. A pole wide is sown at a bout, or in going
and returning. The land is sometimes set out at regular
distances with sticks, and the sowing should be
performed very carefully. The roller should be used to
make the land very fine before it is sown, but not afterwards. The seed is covered by harrows, going and
returning in the same place. The time of sowing is
generally near the end of May, but includes the last
week of May, and the first two of June. It is preferable
to sow when the land is moist, that all the seed may
begin to grow at the same time. The young plants are
often destroyed by the fly, and by slugs.

Pulling and tying, and grassing. The summer, or
cinder hemp, is called femel hemp in some parts of
England, and is the male or barren kind, which
produces no seed. This kind of hemp composes about
one-fourth of the crop; it is pulled up about nine or ten
weeks from the time of sowing, and the proper time of
this operation is shown by the heads becoming yellowish
and dusty, which happens about a fortnight after the
flowers open.

The seed hemp is pulled up about the beginning of
October, and is set up to dry, by fastening together three
small parcels which cross each other near the top. Hemp
is never watered in this county, or put into pits to rot in
some measure, as is the case in other districts, but is
merely dew ripened, by lying three or four weeks on grass
in summer, or on stubbles in the autumn, after the seed
is thrashed out. In very wet weather much care is required
to prevent its being spoiled; sometimes it is set-up

end-ways in a conical form, but it is generally turned two
or three times with a long stick rather bent at the end, and
in the turning, when it is laid close, every swath is put
nearly into the place of that which was previously turned.
The seed is thrashed out on a Dorsetshire flake-hurdle, by
two men with light flails, the parcels of hemp being held
across the hurdle, and turned about by a woman sitting on
a stool. The hurdle is laid on a jib, or frame about 18
inches high, and underneath this is spread a winnowing
sheet, upon some straw.

Breaking and scaling. The strands or stalks of hemp
are broken off about six inches from the root end, and are
then stripped by dextrously slipping the thumbs from
one end to the other, by which means the harle or hemp,
is separated from the scales or remnants of the stalks, in
two operations. The women and children employed in
the winter in this business will scale about 6 pounds of
seed hemp, or 4 pounds of summer hemp, in a day.

Bunching. About eight heads, of 4 pounds each, are
twisted and turned back at the ends, and tied round
with two strings. The bundle is then called a weight.

Balling mills, or more properly, bawling mills, so
called from the noise they make, are employed to separate
the fibres of the hemp, which is laid in hollows, and is
struck repeatedly by heavy pieces of timber (called
stampers, rounded at the end), which are lifted by the
mill-work, and descend by their own weight; a boy
being employed to turn the hemp over in the interval
between each stroke.

Heckling or combing is the next business, which
makes it fit for spinning.

*Cottage outworker of the cordage industry, net-making at
home in her doorway at Burton Bradstock, in the 1960s.*

19

Above: *Taylor's Charity, the South Street almshouse founded by Quaker Daniel Taylor.*

Below: *Stormy seas at West Bay showing the need for the only haven in the eastern part of Lyme Bay.*

Left: *The Tudor 'Castle' in South Street – which may have been St Leonard's Chantry – now houses Bridport Museum.*

Chapter 3
BISHOP BRIDPORT, CHANTRIES & CHARITIES

Many of the earliest mentions of Bridport come with the people who left it. At a time when people were merely called John, Philip or Robert in their home place, they were given its name as an identifying appendage when they moved away. Examples include Master John de Bridport, vicar of Axminster, who witnessed a Newenham Abbey deed in October 1286 and was a Prebend of Crediton in 1288. John de Bridport and Robert de Bridport were the town's members of the first Parliaments through the reigns of Edward I, Edward II and Edward III. William de Bridport appears in the records of Thomas Rymer as a statesman in the era of Edward II.

Another Robert Bridport sat for Dorchester in the Parliament of 1355. Thomas Wainwright, writing about Bridport in 1898, retired to Barnstaple and was told that its earliest Member of Parliament was Robert Brideport. Giles de Bridport was Bishop of Salisbury from 1256 until his death on 13 December 1262.

It is Giles de Bridport who appears in intriguing speculation by Wimborne-born poet and gossip Matthew Prior. This led ecclesiastical historian Stephen Hyde Cassan to infer 'that he was a favourite at court, inasmuch as we find him, in 1256, sent with the Abbot of Westminster beyond the seas, on secret service' to Pope Alexander IV in Rome.

John Leland, Henry VIII's archivist, records that Bishop Bridport founded the College of de Vaulx between the palace wall at Salisbury and Harnham Bridge over the River Avon. The scholars and their two chaplains were 'bound to celebrate the anniversary of Giles their founder at the parish church of Bridport where he was born.' The achievements of Giles – Latinised as 'Egidius' – included having 'covered the new cathedral church with lead'. He received national recognition in 1258 when Boniface, Archbishop of Canterbury, dedicated Salisbury Cathedral at a great service graced by the attendance of King Henry III and his nobles. Locally, in the valleys on each side of his home town, Bishop Bridport owned the rectories at Allington and Walditch.

The importance of Bridport from these early times is shown by the establishment beside East Bridge over the River Asker, at the bottom end of East Street, of the Hospital of St John the Baptist. John Hutchins, the eighteenth-century county historian, gives some of its background but wrongly gives its location as being at West Bridge. The institution was thriving by 1240, largely because medical care for the dying rich guaranteed legacy income, such as the bequest from Helias de Wrockhechel who:

... for the health of his soul and those of his ancestors and successors, granted and confirmed to God and the house of the Blessed John the Baptist that they have ten oxen, four yearling cows, one boar, fifty sheep and one sow, in his pasture throughout Walditch.

In around 1300 he inherited Kelling's Mill, in Killing's Lane, from John Talle and Bartholomew Kelling.

The beginning of the end came when the religious houses were dissolved by Henry VIII. The first to go, in 1535–6, were the smaller ones – defined as those with an income of less than £200 per annum – which included St John's Hospital. It is called St John's Chantry in a document listing valuable items including jewels, silverware and vestments 'in the custody of William Chard, bailiff'. Among 'stuff remaining in the Chantry of Saint Johannus' is 'a pyx of silver' and 'one pax'. Victorian historian Thomas Wainwright tells us about the pax:

East Street, westwards from East Bridge, showing the former Marquis of Granby incorporating the remains of the medieval leper hospital of St John the Baptist (left).

This must not be confounded with the pyx, the box or covered vessel in which the consecrated host was kept, the pax being an entirely different appendage of divine service and devoted to quite another purpose. The pax was a small tablet of metal, wood, or sometimes of glass, bearing a representation of the crucifixion. This after being kissed by the priest and deacon at the celebration of mass was handed by the latter to the faithful laity who all by kissing it were held to express their mutual love in Christ. This was in substitution of the actual salute of each other which was given in early times by Christians in their assemblies and had given rise to scandal.

Closure had taken place but disposal of the building did not occur until after its valuation at £6.15s.4d. by the Chantry Commissioners in 1553. It was then partly demolished. Something remains, however, as sixteenth-century windows are incorporated into the back of the 1768-dated building that used to be the Marquis of Granby public house, on the south side of the street opposite Revd James Rooker's Academy which was built in 1769.

At the other end of the town, Magdalene Almshouses in West Allington survived their visit from the Chantry Commissioners, although its old buildings were destroyed by fire in the nineteenth century and rebuilt in 1877. It was later extended and modernised by the Colfox Trust, into six small flats, in 1955. In all probability there has been a continuity of name and charitable purpose on the same site, on the north side of the main road at West Allington, for nine centuries. Management is now under the auspices of the trustees of Bridport Municipal Charities.

The origin of Magdalene Almshouses was 'a lazer-house' or leper hospital founded by the Legh family, as the de Leyes (both forms of the name are used), early in the thirteenth century. William de Legh, the son of Philip de Legh, and his wife, Dame Nicola de Legh, donated 50 acres of arable land and cultures – as hemp fields were called – at Allington in order to fund the building and the provision of two chaplains. Dedicated as the 'House of St Mary Magdalene of the Lepers of Bridport', it was protected by a royal grant, from Henry III in 1232, and given an additional endowment in 1247. Scotland's Robert Bruce was a famous victim of the disease in 1329, but by the time the Chantry Commissioners visited Bridport in 1553 the crippling affliction was in decline across Europe. The former hospital, valued at £7.8s.4d., had already been converted into a home for poor people living on alms revenue raised in the town. There were still endowed funds but the profits from these went to the incumbent priest, Robert Blakewell, to visit and say mass.

The precise location and manning of St Katherine's Chantry remain a mystery. It is mentioned in mid-fourteenth-century accounts and is commemorated by St Katherine's Drive and St

Pine-topped Colmer's Hill is the distinctive landmark beside the coast road west of Bridport.

Katherine's Avenue between St Andrew's Well and Pymore. As with St Catherine's Chapel on the summit of the rounded hill overlooking Abbotsbury Abbey, the chapel in the woods overlooking Milton Abbey, and a third example that used to look down on Cerne Abbey, it was dedicated to the patron saint of spinsters. The St Katherine's area of Bridport is below the northern of the two hills above the town that are called Watton Hill.

An equivalent spot near Bridport to the monastic examples from elsewhere is Colmer's Hill – part of the Cerne Abbey estates – although this is in the next parish at Symondsbury. It is now topped by distinctive pines and is owned by the Woodland Trust. The Benedictine monks from Cerne Abbas had another outpost in the opposite corner of the county, on Brownsea Island, where they established a chapel and hermitage that was dedicated to St Andrew. The medieval St Andrew's Chapel in Bridport – also giving its name to St Andrew's Well towards Bradpole – is said to have been established by 'White Friars' who built an oratory and priory. These may either be connections or coincidences.

The town's historic Higher Almshouse (also known as the Upper Almshouse) and Lower Almshouse, both on the east side of South Street, had secular origins and were always under the control of the 'bailiffs and burgesses as overseers and trustees thereof'. It was recorded that they had 'time out of mind, repaired the same'. Leases date back to the reigns of Mary Tudor and Queen Elizabeth, and perhaps earlier, but their location has moved over time. Fire destroyed the Higher Almshouse in 1830 but funds in hand of £1,400 and £300 from the Atlas Insurance Company enabled it to be replaced by 'a neat dwelling house and courtyard with accommodation for eight widows, and a house behind capable of receiving two families.' This, however, has since been levelled and the present South Street Almshouses are on the opposite side of the street, north of St Mary's Parish Church.

Daniel Taylor's Almshouse, on the east side of the street opposite St Mary's Church, is a Quaker-run institution beside the Meeting House of the Society of Friends. It was founded on 27 August 1696 and is an exception to the rule about such buildings. Instead of being hidden away where it would not attract attention, a shyness born of persecution, the Quaker buildings of Bridport proudly face the entrance to the Parish Church. It is a characterful collection of historic buildings, grouped around a pump and its stone trough, behind an elegant arch.

There are now eight small flats – occupancy not restricted to Quakers – but in the early-Victorian agricultural depression the community gave refuge to large numbers of homeless people. An inspection by the Charity Commissioners in 1836 found a total of 17 people living rent-free in what were then ten cramped 'compartments'. Even more were grateful just to have a few square feet of roof over them during the 'Hungry Forties'.

Despite Quaker thoughts about alcohol, Daniel Taylor owned the Bull Hotel in East Street, and left it in a charitable trust 'for the purpose of providing an efficient schoolmaster for the poor children of this town.' It remained in trusteeship until 1859 when it was sold with Charity Commission consent, for £2,450, and the money invested in an endowment fund 'to provide bursaries for boys and girls at either general or secondary schools.'

Charles Pitfield, who owned land around Eype and Thorncombe Beacon, created Pitfield's Charity in 1675. His family also owned Pitfield's Marsh on the west side of West Bay and Pitfold Farm – preserving the other version of their name – on the hill towards Burton Bradstock. From the proceeds of Charles Pitfield's charity, penny loaves were distributed every Sunday in St Mary's Parish Church, into the twentieth century. The land had been sold in 1763 but its proceeds continued to fund the preaching of an annual sermon, on 2 March, 'after which a number of petticoats are given away to old women and coats to old men.'

St Michael's Chapel and Chantry, for two chaplains, was founded in 1321. The date, provided by Thomas Wainwright, comes from an inquiry – carried out as a legal search – before Edward II confirmed a grant to Sir Robert de Faringdon. The Faringdon family lands extended from Symondsbury and Allington to Loders. They also rented an estate at Sydling St Nicholas from Milton Abbey. Roger Mortival was the first chaplain, followed by Nicholas Michel after his death in 1329. Both were given the courtesy title 'Sir' which continued to be the term for bishops and clergymen into Shakespeare's time.

Locally, St Michael's Chantry became known as Munden's Chantry, for its contemporary associations with John Munden who represented Dorset in the Parliaments of October 1339, 1346 and 1352. The medievalist Dr K.L. Wood-Leigh, writing in 1956, credits Munden with having founded St Michael's Chapel in 1361 but she also seems to accept that on Wainwright's detailed evidence it must have been already functioning. They have an academic difference of opinion on whether there were two separate chantries servicing St Michael's Chapel – Faringdon's Chantry followed by Munden's Chantry – or whether the first was re-founded as the second. Both chantry or chantries and chapel must have been 'hard by' but Miss Wood-Leigh remains uncommitted about their location.

Thomas Wainwright, however, had no doubt. St Michael's Lane is the obvious clue on the map with the present Chantry, midway along South Street, being of a different date and foundation. St Michael's Chantry appears to have been on the site of the yard of William Fry, the town's Victorian monumental mason, behind 64 West Street. That ties in with the chaplains' description of St Mary's Parish Church as 'the South Church'. That not only distinguished it from St Michael's Chapel but also from St Andrew's Church. The latter stood near the site of the present Town Hall at the T-junction in the centre of the town.

One of St Michael's chaplains was designated as 'Chantry Warden' and made responsible for rendering annual accounts each Michaelmas – the feast of Saint Michael the Archangel – on 29 September. It remains in the calendar as the first university term of the academic year.

The Bridport chaplains had annual stipends of 100 shillings plus an allowance of 10 shillings for expenses. William Savernak, aged about 70, was the warden from 1452. Previously the rector of Ibberton, in the Blackmore Vale, he enjoyed the patronage of Thomas Courtenay, Earl of Devon. From his account book it appears that guests fell into three categories – gentlemen, labourers and strangers. A total of £8.11s.11d. was spent on food in the calendar year between Michaelmas 1454 and Michaelmas 1455.

From their garden, orchard and dovecote came many foodsuffs, including onions, grapes, apples, pears and pigeons and their eggs. Evidence for such things comes into the accounts as labourer John Cleek is paid to prop up the vine or clean out the dovecote. 'One quarter of peas and beans, 2s 8d' would have fed the pigeons. The feed supplier was William Bocher. A carpenter, Henry Witherbroke, turned his hand and saw to pruning the fruit trees. There were definitely pear trees, as pears do not appear in the accounts, but 2$\frac{1}{2}$d. was spent 'for a press to make perry'.

Henry Witherbroke was kept busy, particularly in 1457, when he was paid 5s.6d. for one period of work which took 22 days. The priests had John King as their servant who had additional amounts 'paid for washing' and cleaning.

The itemised expenditure for domestic food in 1454–55 was:

Bread – £1.14s.4d.	Another pig – 0s.5d.
Ale – £2.8s.5d.	Sucking pig – 0s.4d.
Meat – £2.1s.10$\frac{1}{2}$d.	Another sucking pig – 0s.4d.
Fish – £1.10s.8d.	A third sucking pig – 0s.3d.
Butter – 0s.10d.	One goose – 0s.6d.
Eggs – 1s.7d.	One pair of fowls – 0s.4d.
Oatmeal – 3s.4$\frac{1}{2}$d.	One hen – 0s.2d.
Salt – 1s.2d.	Beans – 0s.$\frac{1}{2}$d.
Pepper – 3s.0d.	Peas – 0s.1d.
Milk – 0s.6$\frac{1}{2}$d.	Figs – 0s.6d.
Mustard – 0s.4d.	Cloves, saffron and
One pig – 0s.4d.	powder – 0d.10d.

The following year, 1455–56, the total was £8.15s.2d.:

Bread – £1.16s.0d.	Mustard – 0s.4d.
Ale – £2.11s.0d.	Milk – 0s.3d.
Meat – £2.4s.$\frac{1}{2}$d.	Two hens – 0s.4d.
Fish – £1.10s.10d.	One pullet – 0s.1d.
Oatmeal – 3s.3$\frac{1}{2}$d.	Dates – 0s.3d.
Butter – 0s.8d.	Cheese – 0s.11d.
Eggs – 0s.11d.	Saffron – 0s.9d.
Salt – 1s.10$\frac{1}{2}$d.	Figs – 1s.0d.
Pepper – 0s.1d.	Almonds – 2s.9$\frac{1}{2}$d.

The next year, 1456–57, the total was £8.15s.2d.:

Bread – £1.11s.5d.	Figs – 0s.6d.
Ale – £2.11s.10$\frac{1}{2}$d.	Cheese – 1s.2d.
Meat – £1.15s.8d.	Sucking pig – 0s.5d.
Fish – £1.5s.5$\frac{1}{2}$d.	Six pullets – 0s.7d.
Oatmeal – 2s.7d.	Eight pullets – 0s.6d.
Butter – 0s.6d.	Honey – 0s.1d.
Eggs – 0s.5$\frac{1}{2}$d.	Half a bushel of peas –
Almonds – 1s.4d.	0s.4d.
Salt – 0s.10$\frac{1}{2}$d.	One bushel of peas – 0s.8d.
Saffron – 0s.7d.	Cinnamon – 0s.1$\frac{1}{2}$d.
Milk – 0s.9d.	Mustard – 0s.1d.

For 1458–59 the total was £7.14s.0$\frac{1}{2}$d.:

Bread – £2.3s.9$\frac{1}{2}$d.	Honey – 8d.
Ale – £2.1s.11d.	Salt – 7d.
Meat – £1.13s.3d.	Brawn – 1s.1d.
Fish – £1.4s.7d.	Sucking pig – 4d.
Five pullets – 5d.	Two bushels of peas – 1s.1d.
Butter, cheese, eggs and	Figs – 1d.
milk – 3s.3d.	8$\frac{1}{2}$ ounces of pepper – 1s.3d.
Oatmeal – 1s.6d.	Ginger – 1d.

Wine made its first recorded appearance at the Chantry for the feast of St Dunstan in May 1454. Thomas Wainwright, who transcribed these documents, realised it must have been purchased 'in order to entertain visitors of importance'. He identified one as John Bettischon, an ancestor of the Bettiscombe family of Vere's Wootton – now Vearse Farm – which although in the parish of Symondsbury is less than a mile south-west of St Michael's Lane. A land agent, John Bettischon, rode to Blandford, to represent the chaplains at a meeting with Sir William Stourton. Others included the bailiff and officials making the administrative visitation over Michaelmas. The price of their wine was three pence, which would have bought three pints.

'Best ale' and 'pies made' – by William the Baker – were the special items for the New Year celebrations in 1455, attended by:

> ... the Rector of Bridport, William Oliver and his wife, Richard Burwe and his wife and the Prior of St John's, all of whom came to dinner, and after dinner, many of the tenants and neighbours.

Five purchases a year, at 2$\frac{1}{2}$d. each, were made for rushes which were strewn on the floor in the hall. This was regarded as common courtesy if visitors were expected, so that those who failed to find room to sit on the benches could sit on the floor, and survived as a concept into modern times with the saying that an inadequate host 'did not care a rush or straw for his guest.'

Visiting priests included John Pulter, John Clerk and Thomas Somerset. The chaplains had the company of a boy, apparently as a novice rather than a servant, from March 1458 until June 1460 when William Savernak was seriously ill and could only drink milk. The account book is not accompanied by any journal or diary so information is incidental rather than explanatory. Its great value, extolled by popular historian G.M. Trevelyan, was that it broke Professor Eileen Power's sweeping assertion that 'only the accounts of larger and more aristocratic households' have survived. The exception from Bridport belonged to one of the smallest middle-class institutions for which detailed records can have been compiled. Transcribing them, at the end of the nineteenth century, Thomas Wainwright made comparisons of prices and values:

> From the foregoing details of expenditure on diet various matters worthy of notice will be observed. One point that occurs is the apparently low price at which food was sold; but to estimate this aright, account must be taken of the value of money in the middle of the fifteenth century, and to get a correct idea of this for our purpose we cannot have a better guide than the wages paid to workmen in Bridport at that period. From these St

Michael's accounts then it appears that a master mason or carpenter working at Bridport at the present time is 3 shillings 6 pence per day, it will be apparent that money was worth fourteen times as much in AD1454, as at present, and that the two pence then paid for a hen was equivalent to 2 shillings 8 pence of our money.

Thomas Wainwright would be baffled by his chosen comparison today, a century later. In terms of wages, Victorian labour costs have escalated 500 times, but the price for an oven-ready hen has only risen by a factor of between 15 and 40. The worker I found in nearby St Mary's Parish Church happily admitted he was on £10 an hour for an eight-hour day (£80). As a practising vegetarian I had no idea of the price of a chicken but found myself spoilt for choice in the freezer compartments at Safeway, within easy walking distance of the Chantry. To the bewilderment of a couple of carnivores I noted down the prices on the palm of my hand. Our priest returning from the Middle Ages would have to decide between a 'Medium size, Grade A Chicken' on offer at £1.99 and a similar quality 'Large size' bird at £4.29. Some consultation about their cooking might be necessary as these chicken are smoothly sealed, in a strange clear substance, without advice on the label as to whether this is oven-ready basting or packaging to be removed.

Medieval food for the moderately prosperous household comprised bread, meat and fish as the staple solids. Feast days were enlivened by almonds, sugar, honey and spices. Saffron was partly medicinal, being recommended by herbalist Thomas Gerard 'as it is good for the head and maketh the senses quick and lively.' It was an additive much like salt and pepper, Laurentius writes, being 'in daily use for sprinkling over or cooking with food.' Ale was essential as a drink, before water could be easily purified by heating, as Sir John Fortescue recorded in 1470. Then 'they never vouchsafed to drink water except for penance.' Centuries later the teetotal movement in Dorset towns found it 'a cruel irony' that their members succumbed to cholera and typhoid while 'waisters and drunkards' who stayed on the beer were generally spared.

The Chantry accounts also show that the priests could afford winter fuel. 'Carbo', as carbon, is a word that was applied to both charcoal and coal. The former would be applicable further inland but given the coastal location the importation of coal would have been quite possible by the middle of the fifteenth century. That seems to be borne out by the quantities involved: 'Paid for 31 quarterns of coal, 6s.10d.'

William Savernak's fellow priest, both as predecessor and successor after his death on 20 September 1460, was 80-year-old John Trewen who kept only cursory accounts. William, who left a bequest of 3s.4d. to St Mary's Parish Church, was replaced in October 1460 by Stephen Russell. John Trewen then retired at the end of the year. William Smyth and Hewe Samford were the chaplains a couple of decades later. Expenditure on the chapel included these entries:

Paid for one surplice, 2s 6d.
Paid for wine bought for the celebration, 17d; also for bread, 7d; also for a bolt for the door, 2d; also for wax and making [candles], 7d; also for web bought for making tapers and candles, 1$\frac{1}{2}$d; also for rushes, 4d; also paid for sewing an alb and amice, 1d; also paid for one pound of wax, and making, 7d; also paid for two pounds of candles, 2s 4d; also paid for one pound of wax, and making, 7d. Total, 6s 11d.
To John Clek for making a path to the Chapel, 2d.
To William the mole catcher, 2d.
Also paid for two quart jugs, 1s 0d.
Twelve cressets [lamps], 1s 6d.
Washing the chapel and pantry, 16d.
Also paid to the parish priest, 8d.
Expenditure on the Chapel – Paid Richard the carpenter, for one day's work hanging the bell, 3d; also paid for washing, 1d; also paid for rushes [for floor], $\frac{1}{2}$d; also for rushes for the Feast of St Michael, 1d; also for straps and nails, 8d; also for bread 1d; also for three pounds of wax, 1s 6d; also for making fine candles, 1d; and for making small candles, 2d. Total, 2s. 11$\frac{1}{2}$d.
Expenditure on the Chapel – Paid for bread 6d; also for wine, 8d; also for washing, 1d. Total 1s 3d.

Batches of items tended to be for the key festivals of Easter, Whitsun, Michaelmas and Christmas. They show an active religious life. Properties associated with St Michael's Chantry, providing it with rental income, included the 'penfold' at Walditch – the village pound for impounding stray animals – where John William was paid sixpence for repairing the wall and John Prest received two pence for thatching. Regular purchases of hundreds of lathes and thousands of shingles went towards the maintenance of 'diverse houses' around the town and nearby villages. The beach at West Bay provided free materials but required an outlay of two pence 'for a horse hired to draw sand for one day'. For 'spiking, braiding and daubing a passage' over two and half days John Cleet was paid 5d. A pound of pitch cost a penny. Resin was also a penny.

A wagon load of ash timber was two shillings and the going rate for sawing '885 feet of timber' was 11s.1d. A thousand 'lath nails' were 9d. which was rounded off to a shilling with an unspecified quantity of 'board nails'. The local woodsmen included John Hundyfield or Houndiseld – medieval spellings can be relied upon for inconsistency – and John Stroud 'fyling and spoylyng' alder and poplar from their wagons. Filing and spoiling was the term for loading and unloading. A day's work lopping elms – Dorset's commonest hedgerow tree until it was decimated by fungal disease in the 1970s – cost 4d. The wet western woodlands, in valley bogs or degenerating into

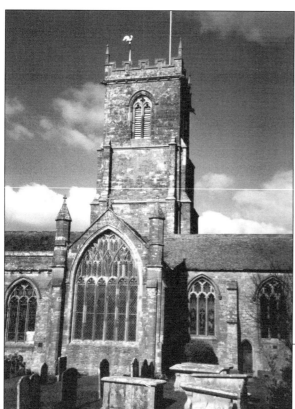

Left: *Lengthened at each end in 1860, and seen here from the south in 1997, the core of St Mary's Church retains its thirteenth-century plan.*

Below: *The Chantry, Bridport's medieval house, facing on to South Street, pictured in 1995.*

scrubby coverts on steep slopes, seldom produced fine timber but 'the Dorsetshire woodwards' – woodsmen – defended the quality of their 'cheap and cheerful alder poles' with an adage that was applied to willows and poplars in the Midland counties:

Thatch me well and keep me dry,
Hearts of oak I will defy.

Richard Marshall was paid two pence for writing out a deed to lease one of the houses. 'John Rogers's collector' received 3s.1d. for acting as the priests' rent collector. One of their tenants was 'William the glover' – a trade already well established in the cattle country between Bridport and Yeovil – whose bread-oven beside the open inglenook fireplace needed repairs, costing sixpence, in 1457. 'Richard the glover' had his chimney rebuilt for a shilling. 'Dionysius the mason' – named for the Greek poet – did most of the skilled work and was paid 3d. per day. 'William the helier' charged 10s.6d. for 42 days' work re-roofing houses and tenements.

As for buying professional time and expertise, legal matters were the most expensive of all services, with attorney John Albayn charging 4s.1d. 'for a brief against John Bishop'. That is unlikely to have required any longer than the day or so taken by the seamstress who charged 3d. 'for repairing napkins and towels'. And he would arguably have needed less skill.

The town's surviving medieval building, known as the Chantry, is on the west side of South Street 200 yards south of St Mary's Church. It is a tall, rambling two-storey stone building, dating from between 1350 and 1450. At its centre are the remains of an original spiral staircase. Numerous other architectural features survive. Despite the name, the Royal Commission on Historical Monuments pronounced that 'its original purpose is unknown' and pointed out that it resembles 'isolated tower houses of semi-defensive nature'.

Rather confusingly, another ancient building in South Street has some claim to have been St Leonard's Chantry, but is known in the town as The Castle. Standing on the east side of the road, 250 yards north of St Mary's Church, it dates from around 1520 and has an impressive porch jutting out towards the street and overhanging the pavement. Damaged by fire in 1876, it was given to the town in 1932, and is now the Bridport Museum.

In pre-Reformation times the churches and chapels of Bridport were generally regarded in the town as a collection of buildings rather than separate entities. This is shown in many wills where the Church of Sarum – Salisbury Cathedral – was listed first, followed by St Mary's Church and St Andrew's Chapel. The Parish Church was invariably left the largest amount. Christian Chilterne, in 1406, among other bequests left:

To Sarum Church, 1s.
To St Mary's, 3s. 4d.
To St Andrew's, 2s. 0d.
To each of the following – St Mary's Church, St Andrew's Chapel, St Michael's Chapel, and St John the Baptist's Hospital, four candles each of four pounds, to burn at the Elevation [Ascension Day].

St Andrew's Chapel was said by John Leland, Henry VIII's archivist, to have been the original Parish Church, but in all other contemporary records it is described as a chapel. Its location, however, beside the T-junction of town streets on the site of the present Town Hall, was certainly the pivot point in the town. By 1349, when St Andrew's was being neglected by the rector, a hearing at the town's Michaelmas Court makes it clear that by custom and tradition it functioned as a chapel-of-ease under the clerical administration of the priest at St Mary's Parish Church:

An inquisition having been held at the said Law Court before Richard Laurence and Robert de Beaminster, the bailiffs, John Gower, William Hitchcock, Richard Coffin, Robert Budd, John Larkstock, John Douk, John Childecombe, John Lom, William Tracy, Hugh Cauff, John Soper, John Whitcombe, Richard Snaward, say on their oath that the Rector of the Church of St Mary at Bridport ought to find a chaplain to celebrate in the Chapel of St Andrew, as his predecessors have done and were accustomed to do, but that he has not done so, but has refrained doing this to the great loss of the town and parishioners. It is therefore ordered that he be compelled to carry this out.

The bequest of a Jane Naper in 1650 enabled the conversion of the thatched former Brewhouse into Miss Gundry's Infant School until it was destroyed by fire in 1906.

Thirteenth-century knight in chain-mail armour, with shield and broken sword, in St Mary's Church.

East Cliff and eastwards, into the mist, as the tide goes out.

The Brit estuary, between rushes as it was from prehistoric times, looking north-eastwards from Pitfield's Marsh.

Chapter 4

HARBOUR ESTUARY & PARISH CONFRATERNITY

Deciphering Norman French, in the medieval records of the Bridport Corporation, Victorian historian Thomas Wainwright found 'culagium' or keelage tolls were being imposed on hulls grounded in 'the estuary at Burport' in 1330. Bridport was already living up to its name and before the construction of a secure Cobb harbour at Lyme it remained the only usable inlet of refuge in the eastern half of Lyme Bay where vessels found themselves driven, by prevailing south-westerly winds, into the miles of swirling shingle along the Chesil Beach. For shipwrecks this stretch of coast is second only to the Goodwin Sands as a notorious graveyard of shipping.

The Old English word 'chesil' means pebble and in ancient times the beach began below Golden Cap at Seatown, under the highest cliff on the South Coast, although the unbroken shingle bank now starts beside the Bridport Arms Hotel on the east side of the River Brit – as a mix of sand and fish-tank-sized pea gravel – and gradually grows in substance and size as it sweeps south-eastwards. It rises to 40 feet above sea level, offshore from the brackish Fleet lagoon, and terminates in pebbles the size of dinner plates in Chesil Cove at Chiswell on Portland. Local fishermen landing on dark nights have been able to fix their position on seeing the size of the pebbles.

The refuge of the estuary of the River Brit, a mile south of Bridport town, was sandwiched between cliffs owned by the Abbot of Cerne around Eype to the west, and those of the Abbot of Caen in the Burton Bradstock direction. The first recorded improvements to the estuary, for the benefit of shipping, were carried out by John Huddersfield in 1385. He constructed 'a haven' beneath East Cliff but lacked the means to complete its quay and asked for Crown approval to levy tolls on boats using the new facilities. By 1401, however, Huddersfield's waterway from the sea into his harbour behind the beach was 'blocked and damaged', and collections were made in Bridport to raise funds for its clearance.

'Rocks and piles' in the estuary were still being described as a hazard to navigation in 1414 and townspeople were urged to resume subscribing towards the rebuilding of their haven. Despite these concerns there was already a thriving town, as other records confirm.

By 1423, middle-class members of the Bridport community were enrolling as 'the brethren and sisters of the Confraternity of St Nicholas' which was based at St Mary's Parish Church and employed Walter Quyntyn and Edward Howden as its wardens. It was a friendly society which guaranteed members mutual insurance. 'The sum of one penny per month' would be provided to pay for care if 'any brother or sister should fall into such poverty as to be unable to maintain him or herself.'

The fund also covered the funeral expenses of any member who:

... departed this life or has been killed outside the town of Bridport, and on account of a distance of more than three miles his body cannot be brought there, then he or she ought to be taken for burial by the brethren where it is most convenient and this at the expense of the brother's or sister's estate, if it will bear the charge.

If this caused impoverishment then the confraternity would meet the cost.

In order to raise funds it levied a charge 'of a mass penny' – on all those who were able to pay – each time one of their fellows died. They had four weeks in which to pay a warden. Failing to attend the annual reading of the accounts on Holy Innocents' Day, after the Nativity, was punished by 'a fine of half a pound of wax'. The same penalty applied if they failed to 'be present at mass on the day of the interment of any brother or sister deceased' without having given 'satisfactory reason for being excused'.

The records of the organisation include membership rolls. The earliest list of the town's traders and gentry (and their spouses) it is also of wider interest for giving us a short-list of the Christian or given names that were popular for children born towards the end of the thirteenth century. William and Johanna top the straw poll:

Peter Alchyn and his wife, Elinor
Robert Alchyn and his wife, Joan
Henry Baker and his wife, Johanna
Thomas Baker and his wife [not named]
William Bowley and his wife, Christine
Richard Brangwyn and his wife, Johanna
John Brode and his wife, Avice

John Burgess and his wife, Avicia
William Butt and his wife, Ammota
Stephen Davy and his wife Johanna
   [followed by second wife Margery]
John Dolle and his wife [not named]
John Gower and his wife, Christine
Thomas Gunnard and his wife, Avicia
Robert Hayvile and his wife, Isabel
John Hooper and his wife, Johanna
Edward Howden and his wife, Edith
William Jane and his wife, Agnes
Thomas Mankeswyll and his wife, Johanna
William Marshall and his wife, Johanna
William Millward and his wife, Johanna
John Mustard
William Pernham and his wife, Letyce
Walter Quynteyne and his wife, Agnes
William Roger and his wife [not named]
William Skinner and his wife, Alice
Roger Sowyntre and his wife, Johanna
John Sterre and his wife, Lucy
William Walter and his wife, Christine
Stephen Webbe and his wife [not named]

Revd John Helyar, the rector from 1421 to 1468, encouraged social works and promoted a harbour-improvement scheme in 1444. Stephen Davy was a prominent member of Bridport society. He and John Biddesgate were the borough's bailiffs who held court in the Guildhall in West Street. Their 'sub-bailiffs', John Smith and John Bennet, gave evidence in 1447 of 'a great dispute' between John Barber and Martin Goldsmith in which the latter was attacked in his jewellery shop in West Street. John Barber, who used the alias John Vincent, appears as a 'leche' (which derives from the Old English word 'laece' for a physician or doctor). He was accused of attacking Goldsmith with a dagger, throwing him on the ground where he 'beat him and wounded him in the head so that his life was despaired of.' The outcome of the legal proceedings is unknown.

The will of Simon Pewterer dates from this time and was preserved as binding material for a book of accounts:

In the name of God, Amen. On the twenty-first day of the month of August, in the year of our Lord 1451, I, Robert Pewterer, being of sound mind and memory, make my will in this manner.

First I bequeath my soul to God Almighty and my body to be buried in the churchyard of St Mary's, Bridport. I also bequeath to the Rector of the said church 8d. I also bequeath to the parish clerk of the said church 4d. I also bequeath to each of my four sons 4d. I also bequeath to the fabric of the church of Sarum [Salisbury Cathedral] 6d.

I also bequeath to my sister Johanna one brass pot with a dish. I also bequeath to my uncle of Wareham a sword with a dagger. I also bequeath to my said uncle

Robert a ewer with a belt. I also bequeath to my said uncle a silver belt.

And the residue of all my goods not demised I give and bequeath to my much loved wife that she may dispose of them for the good of my soul in the best way she can settle.

Bristol used to be known as Bristow, often spelt Bristowe, and one of its merchants bought property in Bridport in the early-fifteenth century. Henry Bristow – Henry from Bristol – had a large thatched house. Robert Mertok, otherwise known as Robert Lely, and his wife Alice were also from Bristol. Their properties in Bridport passed to Robert Skarlet, who was from the town, in 1451. The principal witness to the conveyance was William Canynges, a wealthy Bristol merchant, who founded St Mary Redcliffe Church in the city. Another powerful figure was Bridport merchant William Mountfort, whose family name attaches to one of the vaults and aisles in St Mary's Parish Church. In about 1433, from Walter de Vere, he bought the property of Vere's Wootton, forming the triangle between Allington, Watton and Eype, which is now known as Vearse Farm.

The town had a Confraternity of the Light, which may have been a re-naming of the Confraternity of St Nicholas, perhaps because the dedication caused confusion with its base at St Mary's Parish Church. On the other hand the surviving membership list, which is undated, has a different selection of family names in which John is the main male given name and Alice is coming into fashion, although Johanna remains paramount. Spellings, more bizarre than ever, have been standardised with those in other documents:

Robert Ailward and his wife, Johanna
John Aitkin and his wife, Margaret
Thomas Bailey and his wife, Margery
John Beese and his wife, Margaret
John Borage and his wife, Agnes
John Bowditch
Richard Brangwayn and his wife, Johanna
Alice Brasyheter
John Brody and his wife, Alice
John Bunne, butcher, and his wife, Emmota
Alice Buttes
Walter Calwell
John Chideock and his wife, Florence
John Chiltern and his wife, Avis
Ethelred
Robert Goldhopp and his wife, Avis
Johanna Hemyock
John Hore and his wife, Agnes
Edward Howdey and his wife, Edith
John Keche
Robert Locke
William Marshall and his wife, Johanna

John Maxwell and his wife, Emmota
Thomas Maxwell and his wife, Johanna
William Millward and his wife, Johanna
Rev John Mostarde
John Nithing and his wife, Edith
John Palmer, junior, and his wife, Johanna
William Parnam and his wife, Letice
John Parrok and his wife, Johanna
William Potell and his wife, Alice
John Prout and his wife, Denise
    [followed by second wife, Christine]
Walter Quitayn and his wife, Agnes
Edward Sander and his wife, Margery
Walter Saunders and his wife, Christine
Thomas Shaw and his wife, Avis
William Stour and his wife, Isabel
John Stile and his wife, Christine
Rev John Stirtill
Henry Tite and his wife, Alice
Stephen Webb and his wife, Eleanor
John White and his wife, Christine
John Wydeock
Nicholas Young and his wife, Johanna

Fraternity wardens around the middle of the fifteenth century included John Peers, William House, John Palmer and John Dunn. The wardens represented local leadership. Theirs are names that would continue to flow through the story of Bridport and west Dorset for another six and a half centuries and are still going strong.

The churchwardens' accounts for 1500 record the names of those paying for seats in the Parish Church, including Peter Long (6d.), 'the lame sailor's wife' Mrs Augustin Strong (4d.), John Baulstone (10d.), John Crandon (2d.), Mrs Walter Morne (2s.8d.), Stephen Shaw's wife's mother (1s.0d.), Mrs John Tilly (8d.), Richard Hellier (8d.) and Mrs John Flores (7d.). House rents were due for payment at Christmas (5s.8d.) and again at Easter (13s.3d.).

Payments covered a piece of bell-rope for All Hallows Day (8d.), attendance of the churchwardens (4d.), frankincense (1d.), two pounds of wax for Candlemas Day (2s.0d.), making those candles (3d.), and the 'washing of the church clothes' by Alice Sansom (8d.). There was a new cloth to prepare the high altar for Lent (3s.4d.) and a notebook was bought (1d.). The two organs were given an overhaul for Easter (2s.8d.) and the altar cloth was embellished with a fringe (1s.0d.). A new lamp-glass was needed (2d.). John Hostelry bought a piece of timber (2d.) to mend a seat (2d.).

In 1533, the tower of St Andrew's Chapel was taken down and rebuilt, and the burgesses of Bridport entered into a contract with carpenter Henry Lane from Loders:

This indenture, made the 3rd day of March, in the 24th year of the reign of King Henry the VIIIth, between William Chard the elder, and Robert Hasard the younger, bailiffs of the Borough of Bridport foresaid, with assent and consent of all the burgesses of ye same as hereafter followeth. That is to say – Robert Hasard the elder, Richard Sadler, Richard Davidge, John Bettiscombe, William Trenchard, John Orchard, Nicholas Launsham, Thomas Chard, John Preston, Isaac Preston, William Preston, William Chard junior, Richard Porlock [and] Henry Herman, of Bridport aforesaid on the one party. And Henry Lane of Loders within the county foresaid, carpenter, of the other party. Witnesseth that the said bailiffs and burgesses hath covenanted and bargained with the said Henry Lane to make and set up and take down the steeple of St Andrew Church of Bridport aforesaid and to make and set it up as good as ever it was first made and as high as it was before.

Other items in the accounts show that the rebuilt St Andrew's Chapel continued in use after the Reformation. William Lock was paid £1.3s.4d. in 1614 'for keeping the bells and half a year for the clock' with an additional two shillings for 'mending St Andrew's bell'.

The borough kept abreast of legislative reforms, particularly those relating to consumer affairs, and bought a copy of a statute respecting pins: 'Item for a proclamation for pins, 3s.' This almost gives us a precise date, as there were two such enactments on this functional item of stationery, in 1546 and 1548. The admirable Thomas Wainwright found an echo through the centuries when he wrote up this particular discovery from the records for the *Bridport News* in 1899:

The latter repealed the former which ordered that no person should put to sale any pins but only such as shall be double-headed, and have the heads soldered fast to the shank of the pin well smoothed, the shank well shaven, the point well and round filed, cauted and sharpened. Some of these pins are still to be met with amongst the Bridport documents fastening different papers together.

St Mary's Parish Church before its restoration in 1860.

Replica Elizabethan fire bucket on Thorncombe Beacon, westwards to Golden Cap.

Chapter 5
ELIZABETHAN ARCHERY, LOAVES & PUNISHMENTS

Bridport's Court Leet, the Norman successor to Saxon manorial jurisdiction, continued to supervise life in the borough. Jurors at the Michaelmas Court on 6 October 1556 heard a wide range of complaints. Fines were imposed on those accused of 'neglecting to keep clean gutters'. Others were warned to clear theirs in Church Lane, Honey Lane, Irish Lane, Killing's Lane, St Michael's Lane and South Street. An order was made for the removal of timber left lying on the highway with a penalty of ten shillings for those failing to clear it by All Saints' Day. Walter Moon was fined a shilling for breaking into the parish pound and removing his animals which had been impounded there, either for straying or unauthorised grazing.

Thomas Chard, the miller, was fined a shilling for excessive charges. Other suppliers received lesser fines, generally 4d., for similar offences. The numbers involved indicate a significant degree of friction between the town and its traders – four bakers, sixteen brewers, two glovers, six shoemakers and one tanner. A total of £2.3s.8d. was imposed in fines that day.

Down at the seaside, whatever work had been carried out to improve the estuary at Bridport Haven was failing to impress the authorities in the great Elizabethan seafaring age. In 1558 Bridport suffered the ignominy of relegation, along with even more half-hearted attempts at providing Charmouth with a harbour, and was officially designated as 'a creek' under the jurisdiction of the port of Lyme Regis.

This was the post-monastic age and with it one of Bridport's oldest pieces of architecture came from elsewhere. 'The Abbot's over-mantel', a big chunk of carved Hamstone, was found at No. 13 East Street, but is almost certainly from the Abbot's Hall at Abbotsbury which was demolished after King Henry VIII suppressed the religious houses in 1539. I caught up with it at the Chantry in South Street and later found it had been moved, in 1988, to serve as a monument to the arrival of the Safeway supermarket in the meadow opposite Palmer's Brewery. There it has been mounted outdoors to suffer rain, freezing and other erosion.

A 'stray sheet of cofferer's accounts' in the Bridport borough records for the old-style financial year from September 1574 to September 1575 was transcribed by Thomas Wainwright and gives a snapshot of Elizabethan life. William Bokerell was paid half a crown for a strong rope for the popular pursuit of bull-baiting. George Lumberd also received the same amount for the 'iron-work for the bull ring'. It had been re-paved by a man named Beavis for sixpence. *Hentzner's Itinerary* contains a contemporary account of the importance of such 'sports' in English life:

There is a place built in the form of a theatre which serves for the baiting of bulls and bears. They are fastened behind and then worried by great English bull-dogs; but not without risk to the dogs from the horns of one and the teeth of the other, and it sometimes happens that they are killed on the spot. Fresh ones are immediately supplied in the places of those that are wounded or tired.

Human punishments also provided public performances. Three shillings was spent on 'four yards of course canvas to make a coat when the women were whipped, and the man's labour that whipped them.' Thomas Wainwright, living in Barnstaple by the time he finished working his way through the Bridport archive, found a similar entry in Devon records with the additional instruction 'to whip the women till the blood came', although that may have been merciful in intent as it implies that the lashings were to stop at that point.

The spectacle, previously a punishment by custom, was given legal effect in Henry VIII's reign by the Whipping Act of 1530. This directed that vagrants were to be taken to a market town or other designated place 'and there tied at the end of a cart naked, and beaten with whips throughout such market town, or other place, till the body shall be bloody by the reason of such whipping.' The Act was partially repealed in Elizabethan times, requiring the body to be clad below the waist for punishments in public, and substituting a whipping-post for the cart.

A random leaf from the accounts of 1615 has William Knight carrying out several whippings on behalf of the borough. He was paid 4d. a time. One recipient was 'a stranger'. Another time the punishment was administered to 'a man and a woman', although both for 4d. The third set of offenders were 'two tinkers' but they may have been treated more severely as this time Knight received 8d.

One who probably deserved his whipping, in Torrington if not in Bridport, was the notorious eighteenth-century beggar and confidence trickster Bampfylde Moore Carew from Bickleigh, near Tiverton, who pretended to be a mariner shipwrecked on the Chesil Beach. While travelling between Powderham and Chudleigh, he was confronted by a 'Mrs Oxenham who told him she would have taken him to be Bampfydle Moore Carew, but that she knew he was transported.' Carew instantly thought of Bridport and Tom Jones, the character of Henry Fielding's novel on which he modelled himself:

Bampfylde was not disconcerted at this, but readily told her, with great composure, that his name was Thomas Jones, belonging to Bridport, in Dorsetshire. The ladies gave him each a shilling, and then bid him go into the house, where he had victuals set before him, and before he went away the lady sent him a fine Holland shirt; being thus equipped, he enquires out the churchwardens of the parish, and by the same story gets a crown of them.

For lesser offences there was a cucking-stool, in which 'scolding women' were wheeled to 'a muddy and malodorous pond or a stream' and ducked in the water, and the stocks, for the restraint and ridicule of male 'drunkards and vagabonds'. These two 'instruments of correction' took Bridport carpenter William Locke three days to repair at a cost of 3s.4d. Thomas Wainwright particularly enjoyed his discovery of the entry for the cucking-stool and quoted the contemporary poet Richard West:

No brawling wives, no furious wenches,
No fire so hot but water quenches.

There was also a lock-up called the 'scowl-house'. More seriously, six shillings were paid to Reynold Gage for the upkeep of male prisoners from Bridport who were held in prison at Dorchester Castle.

Fourteen quarts of wine for a civil occasion in 1575 cost 9s.4d. This may well have been linked to the five shillings for the 'minstrels at May Day' which in pre-Puritan times was the great outdoor festival of the year. For public consumption, there was Robin Hood Ale – £10 worth of which was brewed sold during the May games – which took its name from the 'Robin' of the day who presided over the event as the Lord of the May. He had his Maid Marian, his faithful mistress, as the Lady of the May. Bishop Hugh Latimer mentioned this custom in a sermon he preached before Henry VI:

Coming to a certain town on a holiday to preach, I found the church door fast locked. I tarried there for half-an-hour and more, and at last the key was found, and one of the parish comes to me and says, 'Sir, this is a busy day with us, we cannot hear you; it is Robin Hood's day; the parish are gone abroad to gather for Robin Hood; I pray you let [prevent] them not.' I was

Hamstone over-mantel, apparently from Abbotsbury Abbey, now beside the Safeway supermarket.

fain, therefore, to give place to Robin Hood; I thought my rochet [bishop's vestment] *would have been regarded, but it would not serve; it was fain to give place to Robin Hood's men.*

William Kethe, preaching at Blandford in 1570, denounced the 'debauchery' that had spread from this and other festivals to Sundays in general. He blamed the provision of 'Church Ales' for causing the 'holy day' to degenerate into what 'the multitude call their revelling day, which day is spent in bull-baitings, bear-baitings, bowlings, dicing, carding, dancings, drunkenness' and other vices. The result was gallivanting, leaving gentlemen unable to 'keep their servants from lying out of their own houses the same Sabbath day at night.'

Ordinary daily games included handball, traditionally against the church walls (at Eton the chapel wall) in the days when such buildings were treated as functional rather than sacrosanct. This developed into the playing of fives. Its name came from the finger-work required in handling the ball and survives in the expression 'a bunch of fives' for a fighting fist. The town's fives court was built beyond South Bridge, on the west side of the road midway between the Old Brewery and the junction with Flood Lane. The cricket pitch succeeded it, further west, on the other side of the River Brit and the lane leading to Port Mill.

An Elizabethan shilling's worth of bell-ringing celebrated each anniversary of 'the Queen majesty's reign'. The big civil meeting of the year was the Cofferers' Supper early in October, at which the previous year's accounts were approved and the budget discussed for the year ahead. Thresher the ale-maker was paid 8d. for beer but the burgesses and officials preferred their wine, which came to a total of £1.5s.2d. for what must have been a very happy evening. Hogs' heads dominated the feast on the tables – two pigs cost 3s.1d. – and there was also veal (14d.), four capons (3s.6d.), and a 'sheep and a half, 8s'. Rabbit, introduced in Norman warrens, remained a relative delicacy at a shilling for 'one couple of conies'. Miscellaneous victuals and the catering, by Alice Copper, came to 3s.4d. Robert Hoade had delivered 'two loaves of sugar' for 8d., by boat from Lyme Regis. These were given as presents to two of the town's benefactors. One went to the lord of the manor at Hooke and Henry Hody of Pilsdon Manor who had given the town £50, which was invested in buying 'three closes' of pasture at Broad Oak in the Marshwood Vale.

An item to Thomas Vincent, for 1s.4d. 'for fetching the women at Melbury', shows the emergence of the new power base for the area, at Melbury House, from where the Strangways family were in the process of becoming the new lords of most of West Dorset after buying the lands of the former Abbotsbury Abbey. A man named Bryant rebuilt the archery butts in Bridport, over the winter of 1574, for 2s.4d. They received heavy use and another two shillings were spent on 'mending the butts' in the summer. Pitfield or Pitfold had re-laid the surrounding turf – 'three loads' – for three shillings. The butts were erected on rising ground beyond the River Brit on the west side of St Mary's Church where the memory is preserved by Arrow Field at Skilling.

Encouragement of archery was a far cry from Edward III's lament that the national skill was being lost to 'useless and unlawful games'. It was also a mark of troubled times and the fact that Bridport was on England's historic front line. Henry VIII required that every man 'exercised' at the butts and kept a bow and arrows, ready for use, at home. Queen Elizabeth and her ministers were maintaining their guard and the arrow kept its cutting edge long into the age of gunpowder. English archers at the Battle of Crecy in 1346 unleashed fusillades of weaponry that remained unequalled until the American Civil War.

For their protection in warfare, the young Bridport archers were required to train in 'the town corslet' – light sleeveless armour – in exercises which took place in the ancient Iron-Age earthworks of Eggardon Hill between Askerswell and Powerstock. The cost to the borough purse was a reasonable 8d., unless it was the occasion on which a shilling was 'paid to the drummer for his pains in beating the drum.' In preparation for the outing to Eggardon the corslet was provided with 'a new cap' by John Williams for 10d. Thomas Chard covered it with fustian. Afterwards, more repairs were needed, as John Cutler was paid 2s.3d. 'for dressing the town armour'. Thomas Abbot charged 10d. for 'powder and a match' and as an afterthought the ledger has an entry for 9d. 'for a leather bag to put the bullets in'.

Pitfield, who re-laid the turf at the archery butts, also supplied the bailiffs with 'a piece of timber' for 1s.6d. The wood seems to have been used by Batten the carpenter for 'mending the flesh shambles', which was the town's meat market. Bagge the blacksmith made a new key for 4d. Later, the fish shambles needed a new plank, for 9d.

St Michael's Chantry still occurs in the accounts after the reign of Henry III, although in a secular role, as Munden's Court. St Andrew's Church, in the centre of the town, remained in use. Its new bell-rope cost 1s.6d. and it also had a clock, which required a yard of wire, for a penny. Weights and measures were a civic concern with the new post for the yard-arm costing 1s.8d., plus 6d. for carpenters to erect it, and Edward Bellamy supplied its rope for 5d.

In the reign of Queen Elizabeth or earlier the 'common beam and weights' – for weighing goods and products – were leased to Morgan Moon for 21 years. He charged authorised fees, which he retained, and paid the borough bailiffs a rent of £4 per annum. Bridport was already a rope-making town and this was the only public weighing facility in the area.

Each year, on Michaelmas Day, Morgan Moon was required to hand the bailiffs a book listing all the people that had 'hemp growing within five miles of Bridport' and the quantities from each, with the values, that he had weighed. The five-mile hinterland was a statutory area, defined and protected by legislation in the reign of Henry VIII in 1530. This required that all hemp grown there and products made from it had to be sold through the market at Bridport 'upon pain of forfeiture of the said cables, halsers, ropes, traces, halters and other tackle made and to be made contrary to the form and effect of this statute.'

The burgesses also acted as the highway authority, maintaining roads and bridges, with Thomas Vincent being paid 2d. for 'taking up the stones out of the water' which had fallen into the River Asker from East Bridge. An earlier account details the rebuilding of the West Bridge, over the River Brit, in 1555. East and west must have been muddled from time immemorial as the West Bridge tended to be described as 'ye town to Charmouth bridge' in order to avoid confusion. Its 'pavier' was paid five shillings 'for the pitching of the one half', following which Stephen Austen and his brother were paid 6s.8d. to rebuild the parapet walling. The pavier was a visiting craftsman who had to be looked after, with 5d. being spent on 'supper at his first coming' and sixpence 'paid for another pavier's dinner that was sent for from Chard.' Going there – ten miles away in the next county – would be noteworthy for a modern take-away, so perhaps the meal was supplied by Thomas or William Chard of Bridport.

Aggregates were needed for making roads. As ever, using the very method still being carried out by horses until the Second World War, the beach at West Bay provided free sand and shingle. All it cost in 1575 was 3d. a time 'for a man and a horse to go to the seaside to fetch sand.'

The town limits were treated with respect, as 'Beating the Bounds' perambulations took place on Rogation Day when young boys received a symbolic stroke of the cane – as they bent over boundary stones – to impress upon them that freedom of movement stopped at this point and it was potentially dangerous to stray into the next parish, where they may be considered intruders. Bridport borough was always 'hard against its limits' and this caused encroachments.

One such, by Henry Wade in 1594, resulted in a forfeit of £1.10s. and a fine of two shillings for not 'plucking down a wall and setting up a gate in the way of perambulation.' His was a continuing offence with a further penalty of losing another £2 for failing to provide the gate 'by the feast of the Annunciation of the Blessed Virgin Mary.' The jurors determining this and the following misdemeanours were a panel of four, namely Arthur Meynard, Richard Hounsell, William Parker and George Framick.

There is another forfeit – or 'pain' as they called it – of £1 from Peter Long who failed to build 'a mantel or chimney' around his domestic hearth, to the 'great danger of himself and his neighbours' at a time when fire was the greatest urban peril. He was also fined 6s.8d. and warned that there would be an additional 'pain' of £2 if the work was not done by All Saints' Day. A similar offence by Walter George had already cost him a £3 forfeit, plus a fine of 10s., with the prospect of losing another £4. William Elworth faced a subpoena of £1 if he failed 'to make a sufficient mantel in his kitchen or brewhouse for avoiding the danger of fire.'

Fire precautions were also behind this public requirement:

It is further ordered that every inhabitant within this borough shall set forth water at his door within one hour after warning thereof given by the Serjeant and so continue it there during such time as it shall seem good to the bailiffs of this town under the pain for everyone so offending at every time, 3s 4d.

Alice Carhampton was another who had to build a fireplace. She also 'forfeited a pain of 10s for not amending her hedge' which had encroached upon the highway and was 'sunk' into St Michael's Lane. She had also neglected to scour 'a ditch against the same lane being hurtful to the way there.' The fine was 2s., with another forfeit of 13s.4d. being levied for failure to put matters right by Christmas Day, which is described as 'the feast of the birth of our Lord God'.

All the residents in Pound Lane – where stray animals were impounded and released for a fee – came into the penalty zone for failing 'to scour their gutters and ditches in the east side of South Street.' The same applied to 'the house of Watercombe' and each household faced a 'subpoena' of 3s.4d. to do the work by All Saints' Day. Similar orders were given in East Street and South Street and in Church Lane, near St Andrew's Church, where 'soil and earth' had blocked the ditches that functioned as open drains. Licensing laws were also being enforced with 'tippling' at alehouses being brought under control:

All those that keep tippling within this borough shall set out an ale stake or ale pole during such time as they have drink to sell under the pain to forfeit for every person so offending by the space of one week at one time or several times, 3s 4d.

Also it is further ordered that every person within this borough which keepeth tippling in his house shall during all such time as he selleth drink to be drunk within his house shall also sell drink to be drunk out of his or their house, every person keeping one gallon for his own use, under the pain for every person offending to the contrary for every time, 1s 0d.

The accusation that Robert Keat 'had flesh dressed and eaten in his house' at Michaelmas, on Saturday 28 September 1594, was not regarded as serious enough for a fine. Meat was not allowed on the menu on 'prohibited days' in the Church calendar. Neither was gaming on that feast day, in the form of 'unlawful play, viz at tables in his house', resulting in Thomas Gollop being fined 10s. Public house landlord Alexander Primrose was required to provide two sureties of £5 each:

The condition of this present obligation is such that if the above bounden Alexander Primrose do by the space of one whole year next ensuing the date hereof keep good order and honest rule in his house not suffering any unlawful games there to be used, nor to sell any ale, beer, bread or other victuals but such as is wholesome for man's body nor do suffer any persons or person to play, banquet or recreate him or themselves in this house during the time of God's divine service upon the Sabbath and holy days, and also do at all times during the said term keep one sufficient bed with decent furniture for the lodging of the Queen majesty's subjects lawfully repairing to the town, not refusing to lodge any to him sent by the Bailiffs or Constables of the said town of Bridport for the time being without reasonable cause, giving notice likewise to the said officers of all suspected persons before their departure, that then this present obligation be void or else to stand in its full force and effect.

Thomas Wainwright's favourite theory about borough treasurer Richard Tiggin, having transcribed entries from his cofferer's accounts from 1578 through to 1597, was that William Shakespeare's travelling Company of Actors had visited Bath and Bristol and 'took Bridport on the way'. Wainwright detailed the prodigious quantities of 'sack and claret' bought by Tiggin who emerges as 'a decidedly convivial individual'. A total of £6.7s.3$^1/_2$d. had been spent on feasting during one period in which the only instance of charity in Bridport was 'Three dozen of bread for the poor, 3s'. Wainwright thought that 'the fame of Richard Tiggin's lavish expenditure' over those two decades had reached the dramatist and inspired lines at the end of act two, scene four of the play *King Henry the Fourth*. Published in 1598, they read:

Item, sack, two gallons, 5s 8d.
Item anchovies and sack after supper, 2s 6d.
Item bread a half-penny.
(Prince Henry) 'O monstrous! but one half-penny worth of bread to this intolerable deal of sack!'

Shingle gathering for building materials, below East Cliff in 1920. The man leaning on the shovel is Mr Fred Tuck who worked for Norman Goods & Son in West Bay all his life after leaving the Army at the end of the First World War.

37

Right: *Cobbled drive into the Greyhound Hotel, from coaching days, looking northwards across East Street to the old George Inn.*

Below: *'Beach, late Dr Roberts' (left) as the pharmacy on the site of the old George Hotel described itself, in a view eastwards along the north side of East Street in 1895.*

Chapter 6
KINGS, PLAGUE & WAR

In 1620 the town's principal ropers were John Akerman, John Elliot, Giles Hounsell, Richard Hounsell, Thomas Morris, William Morris, John Prince, John Russell and Henry Stone.

The George public house, Bridport's best-known hostelry for several centuries, stood opposite the Town Hall on the north side of East Street in premises that became Beach the Chemists. The George then moved a short distance along the street. Its famous visitor, to the original building in 1626, was the young King Charles I (1600–49).

The George needed all the business it could get that year as 'the sickness' also arrived in Bridport and left 80 dead in four months. In his county history, John Hutchins gives the year as 1623 but the town's parish register shows this is an error. (It also tells us that the average death toll in Bridport for a third of a year was normally less than 14). Bailiffs and burgesses appealed to the privy council for overdue taxation to be converted into a loan in November 1626. The justices of the county of Dorset, sitting in Dorchester, endorsed this request to alleviate 'the destitution to which their town had been reduced by a twenty weeks' visitation of the plague', and prayed they might be 'excused the present payment of the amount subscribed'.

Oliver Cromwell nearly had Charles II captured in Bridport

The bailiffs also sent a quart of wine to each of the town's Members of Parliament, brothers Sir William Strode and Sir Richard Strode of Parnham House, Beaminster, and Newenham Abbey, at Axminster. The bailiffs and 12 burgesses of Bridport 'would have elected Mr Clarke' but having 'passed their promise to Sir Lewis Dive' they received a letter from the Duke of Buckingham who 'recommended' them to return Sir Richard Strode in his place. This they duly did. It may not have been democracy but in the event it turned into the sensible application of practical politics.

Sir William Strode was to become one of King Charles' most determined enemies. Having been imprisoned from 1629 to 1640 he became one of the famous 'five members' impeached by the King in 1642, triggering the Civil War.

Victims of the plague included two members of each of the families of Abbott, Bishop, Dennette, Evans, Gillett, Jones, Elmond Locke, Robert Locke, Long, Shewer, Shoote, Vinson and Whitehead. Three died in each of the Pratt and Smyth families. Four were taken from Robert Miller's middle-class household. The highly contagious nature of the disease is shown by the entries for the Lumbard family. Five children died – Charity, Jane, Lazarus, Peter and Thomas – with their father, George Lumbard, following them. All six were buried over three days at the end of August.

Robert Keat and his family were entirely wiped out. Daughter Edith was buried on 9 September. Son Henry followed on the 11th; wife Elizabeth on the 17th; Robert himself and son Nathaniel on the 24th; and son Philip on the 25th.

The outbreak of the plague was declared over with the death of Amie Shoote who was buried on 31 October 1626. That, however, was immediately disputed. Her entry in the parish register carries the words 'That was the last that died of the plague', to which someone added: 'This is a lie.'

Bridport's church rate for 1641–62, that pivotal year of English history, totalled £10.4s.6d. and the sums collected by churchwardens John Hallett and Alexander Waring give a remarkable insight into the town's householders and their relative wealth. As Thomas Wainwright realised, this 'is a detail of local history which few boroughs in England could furnish.' Some would come to grief in the forthcoming Civil War.

BRIDPORT'S CHURCH RATE FOR 1641–62

(Spellings have been standardised where there is other evidence available.)

Amie Abbott, widow – 0s.4d.
Stephen Akerman – 1s.0d.
William Akerman – 2s.0d.
Mrs Adams, widow – 0s.4d.
Mrs Alford, widow – 0s.6d.
William Alford – 1s.0d.
Christopher Bagge, gentleman – 2s.0d.
Richard Bagge – 1s.0d.
Richard Baggott – 2s.0d.
Henry Balston – 1s.0d.
Simon Balston – 1s.0d.
William Balston – 2s.0d.
Walter Bailey – 2s.0d.
John Bennett – 0s.8d.
Andrew Bettiscombe – 2s.0d.
John Bishop – 3s.0d.
Joseph Bishop – 2s.0d.
Mrs Bishop, widow – 0s.6d.
Thomas Bishop, gentleman – 3s.0d.
William Bishop – 1s.0d.
Morgan Boul – 2s.0d.
Robert Boyce – 0s.6d.
John Boyce – 0s.8d.
Robert Bragge – 0s.6d.
Lionel Brown – 2s.0d.
Nicholas Brown – 2s.0d.
James Brix – 1s.0d.
Mrs Brix, widow – 0s.6d.
Edward Bryant – 0s.6d.
Thomas Carter – 1s.0d.
Nicholas Caswell – 8d.
John Chard, gentleman – 3s.0d.
John Chard [second entry] – 2s.0d.
Angel Churchill – 2s.0d.
John Colfox – 0s.4d.
Lazarus Colfox – 1s.0d.
Stephen Colfox, gentleman – 2s.0d.
William Colfox – 2s.0d.
William Colfox [second entry] – 4d.
William Cooper – 1s.0d.
William Courtney – 6d.
John Cousens – 2s.0d.
John Derby – 2s.0d.
John Douch – 1s.0d.
William Douch – 1s.0d.

William Duck – 0s.8d.
Mrs Fulbrook, widow – 1s.0d.
John Fooks – 1s.0d.
Richard George – 1s.0d.
Richard Gibbs, gentleman – 2s.0d.
Lawrence Gollop – 2s.0d.
Robert Gollop – 0s.6d.
John Gost – 2s.0d.
John Gould – 0s.8d.
Gilbert Grey, gentleman – 2s.0d.
Thomas Gully – 1s.0d.
John Hallett – 2s.0d.
Joseph Hallett – 1s.0d.
Thomas Hallett – 0s.6d.
Morgan Hansford – 0s.8d.
George Hardy – 2s.0d.
Thomas Hardy – 2s.0d.
Robert Harris – 1s.0d.
William Harris – 0s.6d.
John Hill – 1s.6d.
Robert Hill – 1s.8d.
William Holway – 1s.0d.
John Hossard – 0s.6d.
John Hounsell – 0s.4d.
Giles Hounsell – 2s.0d.
Mrs James, widow – 0s.6d.
Richard Knight – 0s.6d.
Henry Lacke – 0s.4d.
Robert Lawrence – 0s.6d.
John Lea, gentleman – 4s.0d.
Harvey Lea – 1s.0d.
Paul Lovelace – 1s.0d.
Old Luther – 1s.0d.
Henry Mabb – 1s.0d.
Joan Man, widow – 0s.6d.
Thomas Mansel, gentleman – 1s.0d.
William Marshall, gentleman – 6s.0d.
Samuel Mather – 3s.0d.
Antony Morris – 0s.6d.
William Morris – 2s.0d.
Matthew Morton – 0s.6d.
William Munden – 0s.6d.
Bartholomew Oram – 0s.6d.
Mrs Orchard, widow – 0s.6d.
Thomas Osborne – 2s.0d.
Robert Panchon – 0s.8d
William Panchon – 1s.0d.
Peter Parkend – 0s.4d.

Alexander Parker – 0s.6d.
Nathaniel Payne – 1s.0d.
Richard Payne – 3s.0d.
John Peach – 0s.6d.
George Petrick – 0s.6d.
Roger Phillips – 0s.6d.
Edward Pillen – 0s.6d.
John Pitfold – 1s.0d.
Mrs Pitt, widow – 1s.0d.
Henry Plucknett, gentleman – 2s.0d.
John Prince – 2s.0d.
Lionel Prince – 0s.4d.
Robert Prince – 0s.8d.
Francis Puckett – 1s.0d.
John Punkfield – 0s.6d.
Philip Rendall – 0s.4d.
Robert Rogers – 1s.0d.
John Rowsell – 0s.6d.
John Russell – 1s.0d.
John Smith – 1s.0d.
Abraham Sprake – 1s.0d.
Richard Sprake – 0s.6d.
John Stevens – 0s.8d.
Henry Stone – 1s.0d.
Stephen Strong – 0s.6d.
Mrs Symes, widow – 1s.0d.
Josias Swasy – 0s.6d.
Mrs Swasy, widow – 2s.0d.
Mrs Thresher, widow – 0s.8d.
Richard Tuck – 1s.0d.
Mrs Wakley, widow – 1s.0d.
Robert Walkey – 0s.6d.
Alexander Waring – 2s.0d.
Alexander Way – 0s.6d.
Bailey [Bailiff] James Way, gentleman – 3s.0d.
John Way – 3s.0d.
Nicholas Way – 2s.0d.
Robert Way – 0s.6d.
William Way, gentleman – 3s.0d.
Thomas Welsh – 1s.0d.
Simon Willis – 0s.0d. [zero entry]
John Wood – 0s.6d.
Nicholas Wood – 1s.0d.
William Woodcock –1s.0d.
Thomas Woolveton – 0s.6d.
John Wrixon – 0s.6d.
John Wyatt – 1s.0d.

⚜ BRIDPORT'S CHURCH RATE DISTRIBUTION FOR 1642 ⚜

This list, certified correct by John Bishop and James Way, is accompanied by an equally rare document naming the recipients of parish largesse which shows that then as now 'the poor are always with us'. As with the previous list, some of the names are still to be found in the town, and I have standardised a few of the spellings. The distribution was made on 27 January 1642:

Lower Almshouse inhabitants (7) at 4d. apiece –
    2s.4d.
Upper Almshouse inhabitants (8) at 2d. each – 1s.4d.
Esekia Bailie – 0s.3d.
William Ball – 0s.3d.
Joan Balston – 1s.0d.
William Balson – 0s.6d.
Jane Bernard – 0s.6d.
Christopher Brinisom's wife – 0s.2d.
Widow Brown – 0s.2d.
Richard Buckerell – 0s.2d.
Robert Buckerell – 0s.2d.
Jane Burnard – 0s.8d.
Morgan Butt – 0s.3d.
Richard Butt – 0s.3d.
Widow Coleman – 0s.3d.
Edward Collier – 0s.3d.
Cope's wife – 0s.2d.
Widow Cunidean – 0s.2d.
Amie Davy – 0s.2d.
William Davis' wife – 0s.4d.
Hannah Doderidge – 0s.6d.
Joan Doderidge – 0s.2d.
William Doderidge – 0s.6d.
William Dollen – 0s.6d.
William Dollinge – 0s.6d.
William Eel – 0s.6d.
John Elliott – 0s.3d.
Henry Ersby's wife – 0s.4d.
Widow Evans – 0s.4d.
Richard Farr, senior – 0s.3d.
Richard Fox – 0s.3d.
Widow George, senior – 0s.3d.
John Gilbert, senior – 0s.3d.
John Giles – 0s.4d.
Gillingham's wife – 0s.4d.
Widow Hakes, senior – 0s.2d.
Hall's children – 0s.4d.
Ann Hearn, widow – 0s.2d.
Alice Hill – 0s.2d.
William Hodder – 0s.9d.
Nicholas Horsford, for the sick – 1s.0d.
Widow Hoskin – 0s.6d.
Henry Huniborn – 0s.4d.
Young Huniborn that is lame – 0s.3d.
Gillim James's wife – 0s.4d.

Robert Jefferys – 0s.6d.
Widow Jones – 0s.4d.
Widow Jones, senior – 0s.3d.
Austis Keech – 0s.2d.
Thomas Knight – 0s.3d.
Old Lake – 0s.6d.
Edmond Locke – 0s.2d.
Old Locke – 0s.3d.
Widow Lupton – 0s.6d.
Richard Lush, senior – 0s.3d.
Widow Lyde – 0s.1d.
Abigail Mabb – 0s.2d.
Dorothy Mabb – 0s.3d.
Widow Mallett – 0s.4d.
Marsh's wife – 0s.2d.
Margaret Mitchell – 0s.4d.
Widow Mitchell – 0s.2d.
Elizabeth Mogeridge – 0s.2d.
Ann Morris – 0s.2d.
John Northover – 0s.4d.
Henry Parker – 0s.6d.
Henry Parker [separate entry] – 0s.4d.
Henry Parker, senior – 0s.6d.
Pheper – 0s.3d.
Widow Poell – 0s.2d.
Widow Powell – 0s.4d.
Nicholas Rodney – 0s.6d.
Old Rodney – 0s.6d.
John Rouswell – 0s.3d.
Stephen Sanders – 0s.4d.
Christopher Saser – 0s.4d.
John Shewer's wife – 0s.4d.
Widow Shorto – 0s.3d.
Old Shut's wife – 0s.3d.
Old Stevens – 0s.2d.
Styles's wife – 0s.2d.
Widow Touchen – 0s.6d.
Widow Turner – 0s.6d.
Widow Wade – 0s.4d.
John Watercomb – 0s.4d.
Mary Webber – 0s.2d.
Widow Welch – 0s.6d.
Grace White – 0s.3d.
White's four children – 0s.4d.
Widow White, senior – 0s.2d.
Old Wood's wife – 0s.2d.

Left: *The old George Inn as a charity shop, seen from the south, in 1997.*

Right: *Broadwindsor plaque where Charles II slept after his narrow escape from Bridport.*

Below: *Charles I on his charger.*

Left: *Charles II whose escape into exile nearly ended at Bridport in September 1651.*

Defeated at the Battle of Worcester, where he fled from the vicinity of St Martin's Gate, Worcester, on the evening of 3 September 1651, vanquished monarch Charles II embarked on one of history's great escapes. The fate of the 'Merry Monarch' and the future of the three kingdoms of these islands 'hung literally on a thread' for three eventful September weeks as he crossed the country and made his way along the Channel coast. History's 'great escape' saw him disguised as a girl servant and hiding in an oak tree – spawning a forest of Royal Oak pub names – and secreted in priest holes, such as that in the Wyndham family's Trent Manor on the borders of Somerset and Dorset.

From there he crossed West Dorset, via Broadwinsor on 22 September, but had to abort his plan to find a boat at Charmouth, waiting in vain at the old Queen's Head until a lookout reported that the vessel they had commissioned had failed to arrive from Lyme Regis. Fearful of attracting suspicion, and afraid their plans had unravelled, they moved eastwards to Bridport where the King and Miss Juliana Conningsby dined in the old George Inn which had received his father in 1626. Charles II dictated the story to Samuel Pepys:

Thomas Fuller of Broadwinsor's History of the Worthies of England.

Just as we came into the town I could see the streets full of red-coats, Cromwell's soldiers, being a regiment of Colonel Haynes, viz fifteen hundred men going to embark to take Jersey, at which Frank Wyndham was much startled and asked me what I would do. I told him impudently that we must go into the best inn in town... so we rode impudently into the best inn in the place.

Up the road, however, his other companion, Lord Wilmot, saw or heard that Cromwell's soldiers were coming in pursuit from both directions. He dashed to the George Inn to impart this 'alarming intelligence' and the royal party rode eastwards up Dorchester Road. At the time they decided to divert inland, northwards into Lee Lane, which is opposite the present-day Bridport Cemetery. From here they escaped into the narrow leafy lanes of the Marshwood Vale, towards the George Inn at Broadwinsor.

The route is commemorated beside the Dorchester Road junction with a rough-hewn block of Bothenhampton stone erected by Alexander Meyrick Broadley on the anniversary in 1901. The last leg of the royal route was then eastwards where they probably passed the Royal Oak in Long Street at Cerne Abbas

and a similar claim can be made for the Royal Oak Inn, West Street, Bere Regis. His flight and plight ended at Shoreham, aboard the *Surprise*, which took him to exile in France. The inscription on the Lee Lane stone is rounded off with a quotation from *The Worthies of England* by Broadwinsor parson Thomas Fuller:

King Charles II
escaped capture through this lane
Sept XXII, MDCLI
'When midst your fiercest foes on every side
For your escape God did a lane provide.'
Erected Sept XXIII, MDCCCCI

The ceremony found a local connection with the event. Miss Lane-Browne, from Walditch, told a reporter from *The Tatler* that she was a descendant 'of the same old Staffordshire family as Jane Lane, whose devotion enabled the fugitive prince to reach the Wyndhams' house at Trent in safety.'

The news spread through Bridport on 18 February 1653 of a major Naval action unfolding in the Channel. People stood listening and watching from the cliffs at West Bay, as what was nearly a disaster for both the English and Dutch fleets unfolded at the eastern end of Lyme Bay, off Portland.

Admiral Robert Blake was lucky to escape with his life, and Maarten Harpertszoon Tromp was fortunate to survive with the bulk of his ships. Blake had blundered by taking his red squadron alone to intercept Tromp's full fleet. The English flagship *Triump* (sic) was heavily engaged, with the loss of the captain, and Blake was severely wounded. Not until the afternoon did Vice-Admiral Sir William Penn arrive with the blue and white squadrons of the English fleet to make an even battle. By the next morning the ships were off St Catherine's Point, Isle of Wight, and Tromp escaped up-Channel. Five of his warships had been sunk and four captured, and 40 merchant ships were also lost, but the main Dutch fleet survived to fight again.

On 20 June 1653 a meteorological phenomenon was regarded with superstitious awe. From a deep black cloud 'it rained warm blood' on the Dorset coast, supposedly from the sea where the British and Dutch fleets fought in the Channel, the blood having somehow been sucked into the sky. Similar red rain fell in the Isle of Wight in 1176. The colour and the fact that the rain in 1653 was warm suggest that the

Lee Lane, along which King Charles II escaped, remains narrow.

event was caused by Saharan dust being blown high into the sky; grey deposits in cold rain would be the fallout of ash from a volcanic eruption.

King Charles II, last seen incognito in Bridport, returned to London in triumph on 29 May 1660 after Puritan republicanism had died with Oliver Cromwell. In the aftermath of the Restoration, the postwar sequesters for Dorset – dealing with land confiscation penalties after 1660 – were John Crabb, John Bishop and Nicholas Samson, all of whom had Bridport associations. A new name arrived in the town around 1665 when felt-maker Samuel Gundry was recorded as living in a West Street house which his father, John Gundry, had leased from the town's almshouse charity.

Dr Thomas Fuller, rector of Broadwindsor, writing in his *History of the Worthies of England* which was published posthumously in 1662, recorded the proverb for which Bridport was synonymous for most of the millennium: 'Stabbed with a Bridport dagger; that is, hanged, or executed at the gallows.' His explanation was that much, if not most, hemp in the region – 'for the quantity of ground' – grows around Bridport.

And hence it is, that there is an ancient Statute (though now disused and neglected) that the cable ropes for the

Navy Royal were to be made thereabouts, as affording the best tackling for that purpose.

Such rope found its way into the kit of the common hangman.

It is a reminder of the severity of old-fashioned winters that the Christmas news at Bridport in 1684 was that five persons from nearby villages had died at Fleet, a coastal hamlet behind the Chesil Beach. They died from exposure after trying to leave Weymouth for home. They were caught in 'a tremendous storm'.

After the upheavals of Civil War, turmoil threatened to return with the death of Charles II on 6 February 1685 and the passing of the crown to James Stuart, Duke of York, the second son of Charles I and Henrietta Maria. His Catholic beliefs and tendency to override Parliament stirred Protestant opponents into persuading and propelling James Scott, Duke of Monmouth – illegitimate son of Charles II – into open rebellion to seize his uncle's crown. He landed at Lyme Regis from a Dutch ship on 11 June 1685 and raised his standard.

The first skirmish in what turned out to be a short campaign took place in Bridport on 14 June 1685. Officers of the Dorset Militia had based themselves in the Bull Inn on East Street. Approaching from the west, Colonel Thomas Venner led the Red Regiment of rebel cavalry through the town. Shots were fired at them from windows at the hostelry. Monmouth's men then broke down its doors but several lives were lost in the process, including those of Dorset gentlemen Edward Coker of Mappowder and Wadham Strangways of Abbotsbury, who were killed by Colonel Venner. Two of the King's men managed to escape, one into an attic and the other hiding in a plot of kidney beans. A shot from the dark wounded Colonel Venner in the stomach, following which he gave the order to retreat and Lord Grey's supporting horsemen also bolted, westwards to Charmouth, at the sound of gunfire. Major Nathaniel Wade restored discipline and prepared to

The Bull Hotel in East Street, scene of the shoot-out during the Monmouth Rebellion.

hold West Bridge, over the River Brit, with his foot-soldiers. The Dorset Militia then contented themselves with an arms-length exchange of insults as Monmouth's men went off in the other direction.

The 3,000 poorly-armed men he led from Lyme Regis to Axminster went on to taste the triumph of walk-overs at Taunton and Bridgwater. Leadership faltered and they balked at the opportunity of taking Bristol – then Britain's second city – and retreated back into the marshy middle of Somerset. Here they were routed in the Battle of Sedgemoor on 6 July 1685. Rebels who escaped the battlefield faced judicial retaliation and revenge as Baron George Jeffreys, the Lord Chief Justice, toured the courts of the Western circuit.

Among those executed by Judge Jeffreys during his Bloody Assize was William Lancaster of Bridport. It is said that, just before he was hanged, he prayed for the Duke of Monmouth, 'who he supposed to be at that time living, notwithstanding the general belief of his death.'

The beheading of Monmouth for treason, on the scaffold beside the Tower of London, had already taken place. The future of James II remained far from secure as 'plotters and statesmen' enraged his son-in-law, Prince William of Orange, to secure his wife's rights to the throne as the elder daughter of James II. He issued a proclamation and eventually landed in England, at Brixham, on 5 November 1688. The Glorious Revolution was under way, to general acclamation, and passed through Crewkerne and Beaminster en route to Sherborne Castle and Westminster.

Local progress met no military opposition but was hampered by poisoned beef pies, ale and cider, allegedly provided by the Strode family from Parnham House, which caused the death of a soldier by the time they arrived in Yetminster. Revd John Whitte reported the incident in *An Exact Diary of the late Expedition of his Illustrious Highness the Prince of Orange*:

The Surgeon, having heard of their evil preparations, prepared immediately an antidote, and gave directions what they must do; whereupon they presently began to vomit, and after some time they waxed a little better, and made shift to get to the wagons which carried sick soldiers, and were under the Surgeon-Major's hand for some time. At the very next town, called Yetminster, one soldier died in the night, and none could tell what was the matter with him, being very well when he went to bed, which soldier I buried there according to our liturgy. The others that were poisoned, were strangely altered, their eyes being swelled after an odd manner.

On a very different medical note, a year later on 29 December 1689, the distinguished physician Thomas Sydenham of Wynford Eagle, north-east of Bridport,

died at his London house, in Pall Mall. He had suffered severely from calculus – a hard stony deposit in his organs. His works contain for the first time adequate descriptions of chronic bronchitis, influenza, chorea, scarlet fever, measles and hysteria, as well as the best account of the gout, from which he had suffered since 1649. He noted the periodic and varying occurrences of epidemic diseases and popularised the cooling method for the relief of the smallpox, as well as the use of bark in agues, which were shivering fevers.

By the time of Prince William's ousting of James II, the power base of Bridport's Royalists had already been undermined, having been unwittingly prejudiced by measures of James II in 1687, which enabled their replacement by a corporation run by dissenters. Bailiffs John Cousens and John Way were supported by burgesses Joseph Brown, Daniel Bull, Robert Bull, John Golding, Samuel Gundry, George Hardy and Thomas Way. In 1690, their principal opponent, Robert Hounsell, was disfranchised 'for abuses in breaking up the town coffer'.

'For your escape God did a lane provide,' saving Charles II in 1651, commemorated beside Lee Lane with this stone in 1901.

The Friend's Meeting House (right) and Daniel Taylor's Almshouse, on the east side of South Street, in 1930.

Right: *The 1814-dated pump, with waterproof plants, in the courtyard of the Friends Meeting House in 1996.*

Below: *J.M.W. Turner's dramatic print of 'Bridport, Dorsetshire' featuring a shipwreck off West Cliff, looking eastwards to East Cliff and Burton Cliff.*

Chapter 7

DISSIDENTS, WRECKERS & THE NEW WEST BAY

Edmund Gibson, in the first English translation of William Camden's *Britannia* in 1695, wrote that Bridport cannot 'maintain the name of a port'. Gibson added that 'the inhabitants have lately attempted it, and failed to in the undertaking; the tides perpetually barring it with sand, against which they could not find any remedy.' The sea soon compounded matters with an exceptional gale which is recorded in many a parish register: 'The great storm, both at sea and land, the greatest ever man knew in England was on the 26th day of November in the year 1703.'

Political initiative in the town was set to remain with the heirs to Cromwellian virtues. Refusing to bear arms, Quakers and their dissident ilk maintained the dignity of silence at their own services but 'felt compelled by the Lord' to interrupt and rave at those of others, and became the fundamentalist rump that took complete control of Bridport Borough in 1717. They won popular support by forcing the abolition of wheat tolls. Male and female alike, they were 'masters of disorder' who in defiance of the Corporation and Test Acts remained in effective control of the town until after the Acts were repealed. Thomas Belsham, from Daventry, visited Weymouth and reported home:

We went to Bridport, a town where the Dissenters are more numerous and powerful than the Establishment. They have introduced a kind of Anti-Test for no man is admitted a member of the Corporation who is not a Dissenter.

In Barrack Street, fronting the old Presbyterian Meeting House, the Liberal Hall rebuilt by Henry Warburton MP is the former Independent Chapel created by Revd John Salteren from a stable-loft which may have been the earliest meeting-house of Bridport's 'multitude of

Quaker rooms, at the Friends Meeting House in South Street, in 1996.

Dissenters'. Revd Thomas Collins was appointed the minister in 1735 and soon found that his private and public utterances were being analysed with increasing suspicion. Mrs Daniel Taylor feared 'that the Saviour was not exalted in his sermons as formerly.' Dr Isaac Watts and Revd John Whitty, from Lyme Regis, planted a trick question: 'Do you believe that Jesus Christ was God equal with the Father for all eternity?' To this Collins candidly answered: 'No, I do not.' On this, 200 of the congregation withdrew.

Things were complicated as the Old Meeting House, John Golding's former home, belonged to Daniel Taylor. Nearby, the New Meeting House, built in 1746, absorbed the break-away congregation. Those of the 'carriage class' took matters in their driver's hands and worshipped in Charmouth instead.

In 1721 an Act of Parliament was passed to enable the River Brit to be diverted from its historic course below East Cliff to the present westerly route through the Basin and into a channel beside a pier that extended seawards. Two decades passed, however, before Chester engineer John Reynolds began the project. The pier was completed in 1742, with a small inner harbour having been dug by Kane Williams in 1741, but the flow of the river proved insufficient to carry away sand that partly blocked the entrance. Ships above 40 tons could not enter, even at high water, and the new entrance became 'dangerously unprotected in a south-west wind, which blows for much of the time.'

Dorset's most famous eighteenth-century wreck was the 350-ton Dutch merchantman *Hope of Amsterdam*, a 30-gun treasure ship returning home from the West Indies with a cargo worth £50,000, mainly in gold. She encountered tempestuous weather in Lyme Bay on the night of 16 January 1749. It was extremely dark and no light appeared from the

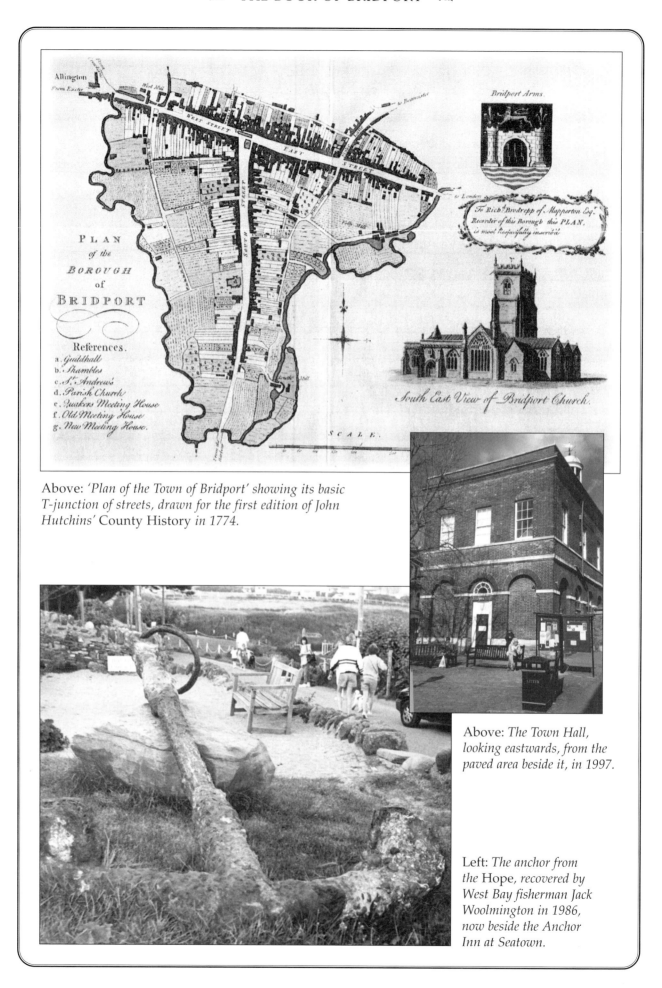

Above: 'Plan of the Town of Bridport' showing its basic T-junction of streets, drawn for the first edition of John Hutchins' County History in 1774.

Above: *The Town Hall, looking eastwards, from the paved area beside it, in 1997.*

Left: *The anchor from the* Hope, *recovered by West Bay fisherman Jack Woolmington in 1986, now beside the Anchor Inn at Seatown.*

lighthouse on Portland. The violent sea stranded the *Hope* on the Chesil Beach, across the Fleet lagoon between Fleet House – now Moonfleet Hotel – and Langton Herring. A 400-strong mob from the coastal villages and Portland gathered for loot as dawn betrayed her predicament:

They came not to rescue but as a merciless battalion that sub-divided into plundering bands each of about 20 in number. In vain did the captain and his company in faltering foreign accents repeat as well as they could – 'No wreck. The goods ours. Bring it to we and we will pay for it' [meaning the salvage]. The winds and waves showed an equal disregard to this language of distress. The pillaging parties threw all they could snatch in one heap, for the security of which Portland labourer Augustin Elliott was posted, as commander of an armed select party. As soon as the reflex of the sea had made the ship accessible, the scattered bands again arrived, in a hostile manner, armed with cutlasses, clubs, hooks, and such like. They marched down to the ship swearing it was a wreck and if not so they could make it a wreck. From curses and menaces they proceeded to offer violence and outrage to those persons, whom even the merciless and furious sea had left unhurt. The injury of strangers in distress is adding barbarity to iniquity and committing an act exceedingly sinful in the sight of both God and man.

Events unfolded differently when the *Reine Gabrielle*, laden with more than 5,000 gallons of honey from Dunkirk, was beached by a storm at Bridport on 25 March 1751. Robert Fowler Coade, a Lyme Regis merchant, organised its floating and brought the ship into the harbour at West Bay. All hands and cargo were saved:

... and re-shipped entire, without the least embezzlement from the country people, though they came down in large numbers to the beach the night the vessel was stranded in hopes of making a prey of both ship and cargo.

On 22 December 1754, Revd Thomas Francklyn addressed his sermons, preached at the churches of Fleet and Chickerell, to the recent shipwrecks along this coast. He reminded parishioners of the Acts of Parliament relating to ships that are stranded on the shore and in particular the penalties they contain for those that plunder the merchant goods:

This has been long looked upon as a thing right and lawful to be done by them who received it from their forebears, and practised it betimes. And, indeed, nothing can reconcile an act as shocking to anyone's reason and conscience, but the frequency of committing.

Further enlargements were made to the pier and basin at Bridport Harbour in 1756 but it remained unsatisfactory in severe weather. The sea was producing other dividends for the seaside communities, particularly in June 1764, when it was reported:

Such a quantity of mackerel was caught at Abbotsbury as the oldest men living don't remember. There were drawn on shore, by twice shooting seine nets, at least 200,000 fish. Thousands of these are still on the beach, there not being sufficient people to carry them away.

By 1 May 1766, a dairyman at Long Bredy, in the hills between Bridport and Dorchester, realised that he had made a bad bargain when he agreed in March to produce, for £5, three square feet of butter for delivery on May Day. 'He has not performed the agreement, which will probably occasion a law suit,' it was reported.

Shipwrecks continued to be normal news from the seaside, with this item dating from 10 August 1767:

Last week three dead bodies were taken up on the shore near Abbotsbury, and one at Portland, with two sides of a boat. The skin was also found of two hands with the nails on. There was a watch and sixpence found on one of the bodies. No account has been received of any vessel lost on this coast.

A lovers' tiff that nearly ended in tragedy provided a miracle on 14 December 1767:

It is reliably reported that two young men of Chideock, near Bridport, have had some words with their sweethearts. They went away together and hanged themselves, both on one tree; but the bough they tied themselves up to broke down before they were quite dead. One of them remained speechless for several days.

The philanthropist Thomas Hollis (1720–74), an admirer of seventeenth-century republican literature, who spent a fortune on books which he gave to the American library at Harvard and those of continental universities including Berne and Zurich, retired from London in 1770 to Urless Farm, Corscombe, near

South Street, northwards to the Town Hall (centre) *from Turner's Corn and Seed Stores* (left) *in 1895.*

Left: *Georgian brick of the 1785-built Town Hall, designed by William Tyler, with the cupola and clock having been added two decades later.*

Below: *West Street, eastwards from Wilfrid Frost's* Bridport News *office* (right), *in 1895.*

Above left: *The beech bole with aerial roots on Lewesdon Hill which was immortalised by the poet William Crowe.*

Left: *Downe Hall and its slopes, looking southwards across the town.*

Beaminster. He gave its fields names with American and libertarian associations.

Hollis died on 1 January 1774 and was buried, it is said, with his horse in a field on Urless Farm. He had lived as a recluse in a frugal manner, abstaining from intoxicating liquors, spices, salt, butter and milk. His estates were left to his friend Thomas Brand from the Hyde, Ingatestone, Essex, who styled himself Thomas Brand Hollis. On his death the estates passed to the Unitarian clergyman Dr John Disney.

Another West Dorset personage who came to fame, in 1770, was Samuel Hearne (1745–92). An explorer, during the previous two years he had found a passage through the icy waters along the north-eastern edge of America for the Hudson's Bay Company. He was remembered in Beaminster, where he lived as a youth, and his book *Journey from Hudson's Bay to the Northern Ocean* was published posthumously in 1795.

Bridport lost medieval links when the Guildhall was burnt down in 1782. Much debate about its replacement was resolved by an Act of Parliament in 1785, which enabled the removal of its ruins and the associated Shambles meat market to bring about clearance of all obstructions within the T-junction. It also introduced building regulations in the cause of fire-prevention measures by prohibiting thatched roofs on new buildings:

An Act for taking down the Market House in the Borough of Bridport in the County of Dorsetshire, and rebuilding the same, together with a Session or Court House in a more convenient Situation; for removing the Shambles or Butcher Row; for better paving, cleansing, lighting, and watching the said Borough, and for removing and preventing nuisances and annoyances, and for prohibiting the covering of any new Houses or Buildings with Thatch. 25 [year of] *George III, chapter 91.*

The replacement Market House and Town Hall, on the site of St Andrew's Chapel, opened in 1786 with 37 butchers' stalls on the ground floor and municipal offices above. One who bought food there was 'the gormandiser' Charles Tyte from Stoke Abbott. It was reported on 13 March 1788 that he had consumed 133 eggs in an hour, plus a large piece of bacon and a quantity of bread. He then complained that he had not eaten a full supper.

Early that year the Clarendon Press at Oxford published anonymously the romantic poem *Lewesdon Hill* which describes a May morning climb to the top of

East Street, looking westwards to the Town Hall, in 1895.

the wooded summit near Broadwindsor and the delightful prospect and its associations. There was such national acclaim for this harmonious blank verse that a second edition has been printed, which identifies its author as William Crowe (1745–1829), the rector of Stoke Abbott, near Beaminster. It was praised by Tom Moore for imagery 'of the highest order' and by Samuel Rogers for 'noble passages'. Wordsworth, Coleridge and Bowles also acknowledged it as an important contribution to the Romantic Movement.

In August 1789, the brig *Endeavour* left Sidmouth to sail up-Channel, en route to Newcastle for a cargo of coal. Her departure coincided with a storm and within a matter of hours she was driven ashore near Bridport Harbour. The crew were eventually saved.

Dating from 1789, Downe Hall is surrounded by its own grounds on the north edge of the town, and rises above it with one of the finest classical elevations in the area. It was built by merchant and mariner Captain William Downe as a rural replica of his London home. He traced his descent from Revd Richard Downe, a Nonconformist minister, and rope-maker John Downe who flourished in Bridport in 1582. The south front is a lofty three storeys faced with Portland stone. One's eye tends to be drawn towards the circular window at the centre of the tympanum between the top of the four pilasters and angled roof line.

Embellishments were added during the nineteenth century. The semi-circular porch of 1807 tends to detract from the flush simplicity of the frontage. Inside, the original main staircase has gone, having been removed to enable the division into flats, in the 1960s. Its time-warp eighteenth-century garden, originally 'cascading across the slope above the town', had gradually been encircled

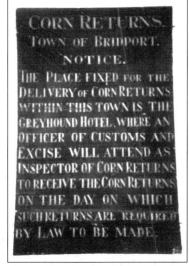

Corn returns were authorised and scrutinised at the Town Hall.

Bridport Brewery and wheel, with bridge, looking north-eastwards, in 1996. The water-wheel operated a pump and is inscribed for its maker, Thomas Helyear at West Allington in 1879.

Water-power at the Bridport Brewery, looking south-eastwards from the bridge, in 1997.

From the brewery the River Brit flows southwards to West Bay.

Right: Bridport Brewery, looking south-eastwards from across the River Brit, in 1970.

Below: J.C. and R.H. Palmer's thatched Old Brewery at Bridport, dating from 1794.

Right: Bridge, wheel and Bridport Brewery from the River Brit, in 1990.

Right: *The thatched roofs of C. & R.H. Palmer's Old Brewery make it unique in Britain, seen from the south-east in 1970.*

Below: *Leo Coats serving Palmer's brew in the Royal Oak at Cerne Abbas.*

Above: *The Literary and Scientific Institute, now Bridport Library, from the pavement of East Street in 1996.*

Left: *Gothic-style frontage of the 1859-built Congregational Chapel in East Street, now the Bridport United Church.*

by development. Three decades later the setting was threatened by plans for house building, the outcome of which will be discussed at the end of our story.

Then as now the weather and transport often made news together. On 31 January 1791 a coach traveller was reported to have frozen to death as he made his way westwards from Bridport:

On Friday last, 28 January, a passenger on the top of the Western coach, bound for Exeter, died of exposure from the cold, between Chideock and Charmouth. He had been taken sick at Chideock, from the excessive cold of the foregoing night, but expired before reaching the next stop, and was removed at Charmouth.

By 1792, an increasing volume of trade was passing through Bridport Harbour, which could now take vessels of up to 300 tons. Considerable quantities of flax were imported from Russia and consumed in the town's cordage and netting industry. Lumber arrived from Norway, Prussia and North America, and grain also came from across the Atlantic. Some eight vessels from the port, each of about 100 tons, operated around the British Isles and crossed the North Sea to Norway.

In 1794 there were 11 coasting vessels, representing a total of over 950 tons, operating from Bridport Harbour. It was the year in which Job Legg, working for Samuel Gundry & Company, established the Bridport Brewery on the corner of South Street and Skilling Hill Road. Brewing in thatched buildings was commonplace then, but fire fears caused all but one of these to be demolished or re-roofed. Bridport Brewery is now unique as Britain's only thatched brewery. All the other buildings of what is now J.C. & R.H. Palmer's Brewery are in later fortress-like stone buildings or under recent tin-clad toppings.

The adjoining water-wheel, beside the River Brit on the seaward side of its confluence with the River Asker, is also an oddity. Sizeable, in cast iron, it is inscribed for 'T. Helyear, Bridport, 1879'. What makes it unusual is that it used the water-power of the river – by then unpleasantly brown – to draw water from a spring two miles away, on the other side of Skilling Head, in the western hills. Pollution was always a threat to town breweries.

Nonconformist Bridport, despite a history of religious persecution and secret services, emerged into a new age of confidence and style when its 'mean meeting house' was replaced by the grand Unitarian Chapel in East Street. The first service was held on Sunday 9 March 1794, but the season was 'inconvenient for the usual meeting of distant friends'. The formal opening was delayed until Wednesday 30 April 1794 and featured sermons 'by Mr Manning, of Exeter, and Dr Toulmin, of Taunton, and devotional services conducted by Mr Gummer, of Ilminster, and Mr Kell, of Wareham.'

The church traced its origin to meetings held by William Eaton before 1662. His successors, through to the Victorian era, were Joseph Hallet (1662–72), Richard Downe (1672–87), Samuel Baker (1687–1727), Robert Drewitt (1729–37), Thomas Collins (1735–64), William Sutton (1764–69), George Waters (1769–87), Thomas Howe (1787–1820), George Barker Wawne (1821–27), Robert Cree (1827–34) and Philip Harwood (from 1835).

South-facing, from rising ground set back from the north side of road, the Unitarian Chapel has an imposing setting but its churchyard vaults are squeezed between the path and the later Literary Institution provided for the borough by Henry Warburton. A tablet over the pulpit records the life of its first minister:

To the memory of
the Rev. Thomas Howe,
the faithful and beloved pastor
of this Christian society
for 32 years,
who died 15th November, 1820,
aged 61.

'Be not slothful, but followers of them who through faith and patience inherit the promises.' – Heb. vi. 12.

By 1835 it claimed equal status with the Anglicans, literally, with 'a roll of half the town'. The list of 2,000 names, comprising 'one of the largest Unitarian societies in the West of England' included the families of Colfox and Hounsell who were descended 'from Mr Collins, and the heterodox section' who once formed a break-away sect. Downe and Gundry are among other distinctly Bridport names. Thomas Howe was credited with having reunited the flock:

His capacious chapel was well filled by a serious and attentive audience, a considerable part of which was formed of labouring mechanics and the industrious poor.

The Unitarian Chapel, seen from the south, in 1996.

Earliest view of the changed layout of West Bay, after 1823, looking westwards to Thorncombe Beacon and Golden Cap.

Left: *Gulls following the catch, out in Lyme Bay.*

Right: *West Bay as viewed from the beach, looking westwards from below East Cliff, in 1997.*

Chapter 8

VISCOUNTS HOOD & BRIDPORT

Events in sight of Bridport over the long years of the Napoleonic Wars, following the French Revolution, started with a calamitous clutch of shipwrecks. On 16 November 1795, Rear-Admiral Sir Hugh Cloberry Christian (1747–98) set sail with his fleet from Spithead, outward bound into a wind that became a hurricane. They were tasked to sail to the West Indies, where Sir Hugh was to be Commander-in-Chief, but few of the vessels reached a point between Portland and Bridport, and none got any further. The flagship, the 98-gun *Prince George*, limped back to Portsmouth on 17 November with her rigging smashed and almost unseaworthy beyond repair. The less fortunate craft foundered or were driven ashore and 1,000 men were estimated to have drowned. A total of 200 bodies were picked up along the Chesil Beach.

Through a combination of growing war needs and restricted flows of imports, disrupted by the French fleet offshore and continental markets being off-limits, the home sailcloth and cordage industry experienced boom times. Erecting the Mill House by the River Bride in 1803, at Burton Bradstock, Richard Roberts founded the first flax-swingling mill in the West of England. This worked in a horizontal mode, with flax being held against the edge of a board, at openings in the frame. There it was struck by the scutchers – pieces of wood which project from a vertical shaft – as that revolved swiftly. This process smashed the stalks to separate them from the flax.

The French Wars gave West Dorset a national hero. Admiral Sir Samuel Hood (1762–1814) served with great distinction under Lord Nelson at Santa Cruz in 1797. He was also in command of the *Zealous* at the Battle of the Nile, and again off Rochefort, where he lost his right arm on 25 September 1805. The son of purser Samuel Hood and his wife Anne of Kingsland, Netherbury, he returned to Dorset and served as Member of Parliament for Bridport. He was

Loders Court was one of the Hood family homes.

back on active service when he died of a sudden fever in Madras on Christmas Eve in 1814, as Commander-in-Chief of the East Indies.

HMS *Hood*, the 42,100-ton battle-cruiser sunk by the *Bismarck* in 1941, was named for him. Hood's elder brother was Captain Alexander Hood (1758–1798) of HMS *Mars*, fatally wounded in the thigh by a musket-shot and among a total of 315 men dead or wounded as the new French warship *Hercule* was pounded into submission off Brest.

There was another Admiral Samuel Hood (1724–1816), eldest son of the vicar of Butleigh in Somerset, Revd Samuel Hood, who was created Viscount Hood in 1796. The family had a second title which was held by the younger brother Admiral Alexander Hood, Viscount Bridport (1727–1814), who blockaded Brest until he was relieved by Lord St Vincent in April 1800. It remains a private joke, told to me by friends of Lord and Lady Hood at Loders Court, that even the family were confused by their two viscounts and differentiated them as Lord Rich (Viscount Bridport) and Lord Poor (Viscount Hood).

On their home coast a shipbuilder's yard opened in 1805 at a site on the west side of the inner pool at Bridport Harbour. Several slipways sloped into the water, to the south-west of the present West Bay harbour, on the west side of the channel to the sea.

The first national census, in 1811, recorded the population of Bridport at 3,567. It was rising and reached 3,742 in 1821 and 4,242 a decade later. In earlier times the story tended to centre around clerics and sailors, but in the nineteenth century crime can have its due, particularly as a changing world would gradually curtail the opportunities for penal transportation and public hangings.

George Hellier, a 37-year-old Bridport patten-maker from Allington, was sentenced to death at the Summer Assize in Dorchester for horse stealing.

This was commuted, however, to transportation for life. He was discharged from Dorchester Castle gaol on 26 October 1814 for the march across Dorset and Hampshire, to the *Laurel* hulk at Gosport and passage to New South Wales. He left behind a wife and three children.

Similar fates awaited 17-year-old Bridport wool-comber John Dalley and 20-year-old sailcloth weaver William Hallsow. Both were born in Broadwindsor and apprehended at Poole on burglary charges. Death sentences were passed but commuted to transportation for life. They began their walk to Gosport for onward passage to the other side of the world on 20 May 1818.

Robert Gaurd, a 60-year-old Allington man with a wife and nine children, was committed to Dorchester Castle on 30 May 1818 after being caught in a field at Bridport 'milking cows to steal milk' to provide for his children. He was 5 feet 8 inches high with 'almost white hair'. His sentence was transportation, for seven years, which began with his forced march to the *Leviathan* hulk at Portsmouth on 17 September 1818.

Briant Paine, a 28-year-old painter of miniature portraits from Southampton, was living in Bridport when he was committed to Dorchester Castle on 18 March 1818 on a forgery charge. It concerned 'a £1 note purporting to be a note of the Bridport Bank.' The artist was sentenced to death at the Summer Assize but this was commuted to transportation for life, and he began his long journey on 15 October 1819, beginning with a static period on the *Leviathan* hulk at Portsmouth.

Disease fears of medieval proportions returned to Bridport in September 1819 when a smallpox epidemic spread through the town and killed 26 people.

Abelardo Staple, a 50-year-old labourer from Stoke Abbott, who had a previous conviction for vagrancy at Bridport, was committed to Dorchester Castle for housebreaking on 27 January 1821. He was transported for seven years and left Dorchester for the *York* hulk at Portsmouth on 1 August 1821.

Crime and unrest caused Chilcombe residents to display one of the earliest recorded instances of security paranoia in West Dorset. They insisted that there was no public trackway across their parish and petitioned against non-residents using the road through its centre, over the hills from Askerswell to Puncknowle:

We the undersigned householders, farmers dwelling in the parishes adjoining the parish of Chilcombe, do declare and make known to whomsoever it does concern that there is not nor ever was to our knowledge a public wagon or cart road through any part of the parish of Chilcombe. And in order to prevent as much as we can any legal claim to that effect we have set our hands this 3rd September 1821.

This track is still an unclassified county-maintained public road, despite a short gated section on the slope between Chilcombe and Rudge Farm not having been tarred until the 1950s. There is a quarter-mile spur from it, also maintained by Dorset County Council as the highway authority, into the hamlet of Chilcombe. The main purpose of the objection was to prevent the through route being diverted along this second track and then out from the cluster of buildings on the other side. In this they were successful as it remains an idyllic cul-de-sac.

Symondsbury farmer Henry Sampson, aged 27 and six feet in height, was apprehended on burglary charges and taken to Dorchester Castle – as the gaol was known – on 30 March 1822. A sentence of death was passed but this was commuted to transportation for life. He left for the *Leviathan* hulk at Portsmouth on 17 September 1822.

From the other side of Bridport, 42-year-old Litton Cheney labourer James Pitman was committed to Dorchester Castle on 30 April 1823. He was convicted of 'entering a dwelling house and stealing wearing apparel'. This was again commuted to transportation for life and he left for the *York* hulk at Portsmouth on 23 September 1823.

Rook pie was a popular Dorset delicacy but in a case reported from the Maidstone Assizes Mr Baron Graham expressed doubts that anyone would eat the birds, and said he had never heard of a such a pie. The *Weymouth Gazette* commented on 24 August 1823:

The good folk in the West of England will be amused by reading this; a strong stomach to encounter a rook pie? If Mr Baron Graham should ever happen to pass through Dorchester when young perchers are beginning to caw, we would engage to provide him with a rook pie equal, if not superior, to any powdered pigeon reared in the kingdom of Cockaigne.

Transportation threat, to those damaging the West Bridge, signed by County Clerk Thomas Fooks in 1828.

Bridport rope-workers 22-year-old William Cook and Daniel Diment, aged 25, stood trial at the Summer Assize in Dorchester in August 1824 for 'stealing money from the person'. Diment, a flax comber from Allington, had a previous conviction for stealing potatoes the year before, for which he served six months' imprisonment with hard labour. This time, for the pair of them, the sentence was death but they were reprieved, with the alternative being the long walk to the *York* hulk in Portsmouth Harbour followed by transportation for life to Australia.

The final evolution of Bridport Harbour and West Bay, into a place we would recognise, occurred in 1824:

A new harbour has been built at Bridport, as a rectangle dug in the marshes of the parish of Bothenhampton, between Mr Good's Ship Yard and the Rope-walk and the premises on the eastern side of the estuary of Messrs Gundry and Ewens. It has now been linked to the sea by a channel to the west of the Bridport Arms Inn and the Revenue Watch House. A crane house has been built on the east side of this run, to the north-west from the inn. The civil engineer is Mr James Green and the work has been carried out under the supervision of Mr Francis Giles. Upwards of 200 men have been working each day for many months and it is estimated that the total cost will be £41,800.

The harbour works at West Bay were still new when they withstood their first test. Storm-force winds coinciding with a high tide on the evening of 22 November 1824 caused a raging sea to break over the top of the Chesil Beach, inundating and destroying much of the coastal villages of Chiswell at Portland and Fleet towards at Bridport. Even on the eastern-facing shores the sea did considerable damage and washed away the Weymouth esplanade. The Wyke Regis parish register records:

This day will ever be memorable for the dreadful catastrophe which caused such destruction along the whole western coast. The village of Chesil [Chiswell] was nearly destroyed, 26 of the inhabitants drowned, and upwards of 80 houses damaged or washed down by a tremendous surf which broke over the Chesil bank

and bore everything away with irresistible violence; there blew a most dreadful hurricane such as never had been before in the memory of man. At 9 o'clock a most horrid scene presented itself. The sea ran down the streets of Chesil with sufficient depth of water to float a vessel of 100 tons and the wrecks of houses and the furniture of the poor inhabitants were everywhere strewn on the shore. The ferry house leading to Portland was washed away and the ferryman drowned. Three quarters of the esplanade at Melcombe [Regis] was entirely thrown down... the waves of sea washed over the high old road and filled all the lower parts of the houses in Gloucester Row and The Crescent with gravel and water... The same storm destroyed the church at Fleet and threw down several houses but fortunately no lives were lost. The Colville, a West Indiaman of 400 tons, was wrecked in the West Bay [off Portland] and every soul on board perished.

In December 1824, *Ebenezer* was the ship that was the talk of the Dorset coast, having achieved a unique claim to fame, by sailing up the English Channel without having passed south of Portland Bill. Instead the 95-ton sailing vessel, a Government sloop carrying stores for the Royal Navy, was left stranded on top of the Chesil Beach by the Great Gale on 22 November. The following month she was tugged down the inland-facing side of the unstable pebble bank and re-launched at high tide into a specially dug trench that saw her safely into the backwater and Portland Roads. From this anchorage she made ready, and resumed her voyage, from Plymouth to Portsmouth.

It was noted at this time that a visitor to Bridport on a Sunday might wonder why the sides of the streets are so far apart, particularly as there was little evidence of cattle or market stalls. The answer that appeared on the Monday morning was home-spinning of yarn for netting, which required a great deal of space. The paths were therefore known as rope walks. By the nineteenth century, the name was being taken indoors, into long sheds that were 15 feet wide and 500 feet long. There would be more than two dozen such sheds across the town by the end of the century.

East Street, westwards to the Town Hall (left) from opposite drapers William Elmes (right) and grocer John Alderton Collins, in 1893.

Below: *St Hilda's School* (left) *and town houses of the 1860s in Victoria Grove, looking southwards in 1895.*

Above: *Bridport's gasometer and the works staff in 1920. Left to right, standing: H. Tuck, C. Hardiman, E. Bishop, F. Legg, H. Legg, E. Burden, E. Hutchings, J. Napthine, W. Hughes, J. Stone, W. Norman, E. Bartlett; seated: S. Hallett, A. Scott, J.L. Reed, R.G. Mabb, W.H. Reed, F. Scott, E.T. Spencer, C. Symes.*

Left: *Bridport Gas Works outing in 1912 with driver J.C. Phillips beside manager's son J.L. Reed, and (left to right, standing) G. Podger, W.H. Reed, E. Hutchings, A. Scott, R, Crabb, J. Ozzard and E. Bartlett.*

Right: *Bridport from Allington Hill, looking south-eastwards to the tower of St Mary's Church and Loders Hill (top left).*

Chapter 9

SUBURBS, REFORM & GAS

In 1826 Allington began its transformation into Bridport's first suburb, with its decayed medieval church on the north side of Parsonage Road being earmarked for replacement. That was achieved with a fine building designed by Charles Wallis of Dorchester. Originally dedicated to St Mary Magdalene, it was re-dedicated to St Swithun when it was consecrated in 1827 on the west side of North Allington. The old church, ruined and roofless by the time it was being pulled down, stood on the west side of the Vicarage where a section of its rubble walls has been retained for a boundary to the grounds.

The replacement, simple and symmetrical, has a splendid portico of Tuscan-Doric exuberance. It was unusual in having its altar in the sanctuary at the west end and represents a rare example of Greek-revival architecture. Church historian Fred Pitfield records a stylistic throw-back to the 'preaching churches' of the eighteenth century, 'in which the clergy shared the same space as the congregation, rather than being separated in a semi-enclosed chancel.'

Stokers Frank Thomas and D. Bugler drawing the last retort in Bridport Gas Works in June 1958 – 126 years after it was first lit.

The painted royal arms are those of Queen Victoria and the font was added during her reign in 1864, with a new altar and reredos being installed in 1975. These are on the south side of the building but the original mahogany altar still stands beside the west wall.

During the nineteenth century, Bridport's Parliamentary representation was reduced in terms of numbers of members but increased in terms of the franchise, although artisans and women had to wait many decades. From 1572 until the passing in 1832 of 'An Act to Amend the Representation of the People of England and Wales', the county of Dorset and its boroughs regularly returned 20 members to Parliament. Two knights were elected for the shire and two members each for the boroughs of Bridport, Corfe Castle, Dorchester, Lyme Regis, Melcombe Regis (now part of Weymouth), Poole, Shaftesbury,

Wareham and Weymouth. These boroughs between them contained 1,225 qualified electors; that was an average of 61 electors to each member.

Modern times for Bridport began in 1831 when it became the first town in Dorset to have a gas supply. The Bridport Gas & Coke Company was incorporated under the chairmanship of W.E. Gundry after a meeting in the Town Hall. Board members were William Battiscombe, William Colfox, George Darby, James Hodder, W. Perham, Dr G.R. Roberts, A. Selwood, John Pike Stephens and Sylvanus Stephens. Bridport Gas Works was built on the west side of South Street, behind the pound, midway between the Chantry and South Bridge.

Dr Giles Roberts (1765–1834) was the figure who was pivotal to the project. His lasting reputation was as the inventor and purveyor of the 'Poor Man's Friend' which generations of country folk swore by for the next century, and more as 'the most efficacious healing ointment known to man or beast.' Roberts claimed it as the 'certain cure for ulcerated legs, even if of twenty years standing, cuts, burns, scalds, bruises, eruptions, pimples, sore eyes, cancerous humours and eruptions that follow vaccinations.' As a 'dispensing chemist and druggist' he had his pharmacy behind the frontage of the former George Inn, on the north side of East Street, opposite the Town Hall. Dr Roberts offered his premises as the trial property for lighting by gas at the time when many feared 'being poisoned and then blown up' by leakage from the pipes. The *Dorset County Chronicle* reported in October 1831:

The fires were lit in the retorts on Friday last and great crowds gathered to watch as the lamps were lit in Dr Roberts's premises, and cries of wonderment were heard at the brilliance of the wondrous illuminations, the Town Band added to the enlivenment of the proceedings.

The Union Workhouse, which became a Public Assistance Institution, is now Port Bredy Hospital.

Loders Parish Church with its early-fifteenth-century south chapel (centre) where the Governor of Bombay, Sir Evan Nepean, was buried in 1822.

The last manager of Bridport Gas Works, J.L. Mayes (left), took over from W.H. Reed in March 1938.

Supply regulations were onerous and strict. All fixtures and fittings had to be installed by the company's own men. Burners had five-inch chimneys and a flame of half that height was allowed. These lights could only be turned on from 'sunset to sunrise' on penalty of disconnection if gas was used in daylight. The main stopcock on the supply had to be turned off before doing the same with those on the burners. Rates were calculated on the assumption of six days' supply for commercial premises, plus a surcharge of a sixth if it was of a domestic nature with a Sunday service also required.

Charges were calculated 'per single Cockspur' light, ranging from £1 per annum for a basic dusk to dawn (8 o'clock) supply to £2.2s.6d. for dusk through to late morning (11 o'clock) after the 'sunrise' restriction had been relaxed. Better-class burners ranged from the Batwing at £2.5s.0d. to a 14-hole Argand lamp at £4.

The company records show that fitter Richard Hayward had offered his services at £1.12s.0d. per week, but was told that £1.10s.0d. was the maximum on offer, although he would find that 'cheap living' was available in Bridport. Robert Gale and William Whittle were the stokers, and John Critchel the lamplighter at just 12s. a week. The secretary, who billed the customers, received 8s. a week.

Removing the gas from coal left coke which could be sold at 11d. per hundredweight and tar worth 4d. per gallon. The gas lamps were 'a wonder of the age for purity and brilliance' and 'the envy of neighbouring towns' which considered similar schemes. These, however, were fraught with difficulties and dilemmas, as a construction company from Neath, in Glamorgan, found when they tried to obtain the £126.17s.11d. outstanding for building Bridport Gas Works. The town also provided an inevitable crop of recalcitrant customers who in 1834 received the first public utility cut-off notices in the county of Dorset. James Hansford, whose horses had collided with one of the town's 49 lamp columns, refused to pay £1.5s.2d. for its reinstatement. Despite the problems, however, the company showed a profit of £133 in 1834 which rose to £278 in 1839. It would have been more if the Town

Council had settled accounts 'with more alacrity'.

Eventually the company went on strike. Gas bills for street lighting had remained unpaid for two years by Bridport's 'feeoffs, who were the town's fiduciary trustees'. In desperation the company cut off the supply in January 1842 and the sides remained deadlocked through the winter gloom. Summer removed the imperative for settlement but as winter returned at the end of the year the councillors capitulated. In future, they agreed, the borough would be responsible for payments.

A new gas holder was constructed in 1841. John Rees supervised the digging of a hole, 36 feet in diameter and 12 feet deep, for £2. It enabled the company to expand the town's mains system north-westwards in 1844 along North Allington, where 636 yards of 3-inch pipe were laid underground and eight lamps erected for £100. In 1857 it was extended by 469 yards into Hounsell's North Mills with the provision of 50 lights in the street and yards. William Hounsell became chairman of Bridport Gas Company in 1879 on the death of Sylvanus Stephens. Another powerful man in Bridport and the world of rope-making, Joseph Pearkes Gundry, eventually adopted 'the wonder of light' and had the supply extended eastwards from Barrack Street to his home in East Road in 1863. His firm also bought 100 tons of coke from the gasworks for £60. Gundry was Bridport's 'most influential Victorian gentleman' whose proudest moment – unknown to most of the town – took place on 7 May 1877 when Montague Guest of Canford House appointed him Deputy Provincial Grand Master of the United Fraternity of Free and Accepted Masons of England.

The story of gas and Bridport continued to have its troubles. News leaking out of the gasworks over the winter of 1844 showed that its management was lax or even non-existent. One of the stokers had died, back in the autumn of 1843, but the foreman neglected to tell the directors, who continued to pay the man's wages of 12s. a week. This was shared between the foreman and the remaining stoker. To compound the fraud they conspired to buy 224 gallons of tar from elsewhere, at $2^{1}/_{2}$d. a gallon, and sold it from the works for 4d. Again the difference was pocketed. These private enterprise initiatives continued for more than a year before word reached the directors.

They showed more acumen in keeping pace with scientific discoveries. White's Hydro-Carbon Process was adopted in 1847. This innovation required four new retorts, costing £21, but soon many customers were refusing to accept a supply – complaining of 'the foul smell' – and output fell by 70,000 cubic feet over a year. Others were placated by discounts of 5s. on their bills. Someone had to sort things out, and there were 54 applications from Bristol and London from those claiming 'a sound knowledge of gas-making, main-laying, meter-fixing, and installation work' for the foreman's job on a salary of £1.8s.6d. a

Powerstock village, eastwards from the track to West Milton,
across to the tower of St Mary's Church.

The 1838-built Wesleyan Methodist Chapel in the town centre, now Bridport Arts Centre, in 1997.

week. David Skinner, the chosen man, turned the situation around and enabled the directors to report record annual profits of £339.17s.5d.

Then 'the demon drink' took its toll on operations. David Skinner was found to be intoxicated after several hours in the White Bull Inn, in East Road, and failed to appear before a special board meeting the following day. He was dismissed and replaced by Peter Crighton who showed a similar weakness and lasted only four months. As a result, the board decided 'that the salary should be reduced to a guinea' – £1.1s. a week – to lessen the opportunity for liquid lapses. The company's annual general meeting on 7 July 1857 heard that there had been a loss over the year of £3.17s.11d. which was blamed on Crighton having fitted 'a defective valve' on the purifiers, causing 'a great loss of gas'. Things were eventually stabilised by James Lowe from Taunton in 1858, who re-negotiated the depleted salary. There were annual increments 'subject to good behaviour'.

Although first in the county with gas, Bridport failed to shake off the horrific medieval scourges that still afflicted Dorset towns – notably the artisan quarter of Fordington at Dorchester – where cholera outbreaks were claiming lives. Polluted water-supplies were to blame. A total of 19 people of varying ages died of cholera in Bridport at the end of the summer in 1831.

The schooner *Jane* was launched at West Bay on 21 August 1834. Her displacement was 200 tons and she was registered in Limerick.

By 31 December 1834 the customs duties collected for the year at Bridport Harbour totalled £6,364, which was a record for the port. It was never to be broken.

Sixteen-year-old Silvester Wilkins was hanged at Dorchester on Saturday 30 March 1833 for arson at Bridport. He was the youngest victim of the notorious hanging judge Sir Joseph Littledale. Even the Governor of Dorchester Gaol was distressed by his youth and diminutive size. Wilkins was such a light boy that weights were cast in lead – inscribed with the word 'MERCY' – and attached to his feet to hasten the execution.

In a manner normally reserved for marking royal commemorations, the name 'Reform Place' appeared on buildings in Bridport's north-west suburb of Allington in 1835. The Reform Act of 1831–32 widened Parliamentary representation to an enlarged male electorate. What the commemorative stone had in common, however, with the majority who celebrate royal events, was that it was in a working-class area. As the Boundary Commission, which came to re-draw the constituency maps in the wake of the expansion of the electorate, noted about Bridport:

The chief trade arises from the manufacture of hemp and flax, and Allington appears to be the resort of the poorer classes of the population engaged in these manufactures.

The town's austere stone-built Union Workhouse – later known as the Poor Law Institution – was built in 1836 and looks down on Barrack Street and St Andrew's Road from Bedford Place. It housed 250 inmates and was managed by a master and matron with the services of a chaplain, medical officer and schoolmistress. Board day for admissions was every other Wednesday at 11 o'clock, and the Bridport Union area included the West Dorset parishes of Allington, Askerswell, Bothenhampton, Bradpole, Bridport, Burton Bradstock, Catherston Leweston, Chideock, Chilcombe, Litton Cheney, Loders, Shipton Gorge, Stanton St Gabriel, Swyre, Symondsbury, Walditch (now part of Bothenhampton), Whitchurch Canonicorum and Wootton Fitzpaine. Together they had a population of 14,000.

Two regular natural scourges made their presence felt. Smallpox again caused an epidemic at Bridport, killing 66 people in six months during 1837. Eight vessels were driven on to the Chesil Beach in a south-westerly gale in 1839 with the loss of all on board, but a ninth ship had a miraculous escape. The force of the waves at the height of the storm threw this 500-ton vessel on to the very top of the beach. There she rested, high and dry, as the winds abated.

The scandal of an alleged 'double murder' unfolded at Powerstock over the summer of 1839. The wife of animal doctor John Hounsell died during the winter. Then the husband of Elizabeth Gale died across the valley in the hamlet of Nettlecombe. The vicar, Revd George Cookson, became suspicious when the surviving spouses asked him to publish the banns for their marriage.

He arranged for the bodies to be exhumed from the churchyard and subjected to post mortem on the altar of St Mary's Parish Church. An inquest was held across the road in the Three Horseshoes alehouse and it was reported that six times the lethal dose of arsenic had been found in Mrs Hounsell's body. It took three weeks for the smell of decomposition to clear from the church before

Bothenhampton Parish Church was built in 1880.

Three-storey brick house in Barrack Street, pictured in 1997.

Left: *The great West Dorset landmark is to Vice-Admiral Sir Thomas Masterman Hardy who was Nelson's flag-captain at the Battle of Trafalgar.*

services could be held again. John Hounsell was arrested and charged with murder but was acquitted at the Summer Assize in Dorchester in July 1839 through lack of evidence. John and Elizabeth then left the district and their marriage took place.

On 20 September 1839 the death occurred of Vice-Admiral Sir Thomas Masterman Hardy, companion in battle and favourite captain of the greatest of all Naval heroes, Lord Nelson. The second son of Joseph Hardy of Portesham, he was born in Martinstown on 15 April 1769 and spent his childhood in Kingston Russell House. It was in his arms that Nelson died, having achieved the destruction of the French and Spanish fleets off Cape Trafalgar on 21 October 1805. Mr Beatty, HMS *Victory*'s surgeon, and Dr Scott, the chaplain, both confirmed Nelson's dying words: 'Kiss me, Hardy.'

His Flag Captain went on to the Govenorship of Greenwich Hospital, being appointed on 6 April 1834, where he did much to improve the lot of the 2,000 Naval pensioners who lived in the hospital and Royal Naval College. He died in the Second Sea Lord's house at Greenwich and his coffin lay in the dining-room before burial in Greenwich Mausoleum. A public subscription was opened to build a suitable monument within sight of his home villages and the sea that had been his life. It was appropriate that a regatta, held at West Bay in 1844, was the first such event in these parts.

In all, during the 1840s, the sum of £609.15s.0d. was raised by the public subscription initiated among the Dorset gentry to commemorate the distinguished life of Vice-Admiral Sir Thomas Hardy. A Gothic column was built on Black Down, between the Hardy family's homes at Martinstown and Portesham, which was designed by Arthur Dyke-Troyte. The first stone was laid by Mrs Floyer, wife of John Floyer MP for Dorset and High Sheriff of the county:

The contract price to Mr Goddard, the builder, was £375 19s 6d; opening quarries at Portesham and quarrying stone, £111 13s 3d; to Mr Glegg and Mr H. Barnes for submitting designs, £5 each; advertisements for donations, £33 10s 11d; for beer £6 1s 8d and £2 19s 8d for bread and cheese, for work people on the occasion of laying the foundation stone in 1844. The base of the tower is at 833 feet above the level of the sea, to an octagonal design which inclines like the batter of a mediaeval castle, into parallel sides with a flared top for the viewing platform. Here the building itself is now 72 feet, making a total height of 905 feet. A circular staircase winds up the middle, around the central pillar; and sparsely lit by narrow slit-windows. From its prominent position it may be seen in every direction, and in clear weather at a considerable distance, from the Isle of Wight eastwards and from the Start Point and Dartmoor westward. It is also a conspicuous object to vessels passing up and down the English Channel, as well as to all the surrounding country.

West Street in the 1890s, after provision of street lights, from the Bull Hotel (left, with coach on pavement) westwards to the Town Hall.

A disputed vote in the Bridport election of March 1846 led a select committee of the House of Commons to consider a petition over many days during June and July of that year. The sitting Tory member, Alexander Dundas Ross Wishart Baillie Cochrane, had been returned by a single vote over Whig candidate John Romilly. Those called from Bridport to give evidence in Westminster included William Salter Gillard (poll clerk), Samuel Bennett (grocer and check clerk for Romilly), George Rasterick (leather seller and check clerk for Cochrane), Samuel Rooker Champ, (superintendent of police at Bridport), William Rockett (petitioner), and James Templer (solicitor, who lived in the Grove and died in 1858). The relevant poll books were produced by James Richard Naylor (clerk to the Crown). Their costs in London, covering two or three days in each case, ranged from £3.15s.0d. for Rockett the voter's travelling, accommodation and meals, to £9.4s.0d. for Templer the solicitor who had more experience at claiming expenses.

It soon emerged that the 'Bribery Oath' was read at the poll as the law required, by Stephen Hussey, but may well have been broken. William Rockett, 'by trade a cordwainer or shoemaker' in South Street, was no stranger to voting altercations. He admitted having had an argument with Joseph Welch, 'a mechanic and engineer', 14 years earlier: 'He struck me, and disabled me, and I put him in prison for three months.'

Before the election, on 7 March 1846, Romilly supporter George Egan took Rockett to the Dolphin. There they met twine-maker Benjey Gill, another Whig, and Rockett tried to get him to pay a long-standing bill. Rockett then went on to the George which he accepted was 'one of Mr Cochrane's houses'. He returned to the Dolphin in the morning, having left his handkerchief there, and admitted having 'a drop of rum and water' before again moving on to the George. From there he crossed the road to the polling-booth in the Town Hall and was back in the George between his two attempts at voting. He denied taking money from 'Mr Cochrane's servant'.

*Sunny view, southwards across the village, from the porch
of Holy Trinity Church at Bothenhampton.*

There was also evidence that Rockett had been heard to say he would be voting for Romilly by 'Mr Coates of the King of Prussia' and 'Mr Penny, at the Pack Horse'. Questioning centred on whether he was sober:

'Had you any drink then?'
'I cannot say now; I had a drink a trifle, but nothing to take away any of my faculties.'

The committee heard from James Coppock that Rockett's vote was 'possibly the last' election matter he intended investigating because he found evidence of corruption to be more alarming:

I meant to take the case of a voter who had been bribed by receiving £10 not to vote, and in a subsequent part of the day had received £10 to vote; I meant to have called that identical man before the Committee, and then get rid of the vote.

The committee accepted there was a *prima facie* case for looking into bribery allegations but regretted that these lay beyond its Parliamentary remit:

Your Committee have felt themselves precluded by the decision of the House, which negatived that part of the original motion, which suggested inquiry, 'whether any compromise or arrangement was entered into by the parties to the petition, their counsel or agents, to prevent the disclosure of bribery and treating; and also whether, and to what extent, bribery and treating were practised at the last election for the borough of Bridport,' from pursuing any further examination into the circumstances of the arrangement spoken of by Mr Coppock and Mr Templer. It is clear that the effect was to prevent the extensive allegations of bribery in this case from being gone into; and Your Committee cannot help expressing their very great regret that these allegations have not been thoroughly investigated.

The election turned on a single vote. William Rockett told the committee that he had voted 'for Mr Cochrane' and 'no person else I ever named'. This claim was disputed. Although he had been entered in the register as voting for Cochrane, it was said he had uttered 'Romilly' whilst inside the polling-booth. The common ground was that he had difficulty speaking and had made two attempts at voting:

It appears that Rockett went twice to the polling booth to vote; that at the time of his first going there was a great crowd and noise in the booth; that Rockett, who is sixty-four years of age, and afflicted with asthma, was, from exhaustion and confusion, almost unable to speak when he had got through the crowd to the poll-clerk, and

Westwards down West Street, in 1890, with the Sun Inn on the south side (left), *the Lily Hotel projecting across the pavement, and the Royal Oak Inn opposite.*

that, having gone away on this occasion without giving his name and address, which were however known to the poll-clerk, he was considered not to have completed his vote; and that he afterwards returned and duly voted for Mr Cochrane.

Joseph Welch 'and other respectable and intelligent witnesses' from Bridport declared that they had heard Rockett say 'Romilly' after he was 'within the bar of the polling-booth for the purpose of voting.' The committee decided that this had happened and that the recording of Rockett's second vote, when he said 'Cochrane', was therefore invalid:

Your Committee think it right to direct attention to the practice, adopted in this case, of altering a vote by arrangement between the contending parties without the knowledge of the voter, and without full investigation. Mr Coppock's evidence shows that the votes have often been exclusively struck off a poll by similar arrangements. In this instance, Rockett's vote was transferred from one poll to another. Your Committee venture to suggest that it be expedient, in order to meet such cases, to make legislative provision requiring notices of all objections to votes to be served on the voters themselves.

The committee resolved: 'That Mr Cochrane was not duly elected. That Mr Romilly was duly elected, and ought to have been returned.'

Shipping from the Channel was turning into West Bay in 1848 on a scale that would never be exceeded. At the high-water mark for the port 26 ships were registered, amounting to a total of 2,465 tons. It turned out to be both the greatest number of ships and the largest tonnage ever recorded from Bridport Harbour. The *Speedy* was launched into the harbour in 1849. Her keel was 182 feet and at 1,460 tons she was the largest ship to be built at Good's Shipyard. She was destined for the nation's great new port, fast usurping Bristol, as the owners registered her in Liverpool.

Left: *Victorian fish-seller at Burton Bradstock.*

Right: *St Mary's Parish Church from the south-west, 1895.*

Left: *Bridport Station seen in its heyday with double platforms, looking northwards in 1906, with the advertisement (right) for Epps's Cocoa.*

Chapter 10

RAILWAY, FIRES & STATE EDUCATION

On 5 May 1855 the proposed Bridport and Maiden Newton Railway, a junction with the Wilts, Somerset and Weymouth line which was in the course of construction, was incorporated in the Bridport Railway Act and given an unopposed Parliamentary passage. The broad-gauge line was to be built by the Bridport Railway Company, which was considering a contract from Kenneth Mathieson, at an estimated cost of £65,000. Progress was swift though building the nine and a quarter mile course, mainly of cuttings snaking through the valleys and hills, sliced into changeable underlying geology and breached the spring line in many places. It was not without engineering difficulties and construction shortcomings were reported by Captain Tyler of the Board of Trade on 9 October 1857. Authorisation for the opening of the line was delayed until they could be rectified.

At nine o'clock on the morning of Thursday 12 November 1857 the first train steamed into Bridport, thereby opening the broad-gauge branch line from Maiden Newton via Powerstock. For Bridport the event was a complete surprise as its operational use had only been sanctioned the previous day by the Board of Trade. There was no time to arrange a proper welcome, so the town celebrated the following Tuesday with a general holiday and a banquet at the Bull Hotel. The operating licence for the line had been awarded by its owners, the Bridport Railway Company, to the Great Western Railway.

The Coronet stagecoach still operated from the Bull Hotel at Bridport through to Parr's Hotel in Exeter but 1859 turned out to be its last full year of operation. A ticket cost 12 shillings for a seat inside, or 8 shillings if you sat outside on the top. The withdrawal of the service, by operators Hewitt & Company, came about as a result of the opening of the London & South Western Railway as a direct line from Waterloo to Exeter on 19 July 1860. Its course was miles inland, via Yeovil and Crewkerne, but the duplication of transport facilities was too close for the last Bridport coach-and-four stagecoach to remain viable.

Horse-buses remained in business. The Defiance was the best remembered of the regular services. It first ran on 3 September 1859 and linked the railway at Bridport Station with the Three Cups Hotel in Lyme Regis. The best-known drivers at the end of the century were William Hounsell and relief-man H.C. Newlyn. Because of the apparent ease with which he dealt with the hills he had to contend with, on roads that frequently slipped over the cliff, Hounsell was reputed to be 'the best coach-and-four driver in the West of England.'

There was another end of an era. Public hanging in Dorset, at Dorchester, ceased with the execution of a 30-year-old thief, James Searle, who committed an horrific crime at remote Puckshore Cottages in Stoke Abbott. They stood 400 yards along Anchor Lane, now a public path, north-westwards from the Anchor Inn (which became Anchor House on being de-licensed in 1958). The spot comprises stones in a small wood that mark the outline of a building and its former garden.

Sarah Ann Guppy – described as 'deformed and diminutive' – had her throat cut on 30 April 1858. The killer then set fire to the cottages. He was identified as James Searle, who was convicted of 'wilful murder' and hanged on 10 August that year. Watching that event, which took place on a scaffold above the lodge at Dorchester Gaol, was impressionable young architect and author Thomas Hardy. He was two miles away with a telescope on Rainbarrow above his cottage birthplace at Higher Bockhampton.

Hardy was Bridport-bound that autumn, on behalf of John Hicks of South Street, Dorchester, who prepared the faculty documents for the restoration and expansion of St Mary's Parish Church. His architectural assistant, 18-year-old Thomas Hardy, measured the building and helped with the plans. These were submitted on 31 December 1858 with the faculty being granted on 7 March 1859 for work estimated at £2,515. Galleries were removed and the work was done with typical Victorian thoroughness, but not at the expense of spoiling the early-thirteenth-century 'basic cruciform plan' of 'a splendid building which has always been the principal, or mother, church of the town.' The work was completed in 1860 and has been documented by ecclesiastical historian Fred Pitfield whose family comes from Bridport:

The main works included the complete rebuilding of the chancel and its aisles (although, according to the faculty documents, it had only been intended to rebuild the outer

St Andrew's Church (right), *built in 1860, in a view north-eastwards along suburban St Andrew's Road in the 1920s.*

Above: *Bradpole Road, now St Andrew's Road, seen northwards in 1903 from the drive into the Delapre estate* (left foreground) *and St Andrew's Church to Roger's Cottage beside Long's Lane.*

Left: *Commercial cart* (left, background) *of 'Matthews and Son, wholesale family butchers' in a view westwards down West Street in 1895.*

walls), and the extension of the nave and its aisles two bays westwards as intended. All this work was carried out in fifteenth-century style with vertical traceried windows and other details to match the main part of the building. At the new west end the lower part of the nave wall is thicker, in order to accommodate a shallow porch.

As far as the roofs were concerned it had been intended to remove skylights, which had presumably been installed in conjunction with the galleries, and to re-tile parts of the roofs of the nave aisles and transepts. In the event it seems that the roofs of the nave and transepts were completely renewed with plaster barrel vaults, divided into panels by ribs with carved and gilded bosses at the ridge intersections. These roofs were probably copied from those already existing, indicating that they had been of fifteenth-century date. It had also been intended to replace the plaster and timber ribbed vaulting over the crossing, in stone, but either this was not done or the replacement was in timber and plaster as before.

Other more minor structural works included the repositioning of the access door to the porch stair turret, the formation of an external door in the west wall of the north transept, and the formation of a communicating doorway between the south chapel and transept.

As well as rebuilding St Mary's Church the town was also provided with a new chapel-of-ease in Bradpole Road. Fred Pitfield points out that the town was expanding north-eastwards beyond the borough boundary into Bradpole, where Holy Trinity Parish Church was a whole village away to the north. There the twelfth-century building had been pulled down and completely rebuilt in 1845–46. It was, however, inadequate for the growing population of new suburbia and the two parishes co-operated in providing northern Bridport with a new St Andrew's Chapel. Nearby was St Andrew's Well and the dedication also preserved the memory of ancient St Andrew's Chapel which stood at the T-junction in the centre of town.

St Andrew's Chapel, in what became St Andrew's Road, was consecrated during the afternoon of 27 September 1860, after which the Bishop of Salisbury and clerical guests were wined and dined in Mountfield House. Workmen, the choir and inhabitants of Bridport's Union Workhouse were treated to supper after the first evening service. Fred Pitfield gives us the construction details:

The architect was Talbot Bury of London and the builders Chick & Son of Beaminster, Mr Gibbs of Bradpole being the mason. The general stonework was from quarries at nearby Loders, but the dressings are Ham Hill stone. The roofs are slated.

The railway was proving popular in Bridport but caused some frustration in villages and hamlets where people saw trains steaming beside their homes but had no means of using them. On 21 March 1862, to meet local requests from the small communities in the valley west of Maiden Newton, an additional station was opened at Toller Porcorum. It was called Toller.

Bridport, Lyme Regis and the villages of West Dorset shuddered from an earthquake at 03.35 hours on the first Tuesday of October in 1863:

The rumbling sound was accompanied by a violent shaking of beds, like the passing of a heavy wagon at a short distance, that lasted about two seconds. Some thought that thieves had broken in; others awoke dizzy. The main oscillation was from east to west with a secondary motion of a whirling nature, producing feelings of dazed terror. Strong doors jumped open, from their catches. The shock was most violent at Bridport Harbour, Burton Bradstock, Chideock, Charmouth, and Lyme Regis. In the latter westward communities many thought that their houses were being taken by a landslip. The fright was considerable though a violent shock in the early hours of the morning comes upon a populace deeply removed from the cares of this world. Even a great noise then is only comparable to a horse rearing in the afternoon, it being impossible to gauge the magnitude of the disaster. Inland the effects were less perceptible but along the Dorset coast most awoke in the middle of that night with a vivid impression of shock.

The railway proved its commercial worth in June 1864 to the seine-net fishermen of West Dorset. An estimated total of 50,000 fine mackerel were pulled ashore at Chideock and Burton Bradstock early on a Wednesday morning. They were brought to Bridport and sent off by train, but for once there was sufficient for a fair quantity to be sold in the town as well, at 10d. per dozen.

Because of its strong dissenting community and their anti-Catholic roots, Bridport could always be relied upon for a lively Bonfire Night. In 1864 'the usual disturbances took place across the county' but in Bridport the Guy Fawkes figure was replaced by a caricature of a well-heeled resident who had made himself unpopular:

The Fifth of November was marked by a not very creditable demonstration in Bridport. In the presence of many hundreds of people an effigy of a gentleman, who rendered himself obnoxious by his assertion that the town needed a new drainage system, was burnt in a field at the bottom of South Street.

Skimmington riding was still prevalent deep in the West Dorset countryside. This carnival of anger took place to show communal disgust at behaviour that had offended the moral code. The *Western Gazette* reported from Melbury Osmond on a Monday night in November 1865 that:

Left: *Westwards along East Street, from opposite the Bull Hotel* (left) *towards the Town Hall* (centre) *which is flying a huge Union Flag for Queen Victoria's golden jubilee, in 1887.*

Right: *South Street looking north in 1895.*

Left: *The main street in Loders to the Farmers' Arms* (centre, right) *and thatched cottages in the centre of the village, looking eastwards in 1895.*

Right: *South Street in 1910, from West's Dairy* (left) *and the pollarded limes* (right), *north to the Town Hall.*

... this usually quiet little place was much excited by men and boys parading to the music of tin kettles, tin whistles, also frying pans, etc. It was ascertained that a married farmer had been misbehaving himself. Effigies were intended to be burnt, but the police stopped it.

Nor was this the last example of the custom that Thomas Hardy was to bring into his novel *The Mayor of Casterbridge*, which he started in 1884. Lucy Taylor (1879–1947) of Stalbridge remembered seeing a procession of local people disguised with sacking over their heads and beating saucepans with tongs and spoons. They escorted a conveyance with caricatures of the guilty pair. These effigies were burnt at The Ring, the village green. The following day no one in Stalbridge was prepared to admit knowing who had taken part in the event.

There were several major fires in West Dorset in 1865. Four buildings were destroyed in a blaze at the West Bay shipyard. Then on a Tuesday in September nearly 20 houses were destroyed by fire at Evershot and 100 people made homeless:

The fire devastated Summer Lane, the narrow thoroughfare leading off the main street, uphill towards Cattistock, where only one or two detached cottages remain. The inferno started at one o'clock when the back of the carpenter's house was enveloped in flames. These spread to the neighbouring thatched roofs, which were tinder dry as a result of the long drought. Police Constable Hare sent for the two fire engines that are kept at Melbury House but by this time sparks were being blown across the street to the barn and slaughter-house of Trenchard, the butcher. The whole lane became a mass of fire. Telegraphic messages were sent to Yeovil for more engines and to Dorchester for a staff of policemen. Before they arrived the wind changed direction and took the fire into the main street, which also became impassable. So great was the heat that the buildings could not be approached until they had burnt out. There was, however, no loss of life nor even any personal injury sustained.

That month, September 1865, there was another public disturbance of the kind known as skimmington riding in a village on the Somerset border. One has the impression that they used to be much more common and were not generally reported until the mid-nineteenth century:

A story had gained currency in East Coker that the wife of a man who had been in America for two years had been on too friendly terms with a married man in the village, with a result that might have been anticipated. The affair was made all the worse by the fact that both parties were connected with the [Plymouth] Brethren and displayed pretensions to superior sanctity. To show

their abhorrence of such cant, some of the inhabitants prepared a couple of effigies which were paraded through the village and burnt in public. The affair created a sensation which is difficult to describe; Coker people will be more than ever suspicious of those who lard their talk with Scripture.

In November 1865 a shipwreck at West Bay confirmed an old adage that 'they chew hemp rather than oats' in Bridport as the latter cash crop was being imported from Ireland:

During the fierce gale of the Monday in the middle of the month, a Cork schooner, the Black Diamond, *was washed ashore on the West Beach at Bridport and is a total wreck, with the cargo being lost. The whole of the crew were safely landed by means of Manley's apparatus. She was carrying oats, consigned to Mr Knight at the Bull Hotel.*

A hurricane-force blizzard swept through Dorset, Somerset and Devon on the Thursday in the middle of January in 1866. A total of 17 ships were blown on to the shore around Portland. Many fine trees were blown over in parks across central Dorset. At Beaminster a lad of 17, who appears to have sat down for a rest, perished of the cold. A group of 87 ewes in a flock of 470 died on Welcome Hill, Bingham's Melcombe. Not in the remembrance of the oldest person in Rampisham has such a fall of snow come so quickly. Roads for miles around were blocked. Then with the thaw the rise of the stream through the village was equally swift. The carpenter's family near the Tiger's Head had to be rescued from their bedroom window after the water had blocked the staircase. From North Dorset the flood waters surged into Somerset where the lands around Glastonbury were flooded for miles. Bread had to be delivered from Wedmore in a boat.

It was reported that spring that fishermen and boys from the villages along the coast near

Southwards along South Street, in 1912, from the Cross Keys (left) and butchers Arthur Lewis, with their cart setting off, and the shops of hosier Frederick Dinham (right) and grocer Samuel Whitemore (with sign for Colman's Starch).

Weymouth still scoured the pebbles of the Chesil Beach for the gold coins that are frequently found washed ashore after a severe gale:

There is always considerable excitement when someone picks up the greater part of the value of a week's hard labour as it glistens from between the pebbles. Mostly, we hear, such coins are Spanish, Mexican, or Dutch.

In May 1866 a fire in the chimney of a beerhouse burnt two cottages to the ground at North Allington, Bridport, and the wind conveyed so many sparks across the street that another dwelling opposite shared their fate.

Archaeology was becoming popular with the equivalent of the 'Time Team' of the day. An 'initiatory restoration' of Hell Stone cromlech on Portesham Hill, a mile north of the village, was completed by Revd Martin Tupper, the author of *Proverbial Philosophy,* on 11 June 1866. Until he started work it was a collapsed burial chamber with a collection of boulders scattered across the highest part of mound about 100 feet long. The sarsen stones were partly hidden by earth. The antiquary Charles Warne described the site:

The supports of the capstone have sunk on the south-west side, and are virtually buried by it, its great weight being now chiefly sustained by a single prop on its north side, so that it rests on a greatly-inclined position. It measures more than ten feet in length, about seven

Forster's Lane (right) *preserves the memory of education reformer W.E. Forster in Bradpole.*

feet in breadth, and has an average thickness of at least two feet and a half. Originally it must have rested upon eight or ten supports.

However, Mr Tupper's workmen failed to replace this massive capstone, which was left lying on the ground until they returned in 1869.

Meanwhile, in 1867 a new brig named *Dora,* which was launched from Cox's Yard at West Bay, left Bridport Harbour for Cadiz, where she loaded quantities of salt and then proceeded direct to Newfoundland for fish. This cargo, duly salted, was taken to Brazil. Most of her hands were from Bridport and 'this neighbourhood'.

The summer of 1869 brought tragedy to West Bay and one of Bridport's principal families when three young men had a wager about who would be first to swim across the harbour entrance, 'in a splash-and-dash', between the piers. The incoming waves were huge but rather irregular. One youth balked at the jump, the second went, and the third followed. The two in the water had misjudged their opportunity. One ended up under the pier, which then had open timbers, and was able to claw his way to safety. The third, Edward Gundry, was drowned in the swell.

On 14 August 1869 eight Portland quarrymen arrived on Portesham Hill to complete the task which Revd Martin Tupper and his workmen had found impossible in their earlier attempt at rebuilding Hell Stone cromlech. Its capstone, estimated to weigh 16 tons, had been left lying on the ground. With the quarrymen, however, the mission was accomplished in a short time. Having brought screw-jacks they were able to raise it on to the nine upright pillars, which are about five feet above the ground. The restoration must be regarded as picturesque rather than accurate. The sarsen stones comprised a Neolithic burial chamber dating from between 3500 and 2500BC.

There were Bridport links with the milestone legislation that was proceeding through Parliament and became the cornerstone of Britain's educational

The spire of Bradpole Parish Church, seen from the south in 1971.

Bradpole Parish Church from the south-east, 1895.

system. The bill was introduced in Parliament on 17 February 1870 by W.E. Forster, who was born at Bradpole, but had to win through after considerable discussion and much opposition from dissenters, including those in Bridport. Two of these families had become inextricably and confusingly linked in the 1860s when brothers Thomas and William Colfox of Bridport married sisters Louisa and Anna Wansey from Warminster. Their interventions, against the concept of State education – arguing that 'it should be left to religious denominations' – were typical of the petitioning and resistance that kept the bill in committee for half the year, but as the Elementary Education Act it received royal assent from Queen Victoria on 9 August 1870. In Bradpole the educational reformer's memory is preserved by Forster's Lane, north-eastwards from the Post Office.

Loss of life in an imminent shipwreck on a stormy night was averted at Stanton St Gabriel by what local people believe to have been a divine premonition in 1872. Isaac Hunter, a Charmouth fisherman, had a violent dream brought on 'by anxiety for his lobster pots'. He was in such a distressed state that he immediately dressed and set off to run eastwards along the coast for two miles, in the teeth of a gale. He found a French ship in distress, off Golden Cap, and was able to raise the Coastguard and effect the successful rescue of the ship's crew. Their vessel became a total wreck.

The antiquary Charles Warne, in manuscript notes made in 1874, recorded the destruction of a major alignment of megaliths about a quarter of a mile north-east from Hell Stone burial chamber, above Portesham (OS map reference SY 608 869):

In a small valley, on the down of Portesham Farm, there stood within these last ten years, four upright stones – each about ten feet high – in a line and nearly equidistant from each other, to which was attached the following doggerel: 'Jeffery and Joan, and their little dog Denty, with Eddy alone.' By the direction of the occupier of the farm, Mr Maufield, these stones were removed and built into an adjoining wall. The

neighbourhood abounding in stone, one would have thought he could have spared these interesting remains; but what is safe against ignorance and avarice combined.

Transport and commerce also took a backward step with the abandonment of Isambard Kingdom Brunel's 7-foot wide track which had enabled larger trains, more room for passengers and greater safety and stability than were possible on George Stephenson's 4 feet $8^1/_2$ inches. The Great Western Railway's Dorset lines, being those from Yeovil to Weymouth and Bridport, were converted from their 7-foot broad gauge to that of the narrower standard track in June 1874. The lines were closed for a few days in the middle of the month.

Mineral exploration along the Bridport coast included searches for coal towards Charmouth and iron ore at Abbotsbury. In 1877 the Portesham Shale Works at Waddon sank a large shaft with the work being carried on day and night by Welshmen and other miners. Two stationary steam engines worked continuously to lift stone and drain water, and the depth reached was 180 feet.

On 29 May 1877 John Lothrop Motley (1814–77), the United States Ambassador to London in 1869–70 and the world authority on the history of the Dutch Republic and the United Netherlands, died at Kingston Russell House, where he was staying with the Duke of Bedford.

Having seen reduced orders for some years and suffered fires and other problems, the shipyard on the west side of West Bay closed in 1879 with the launching and fitting out of the *Lilian*. It was forced out of business by the great yards that were making the new generation of iron-clad vessels in the North. Bridport Harbour had also declined into insignificance, from its thriving trade of the 1830s, and with the arrival of the railway in Bridport town in 1857 its demise seemed inevitable. Sailing ships made in the yard were still trading across the oceans, but by the end of the century they would be a memory as well.

Bradpole, which has become Bridport's northern suburb, looking down on Middle Street and across to Higher Street and Holy Trinity Church (top left) in 1905.

Right: *Lower Eype, with boys on the raised pavement beside Lea Cottage and Honeysuckle Cottage, in a view northwards to the New Inn in 1906.*

Left: *The ill-fated last flight of the military balloon* Saladin *with Captain James Templer, who jumped out at Eype, and the Member of Parliament who disappeared.*

Hydrangea Cottage, named for its flowers, followed by Clematis, Rosemary and Sunset Cottage in Lower Eype.

Chapter 11

SNOW, SALADIN & PORT BREDY

Paddle-steamers arrived in west Dorset in 1875 with the *Commodore* and the *Prince* operated by Cosens & Company from Weymouth. Their loadings were modest, however, and in 1878 it was recorded that a total of 31 passengers had been carried from Bridport to Lyme Regis (1s.6d.), 108 to Seaton (2s.6d.) and 89.5 to Sidmouth (3s.0d.). Then the *Empress* took over the service, in 1879, and by 1880 – with *Premier* sharing the route – there were 3,689.5 passengers from Bridport. The calculations are in adult terms; a child was counted as half a person.

The next year, however, the total fell to 1,857 and it dropped again in 1882 to 686.5. Both years were struck by that perpetual bane of English tourism, 'the inclement weather'. The century's Great Snow began falling on 18 January 1881, deeply and evenly, in quantities larger than anyone can remember. The temperature varied from 25 to 30 degrees Fahrenheit and initially there was not much wind. On 20 January 1881 it was reported:

For the past three days and nights Dorset has endured a blizzard with a strong northerly wind driving the snow into every crevice of buildings and piling it across the lanes until it was level with the tops of the hedgerows. Only the railways continue to function and one of the more fortunate of the otherwise cut-off communities is Bradford Abbas where a wagon of coal is being emptied down the embankment for the benefit of villagers.

In 1881, Bridport Harbour ceased to be a bond port, and the customs duties collected there during its final year were the lowest on record. They totalled only £1,915.

One of the most amazing moments in Bridport and Parliamentary history took place on 10 September 1881 when the War Office's gas-filled balloon *Saladin* drifted out of control and was lost over the sea at West Bay. Alone on board was 'dashing and daring' Walter Powell, Member of Parliament for Malmesbury in Wiltshire, who boasted of becoming 'an aeronautic adventurer'

Walter Powell, MP for Malmesbury, whose last view of English soil was at Eype and West Bay in 1881.

when he accepted the invitation to be a guest on the flight. That wish came tragically true when the two crewmen bounced out of the basket beneath the balloon as it was dragged along the ground above Eype Mouth.

The balloon, 60 feet long by 30 feet wide, had taken off from Bath at 14.00 hours on a weather-research flight. Measurements of cloud temperatures and humidity were taken for the Meteorological Society. They drifted south-westwards, across Glastonbury and Crewkerne, but then underestimated the strength of the northerly wind which took them over Beaminster at 16.00 hours. Cloud prevented visual course correction until someone suddenly spotted Lyme Bay and they realised they were perilously close to the sea. A desperate attempt was made to bring the balloon down but on clipping the ground at Cliff Close, Eype Mouth, at 16.15 hours, crucial elements of vitally-needed ballast were thrown out along with Captain James Templer. He lay on the grass, bruised but safe, as crewman Agg Gardner found himself caught in a rope and dragged for 80 feet along the ground. He broke his leg but survived.

The unlucky third man, Walter Powell MP, gave a wave and rose into the evening clouds. A tiny speck disappeared from view as he floated out across the English Channel. Nothing more was ever heard of

Coalman from Bridport delivering between the cottages of Lower Eype, in a view from 1905.

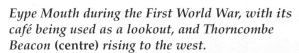

Eype Mouth during the First World War, with its café being used as a lookout, and Thorncombe Beacon (centre) rising to the west.

Right: *Storm-force seas breaking through the ship channel into Bridport Harbour in 1906.*

Left: *Eastwards from Eype Mouth to West Bay (right), with a few of the boats belonging to Charles, Richard and William Warren, in 1921.*

West Bay Station in 1910 with the driver handing over a signalling token.

him, although wreckage of what was presumed to be *Saladin* was found on the slopes of Sierra del Piedroza in the mountains of Spain on 20 January 1882. There were no human remains in the basket or on the hillside and it was thought that the MP may have bailed out over the sea. There were rumours that he had deliberately disappeared, to escape his debts, but publication of his will showed he was worth £40,000 – the equivalent of a modern millionaire. In Wiltshire he is commemorated by the Walter Powell Primary School at Great Somerford, named for him a century later, and the Saladin public house in nearby Little Somerford.

Fire destroyed the crane at Bridport Harbour in 1882. The crane house was to the north-west of the Bridport Arms Inn and the crane used to run on a railway from the end of the east jetty, along the side of the channel, northwards to the harbour. The port's foreign trade ceased the previous year and the crane had become the symbol of past prosperity.

Despite this, 'having missed the boat' as cynics put it, Bridport Railway Company approved a plan to extend their branch line to the seaside. The land was purchased for the extension of the railway from Bridport to the harbour in 1883. A tender was accepted, provided that the cost would be 'within an earlier estimate of £23,000'.

Its extension to West Bay was in anticipation of a growing hotel trade. In the process it gave the town a station in its main street. This was to be built beside the point where the line crosses East Street, east of East Bridge, where the road towards Dorchester becomes East Road. A £12,000 contribution came from the Great Western Railway which held the operating rights. The new terminus by the sea at Bridport Harbour, known as West Bay, opened on 31 March 1884, with an intermediate station as proposed, beside the level crossing where the line intersected the lower end of East Street.

In West Bay the biggest and most distinctive of its buildings – named Pier Terrace but known as Noah's Ark – was built near the site of the former crane house of Bridport Harbour in 1884. Its architect was Edward Schroder Prior (1852–1932) of the Arts and Crafts movement who also built the Esplanade. He designed Pier Terrace to face seawards but moved it by 90 degrees, away from the waves, when he realised the battering it would receive from the elements. It soon found a distinguished detractor in Sir Frederick Treves who condemned it for being 'as out of place as an iron girder in a flower garden.' The double-bayed Moorings – delightful with miniature cupola – and pebble-dashed Querida completed Prior's seaside trio. He had studied under Norman

Lively gulls in the backwater at West Bay, looking south-eastwards across the River Brit, to the George Hotel.

Shaw, who replaced historic Bryanston House with red-brick blandness, and discovered Bridport in 1880 when he was courting Louisa Isabella Maunsell, the rector's daughter from Symondsbury.

Thomas Hardy brought the new West Bay holiday resort into a novel he began writing in 1884, having a character in *The Mayor of Casterbridge* resolving 'to go away to the sea-side for a few days – to Port Bredy.' West Bay also appears in *Life's Little Ironies*: 'The plan was that as soon as they were married they would make out a holiday by driving straight off to Port Bredy to see the ships and the sea.'

The Templer family – headed by Charles Templer (1825–95) who moved from the Grove at Bridport to Surbiton – were among the first to have holiday homes in Pier Terrace. Templer's granddaughter, Mary Horsefell, recalled that 'it was pitch dark' when she arrived at West Bay Station and was directed to her 'comfortable lodgings'. She awoke to the realisation 'that we had a narrow escape from walking into the harbour':

West Bay proved to be a great success with all the family. True, the bathing facilities were not outstandingly good, consisting of three very ancient bathing machines controlled by Harry, the nephew and ever-willing slave of Mrs Slater, the owner, who superintended operations from her wheelchair. Auntie Slater, as everyone called her, wore a black straw hat and black shawl around her shoulders. She was what is today called a character.

The Esplanade, from the west side of the harbour entrance to the foot of West Cliff, was constructed in 1887. A sporting nine-hole golf course was established on the slope (on the opposite side of the valley to the present golf course) in 1891. Morning golfers, who carried bathing tackle, traditionally broke off at the fourth hole and descended to Eype Mouth for a swim. On the other side of West Bay, across East Beach, a Volunteer Review was the great event. Both the Queen's Own Dorset Yeomanry and the 1st Volunteer Battalion of the Dorsetshire Regiment marshalled their

East Street Station (centre) *and the River Asker in a view eastwards along East Road in 1905.*

forces there in the 1890s. A-Company of the 1st Volunteer Battalion, marching from their Drill Hall in St Michael's Lane, were the hosts.

St Andrew's Church, a mission church at West Bay that was manned by visiting clergy from Burton Bradstock, seated 100 people. William Bellingham was the Chief Officer at the Coastguard Station. Old-timers remembered smuggling days and the white-painted markers on the cliff-top path that is now the long-distance coastal path. Their teasing form of address for William Bellingham was 'Mr Preventive Man'.

The police beat was in walking distance of Bridport Police Station, in South Street, where Sergeant Absolem Wiles had four constables. Martin Joseph Briggs, the Harbour Master at West Bay, was followed by Henry Hitchcock. The latter was remembered by Mary Hounsell in her *Life in Bridport* which was published by James Stevens Cox in 1969:

He was well known to all frequenters of the Bay, as he was constantly in the harbour area, either attending to the sluice gates whenever the tide served, night and day, or in readiness to dock arriving ships. The Harbour could take ships of up to 250 tons. The two pilots, John Sheckel and Gale, used to row out to board the ships and bring them safely through the narrow and difficult entrance between the piers to the wharf, where they were hauled alongside to be berthed by ropes pulled by any men available. None of the ships that docked at the port then was driven by engine power. All were sailing vessels, and very beautiful they looked.

All the fishermen wore blue jerseys but John Sheckel stood out as being different, 'always wearing a Sherlock Holmes style deerstalker hat'.

As well as bringing West Bay into contact with Paddington Station (changes at Bath and Maiden Newton) the railway also enabled fast outward transit of two fashionable cash crops from Dorset. 'Up and coming' Victorian society admired one and consumed the other. For a time, more popular than the fabled aspidistra, ferns were the most desirable indoor plant in the land. The other product, for high

Harbour Museum, in the old Salt House at West Bay, with cannon recovered from shipwrecks.

Teas at 6d. through to 9d. with minstrels providing the entertainment West Bay in 1909.

Right: *East Pier at West Bay, eastwards to East Cliff.*

Left: *Seaside architecture at West Bay began with the Moorings, designed by Edward Prior.*

Jaws motif on a boat moored at low tide in the basin of Bridport Harbour in 1995.

Above: *The basin of Bridport Harbour at West Bay, looking south-eastwards across the quay to Pier Terrace and East Cliff.*

Left: *Shingle and thatch seawards by the Bridport Arms (centre) at West Bay.*

Left: *Half timbering, as the present-day descendant of clapper-board cladding, at the old Mission Room in George Street, West Bay, in 1997.*

Right: *Coaster arriving to thrill the crowd during the hot summer of 1959 as the* Lady Jean, *from Rochester on the Medway, works her way into Bridport Harbour.*

Left: *A south-westerly gale making the harbour channel treacherous.*

Right: *Edward Prior's Pier Terrace of 1884 had originally been designed to face southwards and seawards.*

Yachts and sailing ships in the inner harbour in 1903, looking south-eastwards to Pier Terrace (right).

tea, was watercress from clear-water springs beside chalkland streams. The watercress, through fears of parasitic infection, was at least purpose grown but the ferns were stripped from damper parts of the West Dorset countryside in their thousands.

On 17 July 1887 a letter writer to the *Western Gazette* reported that the *Birmingham Daily Post* was carrying regular advertisements for ferns which had been taken from the roadsides of Dorset in a wholesale manner. 'The lanes of Dorset, Somerset and Devon are rightly admired for their beauty and it is distressing to see the huge gaps made in them by the fern robbers,' the reader lamented. The advertisements showed the scale of the demand in the cities for the plants: 'Ferns, Ferns, Ferns. – Fifty lovely Devon and Dorset hardy Ferns, 1s. 3d; 150, 3s. 3d.' and 'Fifty splendid hardy Dorset Fern Roots, being assorted, well packed in moss and carriage paid, 2s.; 100, 3s. 9d.'

On 3 March 1891 all roads across the Dorset Downs were blocked by deep snow. There was a report of a man being lost in the blizzard somewhere between Maiden Newton and Sydling St Nicholas. Searchers recovered the body of John Guppy, near Sydling, and Police Constable James Searley notified the coroner.

This was followed by intensely fine powdery snow, carried by a gale that reached Force 10 during the night, which blanketed the West Country during the early hours of Tuesday 11 March. The blizzard cut off the western peninsula with huge drifts. The hills west of Bridport were worst hit, with 'mountains of snow, twenty feet high' making it impossible to find the main road between Charmouth and Honiton. The hurricane veered from north-east to south-east, and during the Tuesday the temperature varied from 29 to 31$^1/_2$ degrees Fahrenheit but it felt much colder in the strong winds. Westwards, the storm centred on Dartmoor, stopping all trains below Okehampton and Plymouth, and the coasts of Devon and Cornwall also shared this indescribably wretched day. A correspondent from Lyme Regis reported:

One of the heaviest snowstorms ever to visit the south of Dorset was experienced at Lyme on Tuesday. The town lies six miles from the nearest railway station, and the only communication is by two well-appointed three-horse 'busses'. On Tuesday the bus, with an extra horse, left the town at nine in the morning, carrying the mails. The conveyance, with great difficulty, reached the high hill known as Hunter's Lodge, where, notwithstanding all efforts, it was found to be impossible to proceed further. The one lady passenger walked to the hotel at Hunter's Lodge, while the driver, Mr Blake, rode back to Lyme Regis and obtained assistance. By the time the luggage and mails had been transferred to a light wagonette the bus, except for the roof, was invisible, and the roof was only kept clear by the strong winds blowing at the time. Later on the same night, the driver of the mail cart from Ilminster to Lyme started to do the journey on horseback, driving being out of the question. On about the same spot as the bus had been buried, the driver lost his horse, and accomplished the rest of the journey on foot, arriving at Lyme at one o'clock on Wednesday morning. Both horse and bus were eventually recovered and the mail carts resumed running on 17 March.

On the Sunday following the blizzard the body of a man named Bisgood, a labourer, was found near Offwell in Devon. He had not been seen alive after leaving the New Inn, Honiton Hill, on Tuesday evening. The snow held up completion of the greens and bunkers of the first golf links to be laid out in West Dorset. It opened on the West Cliff, between West Bay and Eype, and then migrated across the valley to what is the current West Dorset Golf Club Course on the flatter eastern cliff top towards Burton Bradstock.

Coach travellers brought the news to Bridport on 14 April 1893 that the thatched Chideock Castle, the inn on the north side of Main Street in the centre of the village, had been badly damaged by fire. This had started in the bakery on the opposite side of the road where a long terrace of eight cottages were left completely gutted with only chimneys and front walls

A boat coming into Bridport Harbour with the tide, in 1921, looking northwards from opposite Pier Terrace (right).

Right: *Edwardian West Bay in 1905, seen from East Cliff, with a steamer arriving from Weymouth at the end of the pier.*

Left: *The tidal backwater of the River Brit, looking south to the George Hotel (left), Bridport Arms Hotel (centre) and Pier Terrace in 1925.*

Right: *West Bay and Bridport Harbour, looking westwards across the great expanse of shingle beach from East Cliff in 1930, towards Golden Cap (top left).*

Left: *Chalets and motor cars beside the Esplanade at West Bay in 1922, looking eastwards to Pier Terrace and East Cliff.*

Left: *Grove Iron Works* (right) *at West Allington in 1895.*

Right: *Foundry Cottages and the Foundry House (right) of Richard Robert Sansom's Grove Iron Works, looking eastwards along West Allington in 1900.*

Above: *Bridport Arms Hotel* (left) *and Pier Terrace* (right)*, looking southwards from across Bridport Harbour in 1905.*

Right: *End of East Pier, looking eastwards to Burton Cliff, in the 1920s.*

Above: *Admiration and a photo call for two splendid chauffeur-driven Edwardian motor cars calling at the Anchor Hotel in Burton Bradstock, looking westwards along Barr Lane towards Bridport.*

Above: *Partially paved green lane, romantic and rustic with the name Lovers' Grove, seen in 1935.*

Above: *The town's Merryweather fire-engine, bought in commemoration of Edward VII's coronation, fighting the blaze at the Infants School in 1906.*

Below: *Bridport Infants School, in West Street, on fire on 12 November 1906.*

Below: *Conservative farmer John Wyatt from Powerstock, wearing his smock in Bridport in support of Colonel Robert Williams, during the 1910 Parliamentary election.*

still standing. Some of the furniture was dragged out from beneath an immense cloud of smoke. Over the road, a combination of enthusiasm, the slope and a little more time enabled a remarkable salvage rate for beer barrels from the Chideock Castle. Replacement cottages extend from Corner Cottage, Trefoil, and the Old Bakery to the Old Post Office, Clenston and Jersey Cottage. Sir Frederick Weld also rebuilt Chideock Castle which was re-named the Castle Inn.

To welcome the new century, the specimen of *Magnolia campbellii*, the pink tulip tree from Sikkim that was planted in Abbotsbury Castle grounds by the 4th Earl of Ilchester in 1864, achieved its first flowering in 1900. It was a 30-foot tree. These private grounds are now Abbotsbury Sub-Tropical Gardens, where the tree had reached 90 feet high and was still flowering at the millennium. This species can reach a height of 150 feet in the Himalayas.

The Great Western Railway, the operating company of the Bridport branch line, bought out the Bridport Railway Company which owned the track on 1 July 1901. A price of £6 was paid for each £10 ordinary share. A convenient early-morning service from the East Street station at Bridport to the sea at West Bay had become known as the 'Bathing Train'. At other times the railway had strong competition, from the carriages gathered beside the Greyhound and other post houses, particularly when the shops closed early, at four o'clock on Thursday afternoons.

There was a royal visit on 8 December 1904 when Mary, Princess of Wales, visited Lady Stavordale at Abbotsbury. She stayed at the Ilchester Arms in the village. Her carriage was horse drawn although motor cars had ventured along the coast road and into the hills, but their reception was problematic. On 8 September 1908, the police sent a warning to Martinstown schoolchildren, cautioning them that action would be taken if they continued to throw stones at motor cars. For years the hire-car driver from Bridport, George Bonfield who had a garage in West Street and a 'sales depot' in East Street, flatly refused to allow any of his motor cars to go beyond Swyre and Bexington, through fear of having to climb back up the formidable viewpoint of Abbotsbury Hill. He told the Templer family: 'No I will not drive on that road. It is altogether too rough and steep.'

The town's Merryweather steam fire-pump, purchased in 1902 to commemorate the coronation of King Edward VII, saw action when the thatched Infants' School in West Street caught fire on 12 November 1906. Late lighting of Bonfire Night fireworks were blamed. Fireman Fred Phillips (1880–1966) from No. 49 South Street was the leading horseman, charging ahead with his stoker, Ted Parker, strapped to the back. They were a little too enthusiastic, Fred's son Jack recalled, and 'failed to negotiate the Brewery turning, being compelled to carry on to the Bothenhampton junction, turn and have another go at the Brewery.' Fred Phillips was the living counterpart of Warwick Deeping's fictional Sorrell from the novel *Sorrell and Son*, Jack Phillips told me:

Tory victor of the Bridport count in the West Dorset Parliamentary election of 25 January 1910 was Colonel Robert Williams.

He was born in the horse era and died in the car era, but it would have been more fitting if he had entered this world fifty years earlier, and thus spent his entire working life among the animals he loved. He was a saddened man when the motor car took over from the horse.

Another throw-back from that bygone age, farmer John Wyatt of Manor Farm, Powerstock – one of Colonel Robert Williams' most ardent supporters – 'stole the show by arriving for the count at the Town

Happy Island on the River Asker, between Bradpole and the Dorchester Road, in 1912 when it was popular as the closest inland picnic spot to Bridport town.

Horse-drawn delivery van of ironmongers Charles Edward Bazley, from East Street, in 1910.

Hall in Bridport dressed in a smock, as a yeoman yokel' in the 1910 general election. He was on the winning side as the Conservative and Unionist banker from Bridehead at Littlebredy received 4,011 votes against 2,759 for Liberal candidate William S. Edwards. The latter, the owner of a Bridport net-making works, lived at the Gables in West Allington.

Bridport's first gas explosion occurred in Thomas White's china shop at 22 West Street in 1912. Work was being done by a gas fitter and a lamp failed to light. Mr White then lit a candle. 'A loud report was heard and Mr White could be seen surrounded by flame,' John Rowson reported in the *Bridport News*. Ceilings fell, floors lifted, plate-glass shattered, china became shrapnel, and the great cornice was fragmented. From it all, 'like a bull in

the proverbial china shop,' Thomas White emerged singed but otherwise intact, giving thanks for the 'merciful intervention of Providence'. The cost to the insurance company of Providence and Mr White was £45. The leak was traced to a pipe which had been fractured when fitters laid a new service from the main to a cellar.

On the night of 14 February 1914 the Dutch steamer *Dorothea* from Rotterdam was washed broadside-on to the Chesil Beach off Langton Herring. For once the treacherous bank proved a lifesaver, rather than the ominous threat it must have sounded as the hull crunched and creaked across the pebbles. For hours the sea broke across the deck. Conditions eased after dawn and at low tide the crew walked ashore.

BRIDPORT HOSTELRIES

There were dozens of places where you could enjoy a drink in Bridport and the surrounding countryside. The following list is formidable but by no means comprehensive. These public houses, clubs and their temperance alternatives were in business at the close of the Victorian age and through the Edwardian era:

Anchor Hotel, Burton Bradstock (Mrs Ann Hayward followed by Alfred John Churchouse);
Anchor Inn, Seatown (Reginald George Bugler).

Baker's Arms, Rope Walks (Silvester Dunn followed by Miss Emily Louisa Dunn);
Blue Ball, Dottery (William Webber);
Boot Inn, North Allington (Thomas Turner followed by Albert Edward Steer);
Boot and Shoe Inn, St Andrew's Road (Frederick Lacey followed by George Rendell);
Bradpole Liberal Working Men's Club (Albert Foot);
Bridport Arms Hotel, West Bay (John Eves followed by George C. Plowman);
Bridport Conservative Club and Reading Room, South Street (William Harvey);
Bull Hotel, East Street (William Knight followed by George A. Knight).

Above: *The thatched Bridport Arms Hotel, between Bridport Harbour and the beach at West Bay, seen in 1935.*

Castle Inn, Chideock (James Love followed by William Bugler);
Coffee Rooms, Barrack Street (James Legg);
Crook Inn, Yondover, Netherbury (Charles Woodland);
Cross Keys, South Street (Walter Trump);
Crown Inn, West Bay Road (Mrs Mary Davies followed by George Holt);
Crown Inn, Puncknowle (Frederick Northover followed by Thomas Samways).

Above: *The former Farmers' Arms in Loders.*

Dolphin Inn, East Street (John Hockey Norman followed by Alfred Smith).

Farmers' Arms, Lower Loders (David Stroud followed by Edward Henry Blackler);
Fisherman's Arms, South Street (Denis Shannon);
Five Bells, South Street (Samuel Coombs).

George, The, South Street (John Saunders Harding);
George Hotel, West Bay (Edward Stevens Boucher followed by Henry Lucas);
George Inn, Bothenhampton (Robert Waldron Hawkins);
Globe Inn, East Street (Mrs Mary Anna Russell followed by Charles Edward Walker);

Greyhound Hotel, East Street (Mrs Florence Tucker followed by Walter Trump).

Hare and Hounds, Waytown, Netherbury (Malachi Travers);
Hodder's Temperance Hotel, East Street (Arthur Sylvester Hodder);
Hope and Anchor, St Michael's Lane (Henry Strangway, followed by Ernest Henry Ackerman).

Ilchester Arms, Symondsbury (Benjamin John Knight followed by James Easton).

Greyhound Hotel and the Town Hall in 1996.

King of Prussia, East Street (John Foster followed by Charles John Hoskins, who had it renamed the King of Belgium Hotel in the First World War, which in turn fell out of favour and was replaced by a British hero, Lord Nelson);

King's Arms, North Allington (John Marsh followed by Alfred Harold Lacey);

King's Head, St Andrew's Road, Bradpole (James Coombs followed by James Norman).

Lily Hotel, West Street (James Foss);

Loders Arms, Lower Loders (Wesley Hine);

London Inn, West Road, Symondsbury (Frederick Burton followed by John Walter Gape);

Luncheon Rooms, West Street (Thomas Pavey).

Markethouse Inn, Market Place (Not known);

Masons' Arms, North Street (Thomas Lancashear);

Masons' Arms, Shipton Gorge (Matthew Foot followed by Mrs Emmeline Agnes Hansford).

New Inn, Lower Eype (Walter Gape);

New Inn, Netherbury (John Marsh Morey);

New Inn, Salway Ash, Netherbury (George Chick);

New Inn, Shipton Gorge (John Mannel followed by Miss Mary Ann Gale).

Old Inn, West Allington (John Hart followed by Mrs Frances Biles).

Queen's Head, Netherbury (William Eveleigh).

Public house, school and church (centre) *in a single view from the Ilchester Arms at Symondsbury.*

Downhill from the New Inn at Lower Eype beside the 1860-built Eype School (left).

Pack Horse Inn (previously known as the White Horse), East Street (Richard Cox);

Phoenix Inn, St Micheal's Lane (William Joseph Oxenbury followed by Mrs Elizabeth Oxenbury);

Plymouth Inn, West Allington (Mrs Caroline Eveleigh followed by Mrs Ellen Miller);

Railway Terminus Hotel, Bradpole Road (Richard Miller);

Refreshment Rooms, South Street (John Keily);

Rising Sun, South Bowood, Netherbury (John Warr);

Robin Hood Inn, Folly Mill Lane (Mrs Daisy Battrick);

Royal Oak Hotel, West Street (George Smith followed by Frederick Norris).

Sailors' Home, South Street (Mrs Jane Newman followed by George Pomeroy);

Ship Inn, South Street (the wonderfully named Henry Beer followed by Mrs Lilian May Northover);

Seven Stars Hotel, Barrack Street (Mrs Catherine Dark followed by Henry Walter Trump);

Star Hotel, West Street (Isaac Haines followed by Henry S. Pearse);

Sun Inn, Morcombelake (Mrs Martha Hodder);

Sun Hotel, West Street (James Walter Coombs, followed by William Kingman).

The sign of the Three Horseshoes at Powerstock.

Three Cups Coffee Tavern, East Street (Frank Odell);

Three Horseshoes, Burton Bradstock (Joseph Samuel Day Hawkins followed by James Samways);

Three Horseshoes, Powerstock (Mrs Sophia Palmer);

Three Mariners Inn, East Street (Mrs Jane Legg);

Tiger Inn, Barrack Street (Henry Charles Newlyn);

Travellers' Rest Inn, Upper Loders (Hamilton Rogers followed by Dan Travers).

Volunteer Inn, South Street (William George Hallett).

West Bay Hotel, West Bay (Mrs Patience Yewdall followed by Charles Begg);

West Dorset Club for Gentlemen, East Street (Charles G. Nantes);

White Bull, East Road (Thomas Clark followed by David Sprake);

White Lion Inn, West Allington (William Frampton Hann, followed by Mrs Susannah Osborne);

Woodman Inn, South Street (Frederick Gibbs).

There were also numerous beer retailers at the end of the Victorian age. Frederick Biles, Cornelius Dunn, John Kitcher, George Podger, William Scadding and Matthew Shearman were all in business in South Street, appropriately within yards of the brewery. Charles Albert Gale was in West Street. Levi Richard Gale was in West Bay Road. William John Gale and George Weeks were in Folly Mill Lane.

Miss Rebecca Hart was in West Street. William Kingman serviced West Allington. Mrs Augusta Priest and Mrs Ann Warbin were in North Allington. John Samson attracted the net-workers in St Michael's Lane. Isaac Patten was in Barrack Street.

Slate-clad Tiger Inn, in Barrack Street, in 1997.

The muster of horses in the Square at Broadwindsor on 5 August 1914.

Left: *Eype Down, above Bridport, where the Royal Naval Division dug trenches to prepare for Gallipoli.*

Flying hero William Barnard Rhodes-Moorhouse, from Parnham House, won the Royal Air Force its first Victoria Cross.

Chapter 12
BACKSTAGE AT ARMAGEDDON

During a period of terrible anxiety, when war and peace were hanging in the balance, the uneventful life of Bridport went on. Summer holiday-makers came to West Bay as usual through 1914, by train and on Cosen & Company's 229-ton paddle-steamer *Victoria* from Weymouth. To the town's newspaper reporter there seemed 'no such hateful thing as war to mar and destroy the happiness which God intended for His creatures.' But when the declaration of war was made known, from the *Bridport News* office, all was changed. War against Germany was announced to the House of Commons by Sir Edward Grey, the Secretary of State for Foreign Affairs, on 4 August 1914. The previous day he had spelt out its implications which would see the inherently peaceful people of pleasant places such as Bridport finding themselves backstage at Armageddon: 'The lamps are going out all over Europe; we shall not see them lit again in our lifetime.'

The implications were not widely realised. To most in the seaboard counties the Royal Navy was as powerful and paramount as ever, although the gathering toll of slaughter and sacrifice soon brought home fearful realities to a town of nearly 6,000 people. Hundreds besieged the *Bridport News* offices for the latest news, and all became bustle and excitement, for there was scarcely a fighting ship on the sea but had a Bridport man in her crew. Many men from the town were serving in the Army, and time-expired men had passed into the Reserve. A total of 700 Bridport men would leave the town to play their part for 'King and Country'.

'Reveille rang through the town one morning at five o'clock,' John Rowson reported. It summoned men of the 1st Dorset Battery, Royal Field Artillery, for foreign service. They were mustered by Captain G.D. Nantes as he awaited the arrival of Major Leger Livingstone Learmonth from Child Okeford. The Town Clerk, Charles George Nantes who lived at Delapre, prepared the formal civic goodbyes. These territorial soldiers were already inside the military net. Efforts were immediately under way to convince and cajole their peers to join them. 'Only young farmers without old fathers, who could take over from them, were exempt from going to foreign fields,' Rowson wrote in his war journal which provided the background material for his book on *Bridport and the Great War*.

Rector since 1895 and rural dean for the Bridport area, Canon Henry Richard William Farrer organised a special service of intercession for the first Sunday of the war, in St Mary's Parish Church on 9 August 1914. He led prayers for 'divine mercy and the safety of our empire'. The service ended with the singing of 'God Save the King' and the national anthem would continue to be sung at the end of church services for the duration of the war.

Canon Farrer's services became increasingly patriotic and strident. 'Fight for England, home, and beauty,' he urged from the pulpit. On 30 August 1914 he held what amounted to a recruitment service and lectured from the pulpit on the practicalities of military strategy. Reporter John Rowson recalled that Canon Farrer predicted German intentions and the need for a substantial British Expeditionary Force when he said 'that we ought to be able to put half a million men on the continent at Ostend.' This would have blocked enemy movement down the coast, which was soon taking place, and enabled the German to establish a submarine base at Zeebrugge. Canon Farrer expected everyone to do their duty:

It is no time to think that young men may remain sitting on their office stools in the banks or in the counting-houses and say they are not wanted yet. They are wanted. They are wanted now. Every young man must decide, either to his shame to stay at home, or he must answer his country's call now, at once, and say – 'Here I am; use me for my country's good'.

Lieutenant-Colonel Thomas Alfred Colfox of Coneygar and the Dorset Yeomanry set about erecting a beacon on the East Cliff at West Bay and Captain Alfred Douglas Pass from Wootton Fitzpaine built one on Thorncombe Beacon. Another was made at Abbotsbury, and so on east and west along the line. At that time it was considered possible that a German raiding party might land on our coast and their first move would be to cut the telegraph and telephone wires. In such an event there would have been no means of giving prompt notice to Portland but by those beacon fires. The great heap of 'wood and tar barrels' on East Cliff were to stay in place for the whole of the war that people were led to believe would 'be over by Christmas'.

Colonel Colfox was appointed as Recruiting Officer for the Bridport area. Every evening he went into the countryside, 'speaking and gathering in recruits' for the 5th and 6th Battalions, the Dorsetshire Regiment. It was a poor night if he failed to find 'six to ten sturdy fellows' who promised to present themselves for medical examination and accreditation in the Rifle Drill Hall at Bridport in the morning. From there they were taken to Marabout Barracks in Dorchester. In Bridport, in East Street, Yeoman veteran Walter Trump turned the Greyhound Hotel into a military mess.

The Mayor of Bridport, William George Fowler Cornick, had long doubted there would ever be war with Germany, but soon led the community effort by chairing a recruitment meeting at the Town Hall. So many gathered to attend a later meeting that it had to be held outside in the street and blocked all traffic through the town.

More than 500 men from 'Bridport and the neighbourhood' rallied to Cornick's call to the colours. He was then asked by the War Office to raise the 2-1st Battalion of the Dorset Yeomanry from the countryside around Sherborne. Major Joseph Gundry, from Bridport, was one of its squadron leaders until he was appointed Inspector of Railway Defence in Ireland.

On the coast, those with Naval experience cautioned that Portland was unlikely to be the bulwark that everyone thought. Dorrie Rowson recalled that her father, reporter John William Rowson of 76a West Bay Road (who chronicled Bridport's war effort), was alarmed and exasperated that all the ships of the Royal Navy would be sent into the North Sea. Retired Naval officers and West Bay fishermen warned that this would leave Dorset with an unprotected coast. John Rowson justified these war nerves and admitted that the town was in a state of fear:

We were undoubtedly in very great danger at that time, and it was thought possible that an attacking force might land somewhere in West Bay. So that every precaution might be taken for the saving of life and limb the War Office issued an order that on the notification of the presence of the enemy the inhabitants were at once to make their way inland. Homes were to be abandoned, not a wheel was to be left behind, nor any horses or cattle that might be turned to use by the enemy; they were to be destroyed or sent forward. This was the first thing to bring home to the minds of the people the terrible conditions of war in an invaded land. There was no panic, but so real was it that many actually collected their money and valuables to carry off with them in their flight.

The War Office had already commandeered the best horses in the county:

In this, as in everything else, nothing matters but to win the war, and any trade inconvenience caused by the heavy drafts of horses from the neighbourhood is cheerfully borne in a spirit of patriotism. The Great Western Railway Company has but two dray horses left to do all the carting from the station yard at Bridport. Nearly all the brewery horses were taken, and farmers, carters and tradespeople generally were equally affected. Owners had to bring their horses to the Artillery Parade Ground at the bottom of St Michael's Lane where they [were] tethered in long lines to await veterinary inspection. Mounted Yeomanry gathered in the Square at Broadwindsor as their predecessors had for centuries at moments of national tension.

Refugees began to arrive in Bridport. Forty of 'these derelicts of the war' – as John Rowson described them – stepped off the train on Thursday 26 November 1914. They were 'fleeing from their country homeless and destitute' after the Germans had invaded neutral Belgium in order to sidestep French defences on its border with Holland. In Bridport this 'sad and dejected company' were found empty houses, including holiday accommodation and homes vacated by soldiers going to war, which were taken over and furnished. Men, women and children had fled from Antwerp, Douay and Malines with 'all that remained of their worldly belongings' in bundles, baskets and in one case a galvanised bucket.

On their trek to the Channel ports they had survived on raw turnips. In Bridport, Sister Mary Elizabeth made the Visitation Convent in Pymore Road available as a reception centre and gave them a substantial meal. Some 40 more, already on their way, arrived in time for a morale-boosting concert hosted by the Mayor in the Rifle Drill Hall.

The reality of war was also being brought home to Bridport families. Albert Ernest Greenham, called up on 3 August, became the town's first fatality of the war on 15 October 1914. He went down with HMS *Hawke*, a cruiser with a distinctive profile of twin funnels between tall masts, when she was torpedoed by a U-boat in the North Sea. Walter Cliff was lost with the battleship HMS *Good Hope* and West Bay Coast Guard R.F. Buckler with HMS *Monmouth* when they were torpedoed, also in the North Sea, on 1 November 1914. The loss of such great vessels – to the underhand methods of new warfare – had a great impact on the national psyche as it became clear that not only was Britannia failing to rule the waves but the war was going to continue into the new year. HMS *Bulwark* was blown up on 26 November and the new cruiser HMS *Audacious* was blown up by a German mine in the Irish Sea.

Solace came from far away from Europe with the sinking of four German warships in the South Atlantic, as the European war took on global dimensions. The action off the Falkland Islands on 8 December 1914 showed that the Royal Navy could still 'sweep the seas'. Even further away, honours were even after Vice-Admiral John Collings Taswell Glossop (1871–1934), of Little Wych in Burton Road on the West Bay boundary with Bothenhampton, sank the German raider *Emden*. The brother of Mrs C.F.S. Sanctuary of Mangerton, Glossop, was a veteran of the Samoan troubles of 1899 – as a lieutenant on HMS *Royalist* – and reached the rank of captain in 1911. He was commander of the Australian cruiser HMS *Sydney* at the sinking of the German raider *Emden*, following a lengthy search off the Cocos Keeling Islands in the eastern Indian Ocean. What might have been a total triumph soon became tarnished when it became clear that Kapitanleutnant Hellmuth von Mucke was missing with 48 of his men. They had landed on Direction Island, to attack its wireless telegraph station, and proceeded to capture a schooner, the *Ayesha*. In this they made a rendezvous with a German freighter, took this across the Indian Ocean and evaded a British blockade of Arab dhows off Aden to enter the Red Sea.

They then took to the land, crossing Arabia by camel and suffering recurrent bouts of dysentery, typhus and malaria. They also endured three days of skirmishing with Bedouin tribesmen. Eventually the group reached El Ala and took the train through Turkish-occupied Damascus, to return to Europe after crossing half the world. Finally, at Haidar Pasha, von Mucke proudly presented the survivors, ready for duty, to a beaming Admiral Souchon and staff officers of the Mediterranean division of the Imperial Navy: 'I report the landing squad from the *Emden*, five officers, seven petty officers, and thirty men strong.'

For the British and the Australians John Glossop was the 'sink the *Emden*' hero, but the sequel certainly took the gloss off the achievement and blocked the knighthood he thought he deserved. Despite this he was promoted Rear-Admiral in 1922 and retired Vice-Admiral in 1926 with honours including Companion of the Bath, Officer of the Legion of Honour, and the Order of the Rising Sun (3rd class) from grateful friends in Japan.

Ireland had been on the brink of insurrection, and it was from Victoria Barracks, Belfast, that the 1st Battalion, the Dorsetshire Regiment, sailed to the First World War in the troopship *Anthony* down Belfast Lough at 3.25p.m. on Friday 14 August 1914. Called up in Bridport on 5 August and landing in France to join them a fortnight later, R.G. Tite became the first Bridport fatality in the trenches of the Western Front, on 22 October 1914. He was among the 101 men who fell in the loss of 'a bump in the line' at Violaines during the retreat from Mons, when 'the enemy took the trenches at the point of the bayonet.' Joseph Jeans, also from Bridport, was wounded in France and died in December.

In the Persian Gulf the 2nd Battalion of the Dorsetshire Regiment arrived from India and landed in Mesopotamia (modern Iraq) to secure the Anglo-Persian Oil Company's works beside the Shatt al Arab waterway. As they 'plodded through a rain storm in the date palms' on 17 November 1914, an uneventful

three or four hours was followed by a major engagement, with the Turks and their Arab mercenaries entrenched beside an old fort beyond Sahil. Victory was costly, with the battalion having suffered 23 dead and 149 wounded by the time the Turks were forced to flee from Basra to Amara. Among the dead was Joseph Charles Hoskins from Bridport.

Christmas in Bridport was marked by a special party for the Belgian refugees. Thomas Hervey Beams, master of Bradpole Elementary School, organised the delivery of a cart load of vegetables and other produce which was gathered by the children from their allotment plots. They would repeat the exercise a year later. Other gifts arrived from around the town and surrounding villages. A framed portrait of King Albert of the Belgians dominated the Christmas gathering in the Town Hall. Messages were read from the Prime Minister, the Right Honourable Herbert Henry Asquith, and the novelist Sir Hall Caine who had articulated the nation's tribute to Belgian bravery.

Dorchester author and poet Thomas Hardy made his contribution with a *Sonnet on the Belgian Expatriation* which was also rendered on both occasions. Father Ketele, from the Catholic Church in Victoria Road, translated the work and acted as interpreter. Linguistic difficulties were compounded by the fact that few of the refugees had French as a second language. John Rowson noted that the country travellers from Flemish towns were imagined with their bells, but rather than tinkling sounds of joy, the sound was 'dull vicissitude and frightful outrage':

I dreamt that people from the Land of Chimes,
Arrived one autumn morning with their bells,
To hoist them on the towers and citadels,
Of my own country, that the musical rhymes.

Rung by them into space at measured times,
Amid the market's daily stir and stress,
And the night's empty starlit silentness,
Might solace souls of this and kindred climes.

Then I awoke: and lo, before me stood,
The visioned ones, but pale and full of fear;
From Bruges they came, and Antwerp, and Ostend,

No carillons in their train. Vicissitude
Had left these tinkling to the insiders' ear,
And ravaged street, and smouldering gable-end.

Three 'noble Belgian families' arrived and were housed in three dwellings in the harbourside Pier Terrace at West Bay. For her help throughout this period, in co-ordinating the town's Refugee Committee, the Mayoress, Mrs Cornick, was awarded the Medal of Queen Elizabeth by the King of the Belgians. The Mayor was later given King Albert's Medal, with ribbon, and the Town Clerk,

Newly built destroyers HMS Tyrian *and HMS* Tetrarch *in Lyme Bay, photographed on speed trials off West Bay, at the end of the First World War.*

Charles George Nantes, received the Golden Palms Medal. What embarrassed the town was the name of the King of Prussia public house in East Street and it was renamed the King of Belgium Hotel.

The West Dorset coast became the front line on Friday 1 January 1915. In the face of understandable anxiety that the Royal Navy would quit the Channel, the Admiralty decided to put on a public show immediately after Christmas, to prove that Britannia still ruled the waves. Battleships were to sail along the horizon off the counties of Dorset and Devon. The result, however, was anything but reassuring.

HMS *Formidable*, last in line of the Fifth Battle Squadron from Portland Harbour, became the first Naval casualty of the new year. She was torpedoed at 02.20 hours in Lyme Bay by a German submarine. Her position was 20 miles east of Start Point. An orderly evacuation was carried out for two hours, as the battleship appeared to be stable, but at 04.39 she slipped under quite suddenly. Deteriorating weather had hampered the rescue operation. Of the crew of 780 only 233 were saved, some in their own cutter which took 20 hours to reach the shore at Lyme Regis where six are buried. It had been buffeted by one of the worst south-easterly gales for many years.

Captain Pillar's trawler *Provident* from Brixham carried out heroic rescues, as did the escort cruisers HMS *Topaze* and *Diamond* which together brought a total of 80 survivors into Portland. U-boat *UB-24* was responsible, with two torpedoes from close range, and in the process only narrowly survived, having grazed the heaving keel of the 15,000-ton warship. The ship's dog, an old terrier named Bruce, was also lost; he was last seen standing on duty beside his master, Captain Loxley, on the bridge. Revd G. Brooke Robinson, formerly curate of Burton Bradstock and a prominent member of West Bay Swimming Club, was chaplain on board and also went down with the ship.

Spy paranoia swept the land. The novelist William Le Queux travelled the country lecturing on 'Spies I

have known'. In Bridport he found impressionable acolytes, notably A.N. Stephens of Haddon House at West Bay who spent the rest of the war travelling around West Dorset in his motor car checking on telegraph poles and their wires. Others took it upon themselves to watch for saboteurs on the railway line across the hills from Maiden Newton and Powerstock. Police Sergeant Frank Bishop at Bridport received a report from Superintendent William Saint in Beaminster that the Chief Constable, Captain Dennis Granville, had alerted his men to attempts at polluting water-supplies with cholera germs. This had allegedly taken place at the garrison town of Aldershot and the Naval bases of Plymouth and Portsmouth.

Volunteers were sought to 'keep vigilant observation' over local reservoirs day and night. Even the Boy Scouts – founded in Dorset in 1908 by Lieutenant-General Robert Baden-Powell 'to promote good citizenship in the rising generation' – found themselves mobilised for the war effort. They were given a major role in the task of keeping watch over the reservoirs of Bridport Waterworks. Baden-Powell encouraged their efforts by publishing his memoirs under the title *My Adventures as a Spy*.

In January 1915 William S. Edwards of the Gables at West Allington, principal owner of net manufacturers Messrs W. Edwards & Son, was summoned to London for a conference with Winston Churchill, the First Lord of the Admiralty, and Sir John Fisher, the First Sea Lord. Mr Churchill said that the only thing that could possibly defeat the British Navy was the submarine and with the loss of the Navy there would be the probability of our losing the war. He explained that a Naval officer had thought of using steel-wire nets for catching submarines in precisely the same way as nets were used for catching herrings, the only difference being the use of steel-wire cable instead of cotton thread. A specification was being drawn up for an Indicator (Anti-Submarine) Net.

Submarines took another Bridport life in February when Edward William Gray was lost with a Royal Navy destroyer in the North Sea. Lionel Daubney joined him, in similar circumstances, in August 1915. The oldest enemy – the weather – also remained active, claiming Frederick George Crabb who was washed overboard from the destroyer HMS *Midge* in the North Sea on 18 August 1915.

On Friday 5 February 1915 the last parade took place of the Howe Battalion, 2nd Royal Naval Brigade, of the Royal Naval Division, who arrived in Bridport in January for an intensive course of training. Commanded by Lieutenant-Colonel C.G. Collins, they distinguished themselves during the hurried retreat from Antwerp in October 1914, marching 31 miles during one night to escape an encircling movement:

There are close-on 1,000 fine, smart young fellows. They are digging elaborate entrenchments on Eype Down, skilfully laid out from five to six feet deep, in zig-zag formation. Whole days are spent in the trenches, exactly as in the fighting line, with cooking done under service conditions, and no man showing himself as snipers represent the enemy. On Sundays the trenches are visited by crowds of town and country people. The men are looking forward to renewing 'auld acquaintance' with the town where they spent such pleasant days in their training.

Alas, few of them lived to gratify this desire, as they were bound for the Dardanelles, where nearly all were killed in the fighting at Gallipoli. Winston Churchill's great idea, to 'sweep the Dardanelles and capture Constantinople', had begun to unravel. A succession of letters brought news of the latest Bridport fatalities. Frederick Hoskins and Cecil Patten were killed when HMS *Goliath* was torpedoed offshore on 13 May. William Warren, with the Australian Imperial Force which landed in Anzac Bay on 7 August, was killed the next day. 'Anzac was to deliver the knock-out blow,' official despatches optimistically predicted.

In Suvla Bay, Rupert Stanley Suter landed with the Queen's Own Dorset Yeomanry and was killed on 21 August. Walter Bragg, serving with the 5th Battalion, the Dorsetshire Regiment, died the following day. William Knight, among the Gloucestershire Regiment's casualties, was the son of a landlord of the Bull Hotel.

Casualties from other fronts included Arthur Hann of the Army Service Corps who died at the Military Hospital in Aldershot on 13 April 1915. Arthur William Cook of the 1st Battalion, the Dorsetshire Regiment, was killed at Ypres on 26 March 1915, and his comrade Cecil Caddy succumbed on Hill 60 in Belgium after a notorious chlorine gas attack on 2 May 1915. Jack Macey of the King's Royal Rifles was killed in France on 20 June 1915, and William Moss Challis of the Somerset Light Infantry died on 11 August 1915. Ralph Charles Gale, serving with the 7th Battalion, the Norfolk Regiment, died in October 1915. Albert Thompson of the 5th Battalion, the Dorsetshire Regiment, died of pneumonia in hospital at Grantham on 13 April 1915 and is buried at Londonthorpe, Lincolnshire. By 1915 on the home front there was no longer freedom of movement as we know it, for under the National Registration Act everyone had to be registered – giving name, occupation and postal address – and was required to carry a certificate when away from home for presentation whenever it might be demanded.

West Dorset had a young aviator and adventurer whose story was inspirational. Born in 1888, William Barnard Rhodes-Moorhouse had swept to fame in 1911 by co-designing the Radley-Moorhouse monoplane in which he won air races in the United States and became the first to fly through the Golden Gate at San Francisco. On 12 August 1912, returning from his honeymoon, he was the first to fly across the English Channel with two passengers. Then in 1913 he persuaded his mother to buy the Elizabethan mansion

Wartime class, with the slate telling us they are at Bridport Church of England School, in 1915.

of the Strode family – which provided Bridport with Members of Parliament – at Parnham, near Beaminster.

As Lieutenant Rhodes-Moorhouse of the Royal Flying Corps with No. 2 (Army Co-Operation Squadron), he took off from Merville in France in a BE2b biplane to bomb a railway bridge over the River Lys at Courtrai in Belgium on 26 April 1915. Armed with a single 100-pound bomb he ignored a barrage of machine-gun bullets to descend from 300 feet into a low-level attack in which he delivered a direct hit on the target. In the process he and his aeroplane were ripped apart by bullets, but he managed to return to base and insisted on making his report before being taken to hospital. There he died the following afternoon after being given the rare promise that his body would be shipped to his beloved home beside the River Brit, in a war when the number of casualties generally made this impossible. His other posthumous reward for gallantry, giving him a unique place in the history of the Royal Air Force, was the award of its first Victoria Cross.

In Bridport, Canon Farrer became increasingly belligerent in his sermons from the pulpit of St Mary's Church. 'Tomorrow will be Monday,' he said, 'and my message to all of you of military age is that you must enlist in the morning.' He pointed his finger Kitchener-style – 'Your country needs you' – and quoted extracts from the War Lord's Guildhall speech of 9 July 1915:

Men, materials and money are the immediate necessities. Does the call of duty find no response in you until reinforced – let us say superseded – by the call of compulsion.

In Bridport on 31 December 1915 the extension to the railway from the town to West Bay closed to passenger traffic for the duration of the hostilities. Increasing numbers of casualties led to the women of Bridport forming a Voluntary Aid Detachment of the Red Cross Society under the command of Miss C.A. Colfox. Secondary schools and large country houses were offered for emergency hospital accommodation. More might have been achieved but for the death of

Lady Williams of Bridehead, Littlebredy, who was the original vice-president of the Bridport division of the Dorset Red Cross. Her husband, Colonel Sir Robert Williams, remained Member of Parliament for West Dorset until retirement in 1922.

They had pressed the claim that Bridport was well sited for a convalescent hospital but the economics and scale of total war were such that the authorities could not cater for a location that could accommodate 'only half a train'. They decided that Bridport was at the wrong end of its branch railway – lacking platform space for a full hospital train – and medical equipment earmarked for the project was packed away into the Masonic Hall in East Street.

The closest wartime Red Cross hospitals were at Colliton House, Dorchester – with X-ray facilities and mechano-therapeutic apparatus – and at Chantmarle House, before removal further inland to Holnest. South Dorset convalescent homes included St John's Garden Hospital at Upwey and the Massandra Hospital in the Manor House at Buckland Ripers, as outstations of Weymouth's four military hospitals. The Greenhill Hospital at Sherborne claimed to be the first in Britain to improvise open-air treatment for those suffering from septic wounds and gas poisoning. Para-typhoid was among the exotic diseases imported by the wounded from Gallipoli. Colonel and Mrs Goodden turned Compton House into a Red Cross hospital in 1915, with Caroline Goodden as commandant and Sister Edith Coffey in charge of nursing. They went on to treat hundreds of 'amputations, gas, nephritis, gastric, and neurasthenia cases, and many obstinate and serious wounds' without a single death. Rest and recuperation became their theme, the commandant explained:

From May to October every fine evening was spent on the recreation ground high up on the hill in the park, where the men took their tea, and received friends, afterwards playing tennis and croquet till dark. They had a pony carriage at their disposal which they attended to themselves, and a donkey chair, which was a great source of pleasure to those who had lost a leg.

Orderlies from Bridport served across the county and country. The town responded enthusiastically to Queen Alexandra's appeal for needlework guilds to join the war effort. Bridport Working Party knitted and packed bandages, bedding and clothing for casualties and the dispossessed. Miss Hebe Templer organised 'an army of ladies' to produce a variety of products, initially for delivery to the Dorset Red Cross county supply depot at Kingston Maurward:

We make tail bandages, roller bandages, swabs and fomentation pads. Moist dressings are also required in large quantities and these use sphagnum moss which is collected by boys from mossy grassland valleys and the heathland moors. Special products include pneumonia jackets, to keep fever victims warm, and trench-foot slippers. Davis slings, stump covers and knee caps have brought home to us the fact that some soldiers have been horribly mutilated. Making vests and pants, and lavender bags to freshen the air, can be almost therapeutic.

Mrs C.F.S. Sanctuary, from Mangerton at Netherbury, proceeded to organise Bridport's own supply depot for medical stores. Austen Whetham loaned her a house in South Street which became the West Dorset area headquarters for the second half of the conflict. A total of 1,850 garments and 13,500 surgical dressings were brought to South Street by Mrs Templer's volunteers.

They were 'doing their bit'. People were constantly being exhorted to 'carry on'. The war had already developed its own language. Tommy (full name Tommy Atkins) was the British soldier – and the Hun individually (or Bosche for the German state) being his enemy – with 'dear old Blighty' being the England he had left behind. When he did return to West Bay, on a convalescent trip, what surprised the Dorset-speaking populace was that he spoke a new language. This was soon being imitated by the young of Bridport, Sherborne and Weymouth. The failure of a waitress to respond to a soldier's demand was met with the riposte: 'Guess she's been on a sleigh ride.' That implied she was drugged. The 'snow' of the 'sleigh ride' was cocaine.

Even in the home, flies were no longer swatted – they were 'strafed' – but the popular phrase 'not 'arf' hardly sounded out of place given that men of the Dorsetshire Regiment had never used their aitches before leaving for the war. In Victorian times they brought Hindustani back from India, but the current vogue was for expressions cockney and cosmopolitan, rich in rhyming slang. Following in the tradition of William Barnes, who recorded Dorset dialect words, John Rowson jotted down the new 'war talk' he heard in the street in Bridport.

Almond rocks – socks
Arm – false alarm
ATA wallah – teetotaller (initials of Army Temperance Association)
Buzz – gossip
Cherry ripe – pipe
Chevy Chase – face
Daisy roots – boots
Dora – Defence of the Realm Act, 1916
Home Farm – married quarters (at a garrison)
Jam – good luck
Jammy – lucky sequence
Mince pie – eye
Only a buzz – wild rumour
Plates of meat – feet
Sieda – 'good morning' (Australian usage)
Sieda – socks (Dorset usage)
Whiz-bang – shellfire

They were also repeating, endlessly in some cases, a series of phrases of musical hall or Naval origin:

'Give it the bird.'
'I don't think.'
'Now we shan't be long.'
'Swinging the lead.'
'What ho, she bumps.'

Major William Townley Whetham of 67 Victoria Grove, the pre-war commander of the Bridport Rifles, formed a Town Guard. The determined septuagenarian found other old soldiers who were beyond call-up age and launched an appeal for funds to buy rifles. Calling themselves the Bridport Company they later opened the ranks to younger non-military volunteers and became 'a broader civil defence corps that could respond to any emergency.' Captain J. Suttill and Second-Lieutenant F.W. Knight were its principal officers.

There were moments of hilarity. One band of coast watchers at Seatown went to sleep on the job and were put to shame by having their fish dinner stolen from under their noses. Constant rumours of U-boats surreptitiously slipping into the inhospitable shore around Lyme Regis for supplies all proved groundless but in the process wasted much police time. The only alleged traitor caught on the cliffside turned out to be a fossil collector. Similar false alarms came from the watch ships in Lyme Bay which kept an eye on the shore as well as shipping movements in the English Channel. Their sighting of someone at Eype who was signalling to U-boats in Morse code was found to be a lady 'arranging her tresses before retiring to bed, oblivious of the fact that she had not drawn the blind.'

A harmless crippled man attracted suspicion after making his home in the empty Coastguard Station at Burton Bradstock. One evening he was being kept under police surveillance when a military unit was alerted to something strange going on. They sealed off the coast road and arrested cyclists and pedestrians passing through the village. Among their catch was the police sergeant from Bridport who headed eastwards when he received a secret message that his constable from Burton Bradstock was missing. On his own initiative the man had decided to keep watch upon the disabled man in the Coastguard Station and had himself been observed hiding in the bushes. He was then watched by soldiers. When Sergeant Frank Bishop peddled towards him they closed the net. The muddle was not resolved – and the policemen and other suspects released – until two o'clock in the morning.

Bridport Hospital, then beside Hospital Lane in North Allington, in 1904.

War news in 1916 brought the town more sadness and with increasing frequency. James Sargent was killed on 18 March 1916 when HMS *Paragon* was blown up by a mine in the Straits of Dover. The Royal Navy also fared badly in an old-fashioned set-piece engagement in the middle of the North Sea.

William Abbott was killed on HMS *Black Prince* during the Battle of Jutland on 31 May 1916. Charles Albert Gale and Robert Charles Norman went down with HMS *Invincible*. William John Everleigh was also lost. Edgar John Scadden and Albert Tatershall sank with HMS *Queen Mary*. Albert Tiltman was killed on HMS *Black Prince*. 'There seems to be something wrong with our bloody ships today,' remarked Admiral Sir David Beatty, who very nearly joined them when a shell penetrated the roof of the central turret of his flagship, HMS *Lion*.

Two Bridport men foundered in the next catastrophe, along with the war's highest ranking casualty, the Secretary of State for War, Field-Marshal Lord Kitchener. William George Gale and Ernest John Turner, a chief writer, drowned when the cruiser HMS *Hampshire* was torpedoed off the Orkneys at the start of what should have been a mission to Russia on 5 June 1916. Canon Farrer, one of Kitchener's greatest admirers, organised the town's biggest memorial service of the war in St Mary's Church 'for all creeds and classes'. It was also, as he put it, his 'swan song' before retirement the following month when he handed over the parish to Revd J.W. Coulter. He had a different style, reminding his flock of how close they had come to total disaster and asking for thanksgiving: 'It is of the Lord's mercy we are not consumed.'

Events at sea could certainly have been much worse. Steel-wire submarine nets, manufactured in Bridport by Messrs W. Edwards & Son, were credited with stopping an increasing number of enemy U-boats. Specially designed motor launches, based for a time at West Bay, also played havoc amongst them. The eyes of the launches were airships from Powerstock, floating gracefully over the English Channel, which could locate a submarine lurking in the water below and swoop down to attack it with bombs. The launches would then 'dart out of the harbour like a flash and be over to the spot indicated in no time, drop their destructive depth charge and shoot away again out of danger.' John Rowson witnessed them in action:

The effect of the explosion of these charges under water was terrific and meant destruction to any submarine and death to the crew within a radius of sixty or seventy yards. Naturally much interest was taken in these launches and airships, which were doing far more deadly work than their admirers ever dreamed of, and, unfortunately one of each was lost in the course of their desperate adventures. In two or three instances shipwrecked crews landed on our coast after their ships had been mined or torpedoed by the enemy.

By now nearly everyone in Bridport was mourning losses of friends and family. Philip Alexander Francis of the 2nd Battalion, Dorsetshire Regiment, was killed in the Turkish siege of Kut al Amara, beside the River Tigris, on 7 January 1916. Things there deteriorated as 'an emaciated and exhausted garrison' held out for five months. William Henry Collins of 1-4th Battalion, Dorsetshire Regiment, was killed on 12 April 1916 near Basra on the march to Nasiriyeh before the fall of Kut.

Major-General Sir Charles Vere Townshend's brave men, who had volunteered to go off and fight the Turks while serving in relative safety in India, were force-marched across the desert. Officers were properly treated as prisoners of war but their men, segregated and humiliated, 'had to live off hedgehogs and starlings' through the intense heat of the desert summer. Walter William Bartlett from 1-4th Battalion, Dorsetshire Regiment, was among those who fell with exhaustion and sickness on 8 August 1916 and was left to die. As was Thomas Leonard Phippen on 26 August 1916 and William Walter Gape who was declared 'missing presumed dead' on 31 December 1916.

Stanley George Honey of the 2nd Battalion (the son of J. Honey of East Street) died of heatstroke on 26 September 1916. Bridport's contribution to this ill-fated 'side-show of a side-show' – as far-flung parts of the Middle East tended to be called – was rounded off by the loss of two popular brothers from the town's merchant class. Alfred Bernard Hobbs and William Ernest Hobbs were the sons of South Street draper Ernest Benjamin Hobbs. Serving with the 2nd Battalion, Dorsetshire Regiment, they died within days of each other in the 2nd General Hospital at Amara, Mesopotamia. Albert died from enteric fever on 19 November 1916 and William from dysentery on 28 November 1916. Dudley Roberts of the Queen's Own Dorset Yeomanry was killed in Egypt.

The town's most successful flag-day, raising £400 on Kut Day for the Dorest prisoners of the Turks, was organised by the town's second wartime Mayor, Edward Pratt Rendall. The main event was a fête in the grounds of Downe Hall at the invitation of Captain William Arthur Alexander. Kut's suffering Dorsetmen on the ground had their own Netherbury hero. Captain Campbell Sanctuary volunteered to transfer from the Royal Field Artillery to the Royal Flying Corps and became an air gunner. His role over starving Kut, flying in low, was to drop as much food as the light aircraft could carry. He then qualified as a pilot in what by the Armistice was the Royal Air Force.

On 1 July 1916, William Albert James Samways of West Allington and the 1st Battalion, the Dorsetshire Regiment, was killed on the Somme. The same day Lieutenant Colin Graham Gordon, only son of Mr and Mrs H. Gordon of Westlands, on returning to France with the Gordon Highlanders after being wounded in the charge at Messines with the London Scottish, was also killed: 'He was shot through the head, leading his men gallantly – a fearless soldier whose loss we all mourn.'

Thousands of similar letters were arriving each day all over Britain and Ireland. Eighteen-year-old Reginald George Symes of the 6th Battalion, Dorsetshire Regiment, was killed in France on 7 July 1916. William Ewens, serving with Canadian Forces, was another casualty. William Edwards, with the King's Royal Rifles, was killed on 16 July 1916. Frank Joseph Fowler, second son of water-miller Joseph Fowler of East Mills, was killed on the Somme on 22 July 1916. He was serving with the Australian Imperial Force, having been in Adelaide when war broke out, and outlived his luck by surviving the first wave of landings at Gallipoli. Colleague Alfred Brooks Wadham was accidentally killed before he could leave England.

Another of Bridport's expatriates met his death, at Wailly in 'a quiet quarter' of the Somme, via Gallipoli. Captain Henry Ernest Kitcher of the 5th Battalion, Dorsetshire Regiment, lost his life on 7 August 1916. 'One of the best officers in the battalion,' he was hit by a rifle-grenade, ending a remarkable story. He had left South Street to make his fortune in South America and returned to Europe when war was declared with a contingent of enthusiastic volunteers. Walter John English, in the Somerset Light Infantry, was killed in France on 18 August 1916.

Accidents were also happening. William John Newman drowned in Portsmouth Harbour, where he was training on HMS *Victory*, on 3 April 1916. Young gunner Harry Beer also failed to get further than the next county, being killed with 3-1st Dorset Battery of the Royal Field Artillery in practice firings on Salisbury Plain on 5 September 1916. Thomas Keech of the 1-1st Battalion, Dorsetshire Regiment, was accidentally killed at Bareilly in India on 30 August 1916.

Second-Lieutenant Tom Hollingworth Rowson, serving with the Artists Rifles, attached to the 19th London Regiment, was a casualty of the great Battle of the Somme at High Wood on 15 September 1916. Nearly 40 other officers fell beside him, including his captain and colonel, 'in the face of terrible fire from the German machine-guns.' Back home, in West Bay Road, John William Rowson was the town's best-known newspaper reporter.

The next death he had to record from France was that of William Alexander Poole, with the 5th Battalion, Dorsetshire Regiment, in an assault at Albert while preparing to attack the ridge east of

Ancre. Thomas Harry Spiller of the Rangers – 12th (County of London) Battalion, the London Regiment – was killed in France on 7 October 1916. Spillers could provide every essential service in Bridport, town crier and bill-poster Andrew Spiller declared. Miss Amanda Spiller was the confectioner and milliner in West Street. Mrs Ellen Spiller was a dressmaker in Barrack Street. Simon Spiller was the landlord of the Fisherman's Arms in South Street.

Fred Foord, with the Sherwood Foresters, was killed on 9 October 1916. Robert Laird, serving with the London Rifle Brigade, 'died of shell shock in France' on 15 October 1916. Albert Victor Crespin went down with HMS *Genista* when she was torpedoed while mine-sweeping on 23 October 1916. William Albion Angell, who had transferred from the 1st to 2nd Battalion, the Dorsetshire Regiment, fought at Ypres and on the Somme. He died from his wounds on 29 October 1916.

The third Christmas of the conflict also saw the town's third war Mayor, John Cleeves Palmer, who was no stranger to taking the civic chair in troubled times, having done so in the Boer War from 1899 to 1901. He expressed the hope that it would again be his 'pleasurable duty to read the proclamation of peace'. That was not to be. Instead, while mourning the loss of two of his sons in the conflict, he had to prepare for administration of increasing curbs on civilian life, as the Defence of the Realm Act of 1916 began to bite with rationing of coal, sugar, bread and other essentials. Bread, in particular, became a source of popular bitterness. Its dark, course wholemeal flour was denounced as 'Government dough' with people claiming they could not digest the healthy and husky full-fibre content. By September 1917 potatoes had been added to the mix.

As well as meeting the needs of the town, with its wartime population of 5,200, Bridport traders also handled the ration books of another 5,000 people from the surrounding villages. Coupons were necessary for hotel meals costing in excess of 1s.2d. or teas for sixpence or more. For a time white bread and full cream were put beyond rationing and could only be supplied to children, invalids and patients with the authorisation of a doctor.

Each boatman at West Bay and Lyme Regis – as well as those at Charmouth, Seatown, Eype, Burton Bradstock and Abbotsbury with little more than rowing boats – had to obtain a permit from the Officer in Charge of Coastwatching at Exmouth. Ex-Naval seaman William Farwell of Brook Cottage, Mill Lane, Chideock, preserved his authorisation for *Two Sisters* at Seatown:

This vessel is allowed to proceed within the area sanctioned by Notice to Mariners during daylight hours only. Daylight to be considered from half-an-hour before Sunrise till half-an-hour after Sunset. If caught out by fog the vessel must return to shore at once.

The restrictions also included severe licensing laws, which stayed in force for decades to control and curb opportunities for drinking instead of working. Zeppelin airships brought a new fear and a blackout was imposed and enforced to lessen the chances of 'diabolical air raids on unprotected cities, towns and villages.' None took place over Bridport but Gundry's factory hooter was kept in readiness to sound a 'take cover' warning.

John Rowson remembered it as adding an extra layer of uncertainty to a growing anxiety over the human cost of stalemate in the trenches:

It does not require much effort of the imagination to realise the sadness and desolation of those days, with heart-breaking news coming through week by week of loved ones killed in action, dying in hospitals, wounded, missing or prisoners of war. But the greatness of human character comes out more nobly in the hour of affliction than under normal conditions, and although the old light-heartedness was gone, and the smile had given place in many instances to a grief-stricken countenance, no one lost heart, and there was that quiet determination to go on unfalteringly to the end, so characteristic of the British people and so dreaded by our enemies. Old men were ready, if necessary, to take the place of their fallen sons, and continue the fight so earnestly begun, that those young lives might not have been lost in vain.

Councillor W.E. Bates became the Mayor's faithful lieutenant as they eased the way for the arrival in the town of the East Lancashire Regiment for trench-training exercises on Eype Down. Quarters and accommodation had to be found. The Mayoress, Mrs Palmer, took over fund-raising efforts from the previous Mayor's daughter, Miss Mildred Rendall, and celebrated a particularly successful Alexandra Rose Day.

There was a growing need for such humanitarian efforts. William Henry Stone died on Whale Island, Quebec, while serving with HMS *Excellent* on 7 January 1917. Albert Edward Smith, invalided home from HMS *Mantua*, died in February 1917 after suffering exposure in the North Sea.

Frederick William Eveleigh of the 1st Battalion, Dorsetshire Regiment, was killed in France on 11 January 1917 and is buried at Thiepval. George Oxenbury of the Army Service Corps was accidentally killed at Proven on 5 February 1917. Albert William Hallett of the Royal Flying Corps, the only surviving son of Mr and Mrs J. Hallett, died of pneumonia 'from a chill contracted on his homeward journey'. Arthur John Gale of the 2nd Battalion, Dorsetshire Regiment, was declared missing in Mesopotamia on 25 March 1917. F. Giles of the 1st Dorset Battery, Royal Field Artillery, was also lost in the desert.

Albert Gay of the Devonshire Regiment was killed in France in April 1917. Major Richard Forsey

Royal Navy pilot inspecting the wrecked gondola at the site of the Loders airship crash.

There were exciting moments over Bridport. A new Zero Airship, on an anti-submarine patrol from Mullion, Cornwall, turned inland towards the Admiralty Airship Station at Powerstock. It came in too low after passing over Bridport and clipped tree-tops at Loders, coming down on a grassy slope above the railway line. Bombs were safely jettisoned and the pilot, John Owner, and his crew suffered only minor bruising.

Wartime unemployment was unknown in Bridport and district. The town's netting works and their army of outworkers produced hemp lanyards for the Army and Navy. White lanyards for sailors to wear around their necks and plaited and twisted shoulder lanyards were being delivered in millions, representing something like 300 tons in weight. Likewise, there was a huge demand for tent lines and twines of all descriptions.

The Royal Navy's requirements included fishing seine-nets in large quantities, so that warships could catch fresh fish at sea. The Air Board ordered balloon and aeroplane cordage, with one firm maintaining a continuous supply of six tons per week. In 1917 the idea of camouflage netting was widely adopted, not only for hiding away war material and gun emplacements and so on in France, but for generally disguising the movements of troops. This netting was made in Bridport in huge quantities, both by machine and by hand, so much so that because of the big demand for women workers on the land as an alternative form of National Service, the War Office instructed the manufacturers to issue the copy of a notice to all outworkers and braiders in the district:

It is hoped to reassure them that in braiding these particular nets they are making their highest possible contribution to the war effort. Even such mundane products as potato nets and pea nets have a military application, being used by our troops for boiling these vegetables.

of the Grenadier Guards fell in that month's Arras offensive. Frederick Fursey of 1-4th Battalion, Dorsetshire Regiment, died on 9 April 1917 of the enemy that would kill more than the war – influenza – at the start of the pandemic. Wounded with the Australian Imperial Force in Flanders on 29 April, Bridport expatriate John Lutley died in hospital in Boulogne on 6 May 1917. Warren Edwards, also with the Australians, was killed in May. John William Coombs of the Northamptonshire Regiment was killed on 26 May 1917. Harry Hugh Marsh, the son of Mr and Mrs A. Marsh of West Bay Road, died on 4 June 1917 of wounds received in France while serving with the Dorset Battery of the Royal Field Artillery.

The cruellest irony for a grieving Bridport family was that a year to the day after the death of his brother, Reginald George Samways of West Allington also died in France, on 1 July 1917. Serving with the 6th Battalion, Dorsetshire Regiment, he had been wounded at Arras on 14 May 1917. Another twist of fate for a West Allington family was that Cecil Frank Hannam had been posted missing in the Battle of the Somme, only to make his way back to the British lines where he was reported dead a year later. Equally unfortunate was Alfred George Masters of the 2-1st Dorset Battery of the Royal Field Artillery. Having fought his way across Asia and Europe, via Egypt, from Mesopotamia to France, he was fatally wounded and died in hospital in July 1917.

Clifford Bartlett of the 1st Battalion, Dorsetshire Regiment, was killed at Nieuport, Flanders, on 16 July 1917. Arthur Travers of the Royal Field Artillery was killed at Ypres on 21 July 1917. Albert Nelson Bragg followed in August, along with Albert George Childs, who died of his wounds in France on 5 August 1917. Ernest Bennett of the Royal Warwickshire Regiment was killed at Ypres on 22 August 1917. George Jerrard of the Royal Field Artillery succumbed there on 8 September 1917. Sergeant Herbert John Henning of the 1st Battalion, Dorsetshire Regiment, was killed in Belgium on 12 September 1917. Frederick Coombs, invalided home from HMS *Vernon*, died on 30 September 1917.

Down on East Beach, the horses and carts of Norman Good and Phillips & Son continued to gather sand and shingle for the building of fortifications and other war works. Regular goods trains left the sidings at West Bay Station. One railwayman talked in the town of 'coals to Newcastle' after hearing that a consignment was being shipped to Egypt. Others believed the remark was the purchasing officer's way of telling him to refrain from asking questions in wartime.

Herbert Shepard of the Royal Irish Rifles was killed in France in September 1917. The family then heard that Henry John Shepard, with the 1st Battalion, Duke of Cornwall's Light Infantry, was 'missing presumed dead' on 4 October 1917. Those lost at sea shared a common grave but there were additional agonies for the families of those who had disappeared on land. They felt compelled to cling to the hope that loved ones would return, but when reality was accepted there was no grave for peace-time pilgrimage. The poet Rudyard Kipling did his best to provide substitutes, coming up with the idea of names on cenotaphs, such as the Menin Gate, and giving unidentified bodies the dignified words 'Known unto God'.

Charlie Butler, with the 14th Battalion, Hampshire Regiment, was killed in France on 2 October 1917 'by an enemy aeroplane bomb'. Second-Lieutenant Sidney Stephens, a retired Naval officer who rejoined the infantry ranks and won the Distinguished Conduct Medal and the Military Cross for conspicuous gallantry, was wounded in action in Polygon Wood, Belgium, while serving with the Devonshire Regiment on 9 October 1917. He was then blown up, together with his stretcher bearers, by an artillery shell.

The Dorset Yeomanry took the Mughar Ridge in Palestine from the Turks on 13 November 1917, winning the Distinguished Service Order for Captain G.M. Dammers of Wykes Court, Bridport. He already had a trophy – a Senussi sword – seized on an earlier cavalry charge at Agagia in Egypt. His Palestine citation reads:

For conspicuous gallantry and devotion to duty. He handled his squadron with courage and ability when he was the only officer with the squadron. He charged the enemy's position at the gallop under heavy rifle and machine-gun fire. He succeeded in holding the flank against heavy enfilading fire, thereby enabling the rest of the regiment to advance.

In November 1917, with her headquarters in South Street in Bridport, Mrs C.F.S. Sanctuary of Mangerton organised the Bridport War Hospital Supply Department. Her brother, Captain John Collings Taswell Glossop, was in command of the Australian cruiser *Sydney* when she sank the German raider *Emden* in the Indian Ocean in November 1914.

Naval losses continued on both sides. William Travers from Bridport was killed on HMS *Gurkha* when she struck a mine in the Channel. H.H. Symes was lost while mine-sweeping. E.C. Holwill was torpedoed in a destroyer. Colonial officer George Bernard Morey was lost on board the *Abbosso*, torpedoed off the Irish coast, while returning home from the Gambia. Albert Henry Wheadon, in the 1915-built HMS *Partridge*, was killed when the destroyer was sunk whilst escorting a convoy on 7 December 1917.

The family also lost William Wheadon of the Dorsetshire Regiment who was attached to the 7th Battalion, Royal Sussex Regiment, when he was declared missing in France on 10 August 1917.

The Mayor, John Cleeves Palmer of South Street and the Bridport Brewery, suffered twice during the year. His second son, Sub-Lieutenant Edmund John Palmer, had been turned down for military service on account of defective eyesight, but joined the Quaker-inspired Friends' Ambulance Service on the Western Front. He then talked his way into joining the Nelson Battalion of the Royal Naval Division, trained at Blandford Camp and returned to France, where he was killed on 27 April 1917.

The Mayor's youngest son, Lieutenant Leslie Stuart Palmer of the 4th Battalion, Dorsetshire Regiment, was killed by a German sniper at Zillebeke on 20 September 1917. He was attached to the Machine Gun Corps. Having been gassed he returned home in June 1916 but went back to the Front after recuperation.

Bridport apprentice printer Frederick Hyde from Loders enlisted in the Buckinghamshire Regiment and was killed in France on 1 October 1917. Reynold Robert White of the Duke of Cornwall's Light Infantry died of his wounds on 6 November 1917. The same day, Philip Dicker – born in Bridport in May 1889 – was wounded in action whilst leading a Lewis Gun Section of the Duke of Cornwall's Light infantry. He died two days later. The next Bridport fatality occurred when a shell hit the trench dugout sheltering Richard Stanley Hoare of the 123rd Siege Battery on 12 November 1917.

After two years of driving around the liveliest parts of the Western Front, hauling guns for the Royal Field Artillery, Wilfred Henry Staple Rawlings met 'the whiz-bang with his name upon it' on an unlucky 13 November 1917. James Edgar Rowe of the 9th Lancers, son of fishmongers Mr and Mrs Isaac Rowe of South Street, died of his wounds in France on 26 November 1917. W. Potter of the 1st Battalion, City of London Regiment, and Percy George Ward of the 1st Battalion, Hampshire Regiment, were also killed in France. Charles Henry Huxter of the Devonshire Regiment was lost in 1917, as was Harry Samuel Hallett of the Grenadier Guards, who was killed at Cambrai.

In Bridport, John Cleeves Palmer handed over power to William Saunders Edwards, who became the town's fourth and final war Mayor. He too had held the chair before, three times between 1907 and 1910, and was instrumental in restructuring Bridport's 300 territorial soldiers into Lord Haldane's 'new model army' – to borrow the Cromwellian phrase – of Artillery, Rifles and Yeomanry. Colonel Cecil Henry Law, 6th Baron Ellenborough, from Dorchester, and Afghan war veteran Colonel Henry Spencer Wheatley had joined him in A-Company's Drill Hall to extol the virtues of reforms that were eventually carried out nationally. Lord Ellenborough's claim to fame in 1871 was that he had introduced polo-playing to India.

Aggravating seasonal shortages in December 1917, the German U-boat campaign was having an effect on supplies of food that 'worsened from disruptive to disastrous'. Bridport's Mayor and Mayoress put their efforts into establishing communal kitchens through the local Food Economy Committee. They introduced the school-meals service, particularly for pupils brought in from the countryside, and turned the Artillery Drill Hall into a canteen for the children. These apparently modest efforts met resistance and ridicule. Within a few weeks most youngsters reverted to their standard lunchtime fare of bread and jam.

The casualty list continued to grow. William Frapple of the 2-4th Battalion, Dorsetshire Regiment, died with the Egyptian Expeditionary Force on 11 December 1917 – the very day that General Sir Edmund Allenby marched into Jerusalem without a shot being fired near the city. In January 1918 William Herbert Wheadon of 1-4th Battalion, Dorsetshire Regiment, died of heatstroke in Mesopotamia.

Hilary Charles Gilbert, the only son of house furnisher Edwin Gilbert of South Street, joined up in October 1914 and was a dispatch rider for the Royal Engineers. Having ridden around France for the 16th Division from November 1915, he was hit by a sniper's bullet on the night of 23 February 1918. Joseph Cornelius Bartlett, with the 5th Battalion, Dorsetshire Regiment, died in the second Battle of the Marne. On 14 March 1918 Private T.C. Chard of the 5th Battalion, Dorsetshire Regiment, was killed in France.

The previous week, back at home, Business Men's Week was launched on Monday 4 March 1918. It introduced the idea of War Bonds and Bridport was expected to raise £15,000 for the hard-pressed Chancellor of the Exchequer. It was a jubilant Mayor, celebrating his 50th birthday on 8 March 1918, who proudly announced that the town was set to exceed its target several times over. By that Friday the interim total was £50,400 and the final figure £69,070. To 'salute this handsome achievement' approval was given for an Admiralty airship to fly low over the town and hold its position over the offices of the fund-raising committee.

The need for airships was brought home on 18 March 1918 when the 3,073-ton freighter *Baygitano* was torpedoed by *U-77* just seven miles from West Bay. Built in 1905 and returning in ballast from Le Havre to Cardiff, she was a collier operated by the Bay Steam Ship Company. Close inshore, near Lyme Regis, the ship was more fortunate that most torpedo victims in being within range of almost instant help. Although two of the crew were drowned the remainder were safely taken off by the town's lifeboat and other small craft which swarmed around the sinking steamship. She is now known in Lyme as 'The Wreck'.

One of the few happy stories from the Western Front was that a maid servant at Bridport had put her name and address inside one of the pairs of socks she knitted for the troops. They were amongst the bundles sent to the battery commanded by Major (later Sir) Philip Colfox (1888–1966). The soldier who got them wrote to her full of gratitude, and from this a correspondence grew. The first time he got leave he came to Bridport, proposed to the girl, was accepted, and they were soon afterwards married, 'with a bright and happy prospect in front of them'.

Albert George Marsh, elder son of mechanical engineer Henry Marsh in West Street, was killed on the Somme on 21 Marsh 1918. Lance-Corporal John Guppy of the 6th Battalion, Dorsetshire Regiment, was killed at Villers-au-Foss, near Arras, on 23 March 1918. Having been transferred to the battalion from the Queen's Own Dorset Yeomanry, Bridport clerk John Henry Freeman Parker died at Etaples of wounds sustained at Albert, France, on 27 March 1918. He was the son of Revd Richard Parker, the rector of Hooke, near Beaminster. H. Pearce from the same battalion, taken prisoner by the Germans, died on 29 March 1918.

Bertram Wilkinson of the 3rd Battalion, Coldstream Guards, died on 18 April 1918 of wounds while fighting in Nieppe Forest, France. H.C. Davis of the Royal Middlesex Light Infantry was killed at Zeebrugge in the daring operation to cripple U-boat movements from the Belgian port on 23 April 1918. Jack Stewart Read, second son of Mr and Mrs Percy Read of East Street who ran the town's shoe shop, enlisted in the 7th Battalion, Dorsetshire Regiment. A musketry instructor, he transferred to the 9th Battalion, Cheshire Regiment, and was killed on 29 April 1918 by a heavy shell which fell behind the lines at Ypres and hit his hut while he was asleep.

John Bowden of the Royal Welsh Fusiliers died in the care of 131st Field Ambulance unit, from wounds received in France, on 5 May 1918. Sub-Lieutenant H.J. Clarke of the 1st Battalion, Dorsetshire Regiment, was killed at Hamelincourt near Berles-au-Bois on 21 May 1918 'in one of the finest raids of the war, not from a spectacular point of view but as an example of British spirit.' Born into an Army family, becoming a drummer-boy in the regiment, he had only received his commission a month earlier.

Second-Lieutenant Thomas David Colfox of the Royal Field Artillery, the second son of Lieutenant-Colonel T.A. Colfox, was killed on 14 June 1918. While at Eton he spent his final holidays harvesting and working in a munitions factory. Commissioned in 1917 at the age of 19, he went to France with the 41st Field Battery. Home leave in March was cancelled when he reached Boulogne and he returned to Bethune to help block a German advance, being hit by an artillery shell at Belzace Farm.

West Dorset was finding new heroes. On 28 June 1918, Captain Julian Royds Gribble (1897–1918) of Kingston Russell, fighting with the Royal Warwickshire Regiment, was gazetted for the Victoria Cross. He died of his wounds.

More fortunate was Commander Victor Crutchley (1893–1986) of Mappercombe Manor, Nettlecombe, near Powerstock, who returned to be Bridport's local hero and village patriarch of the inland countryside. He was truly a legend in his own lifetime, surviving a glorious failure and then returning with an heroic second and successful audacious attempt at blocking Ostend Harbour in the face of German guns. For this he was awarded the Victoria Cross.

The valiant first occasion was on 22–23 April 1918 when he was aboard HMS *Brilliant*. For that action the Jutland veteran was awarded the Distinguished Service Cross. Then he returned to Ostend in the repeat operation of 9–10 May aboard the block-ship HMS *Vindictive*, stuffed with explosives, and nearly became part of her sacrifice. Again he narrowly escaped with his life and this time the reward was not only Britain's highest honour but the French Croix de Guerre as well. Admiral Sir Victor Crutchley, as he became, remained at sea between the wars and commanded the 30,600-ton battleship HMS *Warspite* from 1937 to 1940. After a spell ashore as the Commodore at Devonport he returned to the water to command the Australian Naval Squadron, between 1942–44. He was then Flag Officer Gibraltar until retirement in 1947. There followed four decades as the white-bearded village patriarch who appeared on high days and holidays to open fêtes and hand out the commemorative mugs for royal celebrations. Media personalities – such as Kenneth Allsop and Sir Robin Day – had their recognition from the television sets, but when Sir Victor shopped in Bridport he was regarded with awe from two subsequent generations who knew he came from their own valleys and fields and had brought Dorset glory and hope in the darkest days of two world wars.

He is buried in Powerstock churchyard, beneath a striking wooden cross redolent of another age. It is surmounted by the 'For Valour' insignia of the Victoria Cross.

The First World War dragged on through its seemingly endless stalemate with the next batch of casualties. They included Alfred Henry Martin of the Royal Field Artillery who died in hospital in France on 6 July 1918. William Thorne Perrott, son of furniture dealer and grocer William George Perrott in East Street, had been drafted for France but was taken seriously ill. He was invalided home and died on 10 July 1918. Charles George Hallett of the 1st Dorset Battery, Royal Field Artillery, died of heatstroke in Lahore, India.

The fourth anniversary of the declaration of war, 4 August 1918, was designated Remembrance Day. Revd J.W. Coulter conducted a special service in St Mary's Church and Mayor Edwards addressed the people from the Town Hall. He asked them to raise their right hands in silence to endorse the following Borough Council resolution as their personal pledge:

That the citizens of Bridport here assembled, silently paying tribute to the Empire's sons who have fallen in the fight for freedom in the battles of the World War, whether on sea or shore, or in the air, and mindful also of the loyalty, devotion and courage of our sailors and soldiers every day and everywhere, unanimously resolve to do all that in their power lies to achieve the ideals on behalf of which so great a sacrifice has already been made.

Captain Ernest Boon from Bridport, who was serving as a gunner from January 1916 in front-line action with 306 Siege Battery, held the Military Cross and bar. His battles included Messines Ridge, Arras, Passchendaele and St Quientin. In September 1918 his men were the first to cross the seemingly impregnable Canal du Nord. Captain Boon survived the war and spent the rest of his life in Bridport as T.R.G. Lawrence & Sons'

Victoria Cross holder Sir Victor Crutchley with Powerstock schoolchildren in 1977.

auctioneer. The vicar of Loders, Revd Oliver Willmott, told me the story of how they first met in 1947.

Boon was auctioning the possessions of Willmott's predecessor, Revd Charles Palmer, and the vicar was keen to obtain the electric kettle. Out of sight in the kitchen, however, a woman was even more determined and kept outbidding his modest sixpenny advances with rises of half a crown. She won the battle – and gave her name to Captain Boon as Mrs Willmott. Life in the Willmott household was never quite the same again but they became firm friends with the old soldier.

On 29 September 1918, William Butcher of the 1st Battalion, Royal Middlesex Light Infantry, was killed at Cambrai. Government colonial administrator George Richard Wadham drowned while returning from West Africa in the Burutu, in sight of the Mersey, when the troopship was torpedoed by a U-boat. Alfred Hallett of the Somerset Light Infantry was killed at Armentieres on 5 October 1918. The Hallett family suffered again that month. It was a particularly cruel blow as Edgar Hallett, the son of J. Hallett from the town's Post Office, died on 27 October 1918 when he was on his way home after more than four years 'with the colours' from the Dardanelles and Palestine to the Western Front. Charles Gibbs of the Dorset Battery, Royal Field Artillery, who was gassed in France, also died back home in England. Another Bridport gunner, George James Rawles, was killed in France that month.

Lance-Corporal William Hussey of the 6th Battalion, Dorsetshire Regiment, was among the 40 killed or missing under withering shell fire at Neuvilly-en-Argonne on 11 October 1918. Luck also ran out for Major Henry William Francis Blackburne Farrer. The son of Bridport's former rector, Canon H.R.W. Farrer, the 24-year-old ex-Sandroyd boy had played cricket for Dorset. Serving with the Royal Field Artillery he had been wounded on six occasions – seriously so four times – he was mentioned three times in despatches, and received the Military Cross plus two bars and the Belgian Croix de Guerre. He was killed by a shell in France on 30 October 1918. Numerous testimonials included these words from Gunner A. Eley:

He was the bravest officer ever set foot in France. He was loved and adored by all his men of the 30th Battery, and I feel I endorse the sentiments of all my comrades when I say that by his death we lost the best comrade we had in the Great War.

Such words were commonplace but this rose above the automatic responses of officers who had said the same so many times before. The final death-toll hurt the community as much as the first casualties, sometimes more so, as it seemed that if only events had moved a little faster they could have been avoided. The war, for the Germans, fell apart after 'a famous victory' to the east of Amiens on 8 August 1918. It was insignificant in itself, in terms of location and scale, but caused the Kaiser to take stock of the situation: 'We are at the end of our resources. The war must be ended.'

The agreed time was the eleventh hour of the eleventh day of the eleventh month. The first news of the forthcoming eleven o'clock Armistice came by wireless to the Royal Naval Airship Station at Powerstock at 6.30 in the morning, straight from Paris. The message was telephoned to the Mayor of Bridport, who received it at eight o'clock. This had been expected and the streets of the town were already thronged when the new Mayor, Councillor William Saunders Edwards, announced the news. It was received by the people with an outburst of cheering, and the day was made a holiday. The bells of St Mary

Nurses on a cart, passing the home of chimney-sweep Alfred Farwell in Long's Court, West Street, in the peace celebrations of 1919.

Wartime youths on a hard-labour holiday at the Walditch Flax-Pulling Camp of August 1918.

rang out joyous peals and the town clock, which had been silent throughout the war, struck at the hour of 11, marking the official time for the cessation of hostilities.

By the afternoon, thousands thronged across the middle of the town, from East Street to the bank in West Street, opposite the Sun Hotel and the offices of the *Bridport News* which was published by Wilfrid Frost. An offshoot from this dense mass clogged Downes Street. Revd J.W. Coulter joined the Mayor in holding a service of public thanksgiving from the balcony of the Town Hall. Both expressed 'joy and jubilation' but asked for this to be tempered by 'restraint in recognition of the sacrifice by those who cannot celebrate.'

The running sore remained. Arthur William Marsh of the 1st Dorset Battery of the Royal Field Artillery died on 10 December 1918 while undergoing surgery at Umballa Hospital in India. His comrade Stanley George Bishop died of heatstroke in Mesopotamia. Lieutenant Frederick Cooper of the 26th Battalion, Royal Fusiliers, had been badly wounded in France on 16 October 1918. The son of Bridport's borough surveyor, he died on 18 December 1918 at Queen Alexandra's Hospital for Officers. Henry Clapp of the Labour Corps also died in hospital in London. Wilfrid Charles Cliff disembarked from HMS *Empress of India* and died in hospital in Portsmouth in February 1919. Frederick Glyn Fowler, the son the Joseph Fowler of East Mills, went to India with the 2nd Dorset Battery of the Royal Field Artillery. He died on 17 March 1919 in St George's War Hospital, Poona, after an accident. Also in India, Lieutenant Frank Seamark – an instructor in Bridport's own A-Company of the 4th Battalion, Dorsetshire Regiment – transferred to the Somerset Light Infantry holding the troubled North-West Frontier District. He eventually died on 23 July 1920 after being invalided home.

Quite apart from the war dead, an overlapping tragedy was caused by the influenza pandemic which eliminated more than 20 million people worldwide. Not only was it set to kill more than the war but did so with 'cruel irony, picking off young fit and strong men who had come through the conflict unscathed.' They lacked any immunity to the killer virus.

Commemorative tableware of the First World War including a mug to celebrate the peace, carrying the name of Bridport Mayor W.S. Edwards.

In March 1919 it was announced with pride that Bridport had responded magnificently to the national appeal for eggs – for nursing casualties of the fighting forces during the war – over a four-year period from March 1915. These were taken to the receiving station at the Town Hall from where 1,636 eggs were dispatched to military hospitals at Exeter, and a total of 62,793 went to Headquarters for the Base Hospitals in France and other hospitals at home. This represented a donation worth £1,700, given that the top price for eggs had reached 6s.6d. a dozen in 1918. J.E. Smith was the official Egg Collector for Bridport and district.

Holidays tended to be combined with work. Blue had become the colour of southern England at war, with crops of flax for twine which have the odd habit of opening and closing their flowers as clouds scudded across the sky. Boy Scouts from London, led by George Bulmer, came down by train to Bridport and formed the Walditch Flax-Pulling Camp in the hamlet of nearby Bothenhampton parish. F-Gang gathered for a photograph in August 1918 which brought back painful memories to one of the lads of:

> *... the damage tearing up that cheese-wire did to my fingers and palms, which still seemed to be there when we were sent out to pick Brussel sprouts in the frost during Hitler's war.*

A practical symbol of life returning to normal was that Bridport's holiday line, the extension railway from the town to its seaside resort of West Bay, reopened to passenger traffic on 7 July 1919 after having been closed during the war. The Treaty of Versailles was signed on 28 June 1919 – five years to the day after the assassination of Archduke Ferdinald which had been the catalyst for conflict – and King George V declared a National Thanksgiving Day on 6 July 1919.

Many combatants complained that demobilisation was a slow process, spread across months, whereas they had been mobilised in as many days. The absence of so many of them marred the public Peace Days of 1919. Dozens of children treated to tea in the town's two Drill Halls on 19 July 1919 were still awaiting the return of their fathers.

The next strategic date, the fifth anniversary of the outbreak of war, was declared a bank holiday on 4 August 1919 and ambitiously promoted as 'the Peace Day in a land fit for heroes.' A total of 450 of them gathered for dinner in the Artillery Drill Hall. The catering, cleverly circumventing continuing rationing and shortages, amazed everyone. 'Bountiful supplies' were coupled with Mayor Edwards's 'warm hearted liberality'. In thanks the men raised £50 at a sports meeting, which was split between Bridport Hospital, Bridport Comrades of the Great War and the Women's Institute branches that had done so much to procure their feast.

Edward Reynolds of the Homestead in West Bay Road became the new Mayor on 9 November 1919 and led the civic procession to an Armistice Day service in St Mary's Church two days later. All stood with bowed heads for two minutes of silent prayer at the moment of the anniversary at 11 o'clock. Men were still on their way home from the war and a formal civic ceremony for those who had served was postponed until 27 December 1919, when both drill halls were needed to accommodate them in a two-tier event.

A 'smoking concert' took place in A-Company's Drill Hall while a total of 700 men trooped through the Artillery Drill Hall to receive certificates from the Mayor. He also completed the handing out of 2,500 commemorative mugs, carrying the name of his predecessor, which gave 28 June 1919 – the day of the peace treaty at Versailles – as the official date for the end of the war.

A line was drawn under the Kaiser's war on 27 May 1920 when a Union Flag was draped across Bridport's newly erected war memorial, beside the Parish Church in South Street. This was unveiled by Lieutenant-Colonel Colfox, High Sheriff of Dorset. His younger son appeared on the list of the fallen under Rudyard Kipling's immortal words: 'Their name liveth for evermore.'

St Mary's Parish Church and the war memorial (right) *in South Street*

Above: *Visiting Scout
troop from Richmond in
the 1920s.*

Above: *Richard
Tucker's Post Bus
preparing to leave
Bridport, for
Beaminster, in
1925.*

Left: *East Road
flooded on 28
November 1929
with the approaching
car crossing the
railway line at the
level-crossing.*

Chapter 13
BUSES, SUBMARINES & TRAGEDIES

Bus wars broke out in Bridport after the First World War. Returning from the conflict, Major F.C. Butler and his brother established the first regular motor bus service in the area, from West Street in Bridport, in February 1920. They called it service 1A and ran from Bridport Post Office to Axminster in an ex-Royal Air Force lorry fitted out with longitudinal seats, shielded by coconut matting, and steps at the back. They soon augmented the service and bought modern vehicles. The 30-seater charabancs had six doors per side.

As Butler Bros (Bridport) Limited they were pioneers who responded fast to growing market demand. The seaside was reopening for business and people started flocking to it again, so a holiday route was created from West Bay to the Pilot Boat Inn in the centre of Lyme Regis. Services were expanded as others copied their efforts.

First to head for the western seaboard, on 8 July 1922, were the National Omnibus & Transport Company from the Nautilus Works in Yeovil. Their forte was frequency – 'ideally an hourly bus' – and co-ordination with train times. They realised the importance of linking the Bridport branch railway with the closest station on the Exeter-Waterloo mainline which is at Axminster. Soon they were one of the first companies to have their services listed in railway timetables and boasted of tickets 'with road-rail inter-availability'. National Omnibus continued to force the pace with 35-seater AEC Regal single-deck buses, and then the first double-deckers in 1951.

Bonfield's Royal Mail Bus, operating from the Post Office in West Street, began its run to Chideock, Morcombelake and Charmouth Post Office (then in Wisteria House) at 06.15 hours on 13 April 1923. Four runs were made in each direction on each weekday by G. Bonfield & Son. There was only one Sunday service, in the afternoon, but it was extended from Charmouth to Lyme Regis and returned to Bridport at 18.30. Through the decade the 20-horsepower Renault, with two rows of seats accommodating six passengers, was the most familiar vehicle in the area. Its registration number was PR 328.

The next service to link the rail stations of Bridport and Axminster was introduced by Kitcher & Dunham of Bridport in 1923 but only lasted until 1926. From 1924 Southern National Omnibus Company's service 42 and Devon General Omnibus & Touring Company's service 47 shared the route between Bridport and Axminster. Frank Clarke, based at the Coach and Horses in Charmouth, arrived at the Daffodil Café in Bridport and instigated the service that evolved into Southern National route 32A. He endeared himself to villagers by diverting through Symondsbury, Ryall, Whitchurch Canonicorum and Wootton Fitzpaine.

The return to peace was interrupted as the nation mourned on 10 January 1924 when HM Submarine *L24* was rammed by the battle-cruiser HMS *Resolution* and sank with all hands. The collision occurred in Lyme Bay, south-west of West Bay, between Portland Bill and Start Point. The captain, Lieutenant-Commander Paul L. Eddis, drowned with his 42 officers and men.

Paddle-steamer services were back on the summer menu, only on Tuesdays and Thursdays, from Weymouth to West Bay. The route was then onwards around Lyme Bay to Lyme Regis, Seaton, Sidmouth and Torquay. Then, in 1925, Cosens & Company discontinued the service, citing as their reason 'these days visitors to Weymouth are unwilling to get up early in the morning'.

Educational life resumed in the Visitation Convent in Pymore Road, opposite the junction with Coneygar Road, which was a Catholic preparatory school. One of the old boys from the 1920s, a retired merchant banker, would only give a number – 41, as if it was the answer to everything – rather than his name, on a nostalgic return to Bridport at the time of its demolition in 2001. He explained the significance of the number:

It was a boys' school for both day pupils from the town and boarders like us. We worshipped in the Catholic Church in Victoria Grove. The nuns never allowed us to use our names and gave us numbers instead. To this day I remember my friends by numbers. Even when they phone you say 'Hullo 6' or 'How are you doing, 23?'. Discipline was instant and strict. From age five onwards, for any misconduct, we stepped forwards to receive six strokes of a bamboo cane across the palm of the hand.

A different kind of sect and discipline grew out of the women's suffrage movement. Adela Curtis (1864–1960), the author in 1907 of *The New Mysticism*, established a celibate and contemplative vegetarian Christian commune for women, to work the land

Above: *Bridport Post Office, in West Street, with delivery and counter staff in 1925.*

Right: *Windfall tree blocking Common Lane, on the corner with the High Street, in a view northwards into Burton Bradstock in the 1920s.*

Left: *Bridport Harbour, looking north-eastwards towards the George Hotel (left) and Loders Hill above Bothenhampton (centre) in the 1920s.*

Right: *Bridport Harbour in 1960, looking westwards from the quayside near the Bridport Arms Hotel, with as wide a range of vessels as the century could offer.*

Right: The Esplanade and western beach at West Bay busy in 1927, looking eastwards, with parked cars including TA 1591 and Dorset-registered FX 5222 parked behind.

Westwards along the Esplanade, to West Cliff, in 1947.

Above: *Chalets and motor cars beside the Esplanade at West Bay in 1922, looking eastwards to Pier Terrace (centre) and East Cliff.*

Left: *Timber groynes at West Bay in 1955, in a view westwards to West Cliff (centre) and Thorncombe Beacon (left).*

Left: *AFX 335 parked on the corner of South Street, in this view down West Street in 1947, looking across to the Royal Oak, Lloyds Bank and Samsons.*

Above: *Staff at Bridport Gas Works in 1932. Left to right, standing: E.P. Sue, F. Legg, E. Bartlett, W. Norman, W. Hughes, H. White, C. Loveday, W. Canterbury, J. Stone, C. Symes, A. Burden, W.G. Scott, A. Bartlett, S.R. Gardener, T. Young, H. Brown, H. Legg, E.T. Spencer; seated: E.W. Hutchings, F. Scott, W.H. Reed, R.G. Mabb, A. Scott.*

Above: *East Street in 1930, westwards from Hine & Son newsagents (left) to the Town Hall, with ironmongers Cox & Humphries opposite.*

Right: *Street market in progress between the lime trees on the north side of West Street in a view eastwards to the Town Hall in 1937.*

Second-hand Trojan van VB 4256, seen in 1932 with S. Hoskins and J. Goodall, was the first motorised transport of the Bridport Gas Company.

around the newly-built St Bride's Farm, Burton Bradstock, in 1928. She had lectured and written of her experiences with a community, the Order of Silence, which she founded at Coldash, Berkshire, in 1912.

The Poor Law Institution, overlooking Barrack Street from Bedford Place, became The Institution. It housed 114 inmates – less than half its Victorian capacity – and is now Port Bredy Hospital.

In about 1927 the management at Bridport Gas Works decided to move with the times and pension off their maintenance handcart and the horse and cart used to deliver boilers and cookers; the horse was borrowed when needed from a farmer 'up Watton Hill behind us, which we called Brewery Hill to avoid confusion with the other Watton Hill towards Bradpole.' Second-hand Trojan van VB 4256, for a time still carrying its previous owner's advertisement for Homeland Dairy Farm, became their first motorised vehicle. 'Gas, Buy Now,' was the new logo of Bridport Gas Company.

The attempt to establish a seaside resort at West Bay received a setback on 22 September 1930. Passenger trains to West Bay ceased on that day, the extension line from Bridport town to the coast having failed to coincide with development of a strong hotel trade, although the line was kept open for goods working.

In January 1937 old people recalled 'the white winters' of the last two Victorian decades. At the end of the month the worst snowstorm for many years raged across west Dorset, leaving huge drifts between Bridport and Dorchester. Cars were stranded along the main road and 100 people spent the night at the Askers Road House on the crest of the downs.

That summer Fred Welch, Bridport's town crier since 1925, won the National Town Criers Competition.

'The White Ladies' as they were locally known – because of their cream veils and robes – were now causing much comment in Burton Bradstock. St Bride's Christian Contemplatives' Community at Burton Bradstock, formed by the mystic writer Adela Curtis in 1928, was being provided with its own large chapel. The community's rules and constitution, enshrined in a trust deed signed on 21 December 1938, precluded 'papists and Christian Scientists' from the commune and also banned the installation of water closets 'because sewerage is at the basis of their organic methods of growing produce.' Piped water was also prohibited, as were electricity and fossil fuels. There were seven periods of prayer each day, beginning at five o'clock in the morning.

The Star Hotel (left) *and the south side of West Street, with long shadows in the evening sun, in 1956.*

117

Above, on and below ground at the underground Nissen hut of a bunker of British Resistance Forces, surviving near Bridport in a time warp from 1940.

Chapter 14

FRONT-LINE BRIDPORT

On Monday 13 February 1939, returning from Chequers to No. 10 Downing Street, Prime Minister Neville Chamberlain felt much the same about life, despite the strain and stresses of brinkmanship on the edge of diplomatic disaster:

... with a thrush singing in the garden, the sun shining, and the rooks beginning to discuss among themselves the prospects of the coming nesting season, I feel as though spring were getting near ... All the information I get seems to point in the direction of peace.

Hitler marked Chamberlain's 70th birthday, on 16 March 1937, by marching into Prague the previous day. Appeasement ended at that moment. By August 1939 the Lyme Regis Bombing Range, covering 16 square miles of sea, had been designated by the Air Ministry for daylight use. An initial limit of 120lbs was imposed on live bombs that could be dropped.

The famous speech, from the Cabinet Room in No. 10 Downing Street, was broadcast to the nation on the morning of Sunday 3 September 1939. On the Tuesday, just two days into the new war, in *K Destroyer Flotilla News* – the daily newspaper of the 5th Destroyer Flotilla – Bob Knight reported to the crew of HMS *Kelly* on the fishy sequel resulting from anti-submarine depth-charges that claimed a U-boat off Bridport the previous day:

That's war – that was; but we must not lead ourselves to believe that some of the catch will always appear on the breakfast table. The presence of mind of Posty in producing a gaff to lift the whales inboard while the ship had stopped to obtain a sample of the oil on the sea

is much to be admired. We all hope that the Kelly*'s and* Acheron*'s efforts* [another destroyer] *did away with one of the pests that sank, without warning, the liner* Athenia *on Sunday night* [3 September, off Ireland] *– and, of course, we hope that the lucky messes in the* Kelly *enjoyed their breakfast. There is plenty of corroborative evidence to show that there were two U-boats here yesterday, one in Weymouth Bay and one in West Bay. The periscope of the former was seen from the signal bridge of the* Resolution *and the M.A.S.B. and the tracks of two torpedoes fired at the* Kelly. *They missed us by 30 or 40 yards, so certainly we were lucky. To be missed by one submarine and bag another* [later, in Lyme Bay] *all in the first day* [at sea, from Portland] *is good going.*

Naval losses over the winter, on both sides, were followed by the next move on the chequer-board of Europe as German troops poured into Norway. On 12 April 1940 a laurel wreath was attached to the door of the Hardy Monument, the memorial to Nelson's flag captain on the hills above Portesham – the village known to Thomas Hardy as 'Possum' – in memory of the men of the Royal Navy who lost their lives two days before in Narvik fjord. A card read: 'To the unfading memory of Captain Warburton-Lee, RN, HMS Hardy, and the gallant men who died at Narvik. Nelson's Hardy and Hardy's Possum salute you.'

The situation around Narvik stabilised towards the end of May but became impossible after Hitler's march into the Low Countries was followed by the fall of France. The evacuation of 27,000 men from Norway was as much of a miracle as that from Dunkirk. One questionable deployment, however,

Pillbox peeking through a hedge from Highlands End Caravan Park at Eype.

Left: *Machine-gun post in the rushes, overlooking the stream at Eype Mouth.*

Right: *Wartime radar station at Cain's Folly carried seawards by a landslip in 1942.*

The main buildings of the coastal radar station on Stonebarrow Hill are now a shop and sleeping quarters on the National Trust's Golden Cap estate.

was the use of an aircraft-carrier to evacuate ten obsolete biplanes and seven modern fighters. Lieutenant-Commander Charles John Thompson Stephens was lost on the afternoon of 8 June 1940 during the sinking of the aircraft-carrier *Glorious*, off Narvik, by gunfire from the German battle-cruisers *Scharnhorst* and *Gneisenau*. Commander Stephens, aged 35, was the son of Major John August Stephens of Evershot, who served in the Royal Field Artillery and died in 1925 after a prolonged illness that resulted from injuries suffered in the First World War. Two escort vessels, the destroyers HMS *Acasta* and HMS *Ardent*, were sunk off Narvik in the same action.

Sometimes pub names have to move with events. Such was the fate of Bridport's King of Prussia, at 52 East Street, which became the King of Belgium when he was the nation's darling for standing up to the Kaiser in 1915. In June 1940, however, he capitulated to the next wave of invading Germans. This time Palmer's Brewery chose a hero who could not be deposed – they decided that Lord Nelson had stood the test of time.

By July 1940, 32 underground hideouts had been established secretly by the Royal Engineers in woods and commons scattered through the Dorset countryside to conceal the weapons, explosives and food necessary for Auxiliary Units of British Resistance to operate behind German lines in the event of an invasion. Several were close to Bridport in the wild and tumbling countryside around Beaminster and Marshwood.

The Western Front in the Battle of Britain – literally overhead at Bridport – was shared between Spitfires from RAF Warmwell, near Dorchester, and Hurricanes from RAF Exeter. On 15 August 1940, 27-year-old Squadron Leader Terence Lovell-Gregg of 87 Squadron from RAF Exeter failed in a desperate attempt to make a crash landing in The Fleet lagoon in the late afternoon. The Hurricane came in blazing over the sea but was brought into a controlled descent for a forced landing. It then clipped a tree beside Abbotsbury Swannery and its wounded pilot fell to his death.

Flying Officer Roland Prosper Beamont, one of the Exeter pilots, returned with the story of how Lovell-Gregg had led his squadron into the midst of a mass of German aircraft at 18,000 feet over the English Channel:

We saw the 'Beehive' almost straight ahead at the same height, and with his Hurricanes, Lovell-Gregg flew straight at the centre of the formation without hesitation or deviation in any way.

A total of 120 enemy aircraft were heading towards Portland. Lovell-Gregg was a quiet pre-war professional from Marlborough in New Zealand, who had taught many of the emergent generation of flyers.

His courage was never in any doubt, although he had led his squadron for only a month, since 12 July. The pilots knew him as 'Shovel'. There were only four of them with his plane when they scrambled at 16.00 hours. Five Hurricanes were all the air-worthy machines that 87 Squadron could muster. Undaunted by the adverse odds of fifteen-to-one that loomed in front, Lovell-Gregg asked the impossible of his men: 'Come on chaps, let's surround them!'

Writing in *The Two Edged Sword*, Adela Curtis, leader of the Christian Contemplatives' Community at Burton Bradstock, advised in August on methods of furthering the war effort through positive prayer:

We are to summon each enemy leader by name. For cumulative effect the message should be spoken three times – Adolf Hitler! Adolf Hitler! Adolf Hitler! Hear the Truth!

The German invasion appeared to have started on Saturday 7 September 1940. Reports were received of a seven-mile convoy heading towards the Dorset coast and there was 'a general flap on that Operation Sealion [was] taking place'. Field-Marshal Fedor von Bock was on his way with the victors of Poland, the Wehrmacht's Army Group B. An order was given for fuel tanks to be fired, to set beaches ablaze, and an aircraft from Gosport dropped incendiaries to start them off. Troops at Bournemouth manned the cliffs and kept emphasising that this was 'not an exercise'. At 20.07 hours that Saturday night a national alert was issued by the War Office: 'Condition Cromwell'. That was the code for an invasion being 'regarded as imminent and probable within 12 hours.' Nothing happened. Despite that, invasion fears reached fever-pitch, although not without reason, for aerial reconnaissances were showing concentrations of ships and barges from Brest to Calais. It might have been reassuring to people north of the border that a photograph was issued showing a single soldier with a Lee-Enfield rifle patrolling a coil of cliffside barbed wire 'somewhere on the Scottish coast'. What would have reduced its credibility between Bridport and Lyme Regis was that the background showed Seatown and the distinctive 617-foot profile of Golden Cap. That was deliberate misinformation – what might have been a regarded as adequate several hundred miles away from the nearest German troops was hardly a reassurance for those facing occupied France.

The tall 1873-built tower of Cattistock Parish Church was gutted by fire at 14.30 hours on 15 September 1940, destroying its famous carillon of 35 bells. The village missed the tunes. Officially the cause was not known, but locally it was blamed on a cigarette discarded by a member of the Home Guard who was in the tower fire-watching.

On 8 October 1940, Pilot Officer Harold John Akroyd of 152 Squadron from RAF Warmwell died at

121

Dorset County Hospital, Dorchester, from burns received the previous day when his damaged Spitfire, N3039, burst into flames on crashing at Shatcombe Farm, Wynford Eagle. It had been crippled by enemy fire in dogfights over West Dorset. Aged 27, he was buried in the RAF plot at Warmwell churchyard.

Bombers crossing the coast from Lyme Bay often had Bristol as their target but Yeovil had its turn on 7 October 1940. A Junkers Ju.88 bomber (9K+SN), heading for the Westland Aircraft Factory, was brought down at 16.20 hours on Tappers Hill, above the hamlet of Up Sydling, near Sydling St Nicholas. The kill was claimed jointly by Sergeant Pilot Edmund Shepperd of 152 Squadron from Warmwell and Flying Officer Bob Doe in a Hurricane of 238 Squadron from RAF Chilbolton. All four members of the German crew baled out successfully and were taken prisoners of war after being rounded up by shotgun, following which the farm labourers performed a victory dance around the wreckage. The crewmen were Oberfeldwebel Sigurd Hey, Leutnant Friedrich Bein, Oberfeldwebel Christian Koenig, and Oberfeldwebel Josef Troll. The bomber belonged to the 5th Staffel of II Gruppe Kamfgruppe 51.

Then a Messerchmitt Bf.110C (3U+JP) of the 6th Staffel of Zerstorergeschwader 26, which had been defending the bombers en route to Yeovil, crashed at Brickhills Field near Kingston Russell House. Crewmen Obergefreiter Herbert Schilling and Oberfeldwebel Karl Herzog were killed on impact. Human remains were removed, together with wreckage and identification papers, during an excavation carried out by Andy Saunders in 1976. The flyers' graves are in the German War Cemetery at Cannock Chase. A camouflage-painted propeller from the fighter-bomber stands behind me, beside the office door, as I type this manuscript.

On 14 October 1940 the British armed trawler HMT *Lord Stamp* sank after striking a mine in Lyme Bay. The Royal Navy's losses of armed trawlers to the German minefield off West Dorset continued on 17 October 1940 when HMT *Kingston Cairngorm* blew up off Portland Bill.

In the early morning of 6 November 1940 a Heinkel He.111 of Kampfgruppe 100, the elite two per cent of German bombers operating from Vannes, Brittany, suffered a compass failure. It was acting as a pathfinder for the attacking formations. The navigator was confused by the British masking of German radio beacons into thinking it was back over France when in fact it was running out of fuel above Dorset. The pilot landed on the shingle beach at West Bay and three out of the four crew survived – although they soon had their illusions shattered regarding France and found themselves in captivity.

Soldiers guarded the aircraft, which carried the identification code '6N', and had some difference of opinion with a Naval detachment that came to drag the plane up the beach. The soldiers followed orders not to let anyone touch the bomber and it was engulfed by the incoming tide. The aircraft had three vertical aerials and related radio equipment. This apparatus was salvaged for inspection by Air Ministry experts.

By 21 November 1940, scientists at the Royal Aircraft Establishment, Farnborough, had reassembled radio beam-flying equipment removed from the bomber. The aircraft had an intact X-Gerat radio receiver, also known as Wotan I, which was used for precision bombing by enabling the aircraft to follow a radio direction beam emanating from the Cherbourg peninsula. What surprised the Air Ministry experts was that the apparatus was tuned to 2,000 cycles per second (approximating to the 'C' which is two octaves above standard-pitch middle 'C'), whereas British jamming counter-measures had assumed a note of 1,500 cycles (approximating to the 'G' below this upper 'C').

They were less than pleased that the vital equipment was corroded and full of sand, this avoidable damage to the delicate light-alloy components being due 'to the crass folly of the Dorset soldiers who prevented sailors from pulling the aircraft up the beach to safety.' Particular anger was expressed that the secret could have been cracked in time to foil the Coventry raid, which took place a week before: 'Someone in Dorset should be shot!'

Secret war work in Bridport itself included the precision cutting of quartz chips for the transducers of Asdic submarine detectors carried by destroyers and other escort vessels. This work was carried out by eight men on contract work for the Admiralty Underwater Weapons Establishment, using the tombstone-engraving equipment of monumental masons Appleby & Childs at 64 West Street.

An RAF Blenheim, returning from Bomber Command's raid on the port of Brest, crashed at Frampton on the night of 3–4 April 1941. The three crewmen, Sergeants P.I. Burrows, G.B.H. Birdsell and H.R. Perry, were killed instantaneously as the aeroplane exploded on hitting the ground. The aircraft belonged to 101 Squadron and had taken off from RAF West Raynham, Norfolk, at 19.15 hours. The crew came over the coast near Bridport and crashed while trying to chart a course to RAF Boscombe Down which is 45 miles north-east of Frampton.

On 10 May 1941 it was announced that the 'Wings for Victory' appeal in West Dorset – which raised nearly £6,000 – had paid for Spitfire R7062 which was handed over to 308 Squadron. It was named 'The Brit' after Bridport's river. The fighter was transferred to 403 Squadron on 28 May 1941 and later to a training unit near Chester. It was lost in a flying accident on 21 December 1941.

There was a local reminder of the wider war on 10 December 1941 when Seaman John Henry Brabant from Powerstock was among those killed when Japanese aircraft sank the battle-cruiser HMS *Repulse* in the Indian Ocean.

The Star Hotel (right) *on the south side of West Street, showing its best side after German bombing in August 1942.*

On 17 December 1941, when their starboard engine failed, five crewmen of Wellington X9785 baled out over Chilfrome, eight miles north-west of Dorchester. The pilot, Sergeant Vezina, continued on a course towards Bridport and successfully brought his crippled bomber to a crash landing at Holm Farm, above West Milton, near Powerstock. The Wellington, belonging to 218 Squadron, had taken off from RAF Marham, Norfolk, at 18.40 hours to attack the German capital ships in the French Atlantic port of Brest.

Radar rather than carrots accounted for the night sight and over-the-horizon vision that enabled the RAF to intercept the Luftwaffe. Nature did more damage to a Dorset coastal radar station than enemy action on 14 May 1942. The occupants of the secret installation at Cain's Folly, on the cliffs east of Charmouth, had a shock when the ground literally opened up beneath them. A landslip carried away concrete buildings and deposited them on the tumbled undercliff some 50 feet below. This may well have disrupted radar coverage as a number of approaches by enemy aircraft crossed the coast before being detected.

One made a quick attack on West Bay on Wednesday 1 July 1942, spraying machine-gun bullets around a Royal Artillery Coast Defence Battery. The following day a bomber dropped a stick of four bombs on Chideock village at 14.35 hours,

with mainly light damage to a total of 82 buildings and disruption to electricity supplies.

What was known as the Battle of Lyme Bay took place on 9 July 1942. It was carried out by the German 1st Schnellboot Flotilla (S48, S50, S63, S67, S70, S104, S109) against Allied Coast Convoy E/P 91. A total of 12,192 tons of shipping was sunk; the tanker SS *Pomella* and four freighters. One of the British escorts, armed trawler HMT *Manor*, was also lost.

Two German Focke-Wulf fighter-bombers carried out a hit-and-run raid on Bridport at 18.33 hours on the clear evening of 2 August 1942. They had not been detected by radar and it took a couple of minutes for the air-raid sirens to screech into action. By this time the Star Hotel at 14 West Street was devastated, although John Hembrow Hecks and his customers and staff were unhurt.

One of the great stories of wartime initiative, skill and bravery began in Dorset on 4 December 1942. Barnes Neville Wallis, the assistant chief designer at the aviation section of Vickers-Armstrongs Limited, flew from their Weybridge works to the Chesil Beach Bombing Range. He was in Wellington BJ895/G, an aeroplane he designed, and acted as the bomb aimer when the pilot, Captain J. 'Mutt' Summers – famous as a test pilot of the Spitfire – came in low over the flat waters of The Fleet lagoon, which lies between the offshore pebble

123

Bridport bombed, looking northwards from the gardens at the back of Numbers 92–102 East Street, showing the scale of destruction on 16 December 1942.

Bridport's wartime Air Raid Precautions wardens in Civil Defence uniforms.

bank and the inshore coast of Langton Herring and Abbotsbury. Captain R.C. Handasyde acted as the observer. Two steel spheres were dropped, with the hope that they might bounce along the surface of the water, but both burst upon impact. Neither carried explosives.

The Wellington returned with two more spheres, via Warmwell Aerodrome, on 15 December 1942. As with the first test both drops failed, and it was decided to try again after Christmas.

The air-raid sirens in Bridport sounded at 13.17, during the cloudy lunch-time of 16 December 1942, as a single Dornier Do.127 approached the town. It had been detected by radar. A total of 33 rounds were fired from the eight 40mm Bofors guns of 439 Light Anti-Aircraft Battery, which opened up after the German bomber crossed the coast at Cogden Beach at 1,000 feet and turned north-westwards to circle the town.

It then approached from the west, dropping to 600 feet, and dropped four 500kg bombs along East Street. The first, which fell into the entrance of the Westminster Bank at 22 East Street – spreading nearly £1,000 in cash into the street – failed to explode. The second fell to the south into gardens behind East Street and King Street. The third hit buildings between 92 and 102 East Street, killing two women and a child and injuring 16 people. The fourth landed in the meadow north-east of East Bridge. The bomber continued south-eastwards, machine-gunning Walditch before turning south at Abbotsbury and heading for home. East Street was sealed off beside the Town Hall until the Westminster Bank bomb was defused. Nearly all of its missing money was recovered and returned to a by-now doubly-relieved manager, Herbert Langdon.

The town was fighting back with its traditional products, with camouflage netting added to the list, and the shingle from West Bay was leaving in long ballast trains for the building of defences and as hard-core for the dozens of new 'hardened' airfields that were replacing the grass aerodromes of the Battle of Britain. These were appearing across the Dorset countryside – at Hurn and Tarrant Rushton – and in the New Forest for airborne forces and night-fighters. Bomber bases were concentrated in the Midlands and East Anglia.

On 9 January 1943 two more steel spheres were dropped by Wellington BJ895/G from the Vickers-Armstrongs Weybridge works on the Chesil Beach Bombing Range. The tests were once again a failure. The aim of aircraft designer Barnes Wallis was to devise a bomb that could bounce across the water and have a dam-breaking capability. So far, of six dummy bombs that had been dropped, five had fragmented on touching The Fleet lagoon and the other was incorrectly released and hit the land.

That night Barnes Wallis carried out modifications to one of his prototype bouncing bombs at Warmwell Aerodrome. The Wellington lifted off with it on 10 January for another low-level drop over The Fleet lagoon. The boffin and his crew were jubilant! For the first time their bomb, which had been strengthened, skimmed the surface of the water. It spun for 50 feet and then shattered – but the principle had been proved.

They were back again on 23 January 1943. Wellington BJ895/G dropped a wooden version of the bouncing bomb. It achieved 13 bounces on the inshore lagoon of The Fleet to the east of Langton Hive Point, Langton Herring, on the RAF's Chesil Beach Bombing Range. Things were even better the following morning.

This time 20 bounces were recorded by scientist Barnes Wallis as his revolutionary bomb zipped across The Fleet lagoon at Langton Herring. Once again it had been dropped from Wellington bomber BJ895/G which then flew back to Warmwell Aerodrome. The team from the Vickers-Armstrongs Weybridge works then prepared a boom across the shallow waters. This was intended to simulate the wall of a dam. The evening saw another successful trial when the Wellington returned to the Chesil Beach Bombing Range. It again turned over the sea and came in across the lake-like waters of The Fleet. The bomb was dropped, and bounced, and proceeded to jump the boom.

The trials of wooden prototypes of Barnes Wallis' bouncing bomb resumed on The Fleet on 5 February 1943. They were dropped from Wellington BJ895/G, coming from Weybridge and operating for the day out of Warmwell Aerodrome. The bomber was now making faster approach runs. It swept in across the Chesil Beach Bombing Range at 300 miles per hour and succeeded in sending bombs jumping across the sheltered and waveless inshore water for distances of around 4,000 feet.

Offshore there was still a real war raging on 28 February 1943. In the previous four days the 5th Schnellboot Flotilla had been harrying a Channel convoy in Lyme Bay and then onwards between Portland and the Isle of Wight. Two of the escorts protecting Convoy CHA 172, the armed trawlers HMT *Harstad* and HMT *Lord Hailsham*, were sunk. The freighter *Moldavia* (4,858 tons) was also lost, together with a new 658-ton tank landing craft, *LCT381*.

That month a Dornier Do.17 bomber was shot down at night over South Buckham Farm near Beaminster. Its destruction was claimed by Wing Commander Rupert Clerke, flying a Beaufighter of 125 (Newfoundland) Squadron from RAF Fairwood Common, Glamorgan.

The bouncing-bomb story resumed on 8 March 1943. Carrying fully-weighted steel versions of the prototype, Barnes Wallis and Wellington BJ895/G returned to Warmwell Aerodrome and the Chesil Beach Bombing Range for an extended series of trial runs over The Fleet lagoon. The dummy

Blacksmith Benjamin Burton of Burton Bradstock, chatting to an American officer in the winter of 1943.

Above right: *Shared history of a pre-1783 tombstone being pointed out by Revd Arthur Dittmer in Burton Bradstock churchyard, to Major E.M. Beebe and Lieutenant S.M. Weitzner of the United States Army.*

Petty Officer Podger, RN, retired, giving directions to Private 1st-Class Roy St Jean of Springfield, Massachusetts, in Burton Bradstock.

Forging bonds of friendship – between American GIs, village boy, blacksmith Benjamin Burton and a docile customer – in the Smithy at Burton Bradstock.

bombs, re-designed like dimpled golf balls with two flat edges on each side, from which they spun on an axle, were released to skim over the water with a precision that suggested their use as an effective weapon was feasible. These trials concluded on the evening of 9 March 1943.

Locally there had been complaints that the Wellington's approach flight, at 300 miles per hour over the West Fleet towards Langton Hive Point and the uninhabited Herbury peninsula, was upsetting nest-building at the famous Abbotsbury Swannery. Ironically, one of dimpled bombs – recovered from the Fleet – is now displayed at the Swannery. The next set of tests, to determine the handling behaviour of the bomb on choppier water, took place off Reculver, Kent.

The actual practice runs for Operation Chastise were carried out by Lancaster bombers of 617 Squadron over the Elan valley reservoir in the mountains of mid-Wales. On the night of 16 May 1943 precision low flying delivered the novel weapon and breached the Mohne and Eder dams in the Ruhr. Air Marshal Sir Arthur Harris, Commander-in-Chief Bomber Command, recalled that he encountered problems giving the 'good news' to the Prime Minister, Air Marshal Portal and General Sir Alan Brooke, Chief of the Imperial General Staff. They had sailed to New York on the *Queen Mary* and were about to meet President Roosevelt:

I rang up Washington, where Churchill and Portal were at the time, and there was some little difficulty. When I did get through I was intercepted and asked for an assurance that the person I was calling was reliable. I don't know whether she was persuaded that Winston Churchill came into that category, but I got through to Portal in the end and told him that the two dams had gone.

Eight of the 19 Lancasters involved in the bombing failed to return. Squadron Leader Guy Gibson won the Victoria Cross. The main aim had been to cause a water shortage for industrial purposes in the Ruhr, rather than sweeping everything away in a flood, which is how we tend to remember the exploit. Not that there were many happy farmers in Kassel when 330 million tons of water spread across their fields. Several hundred Ukranian prisoners of war were among the 1,294 people who drowned.

In December 1943 one of kindest sequels to a war story was that of RAF Sergeant Pilot Ronald Foss from Bridport who was lost on a Coastal Command flight over the Bay of Biscay. The first person to know he was missing happened to be his wife, whom he married in April 1942, as she was serving in the operations room of the same air station. Ronald, in fact, was still alive and would be picked up from the sea a week later with enough experiences of war to fill a book. Or, rather, three of them. The titles were *In the Drink*, *Three of us Live*, and *Famous War Stories*.

'It is true you have made a score of enemies,' General Sir Bernard Montgomery was told by a friend when he returned to England, after visiting Prime Minister Winston Churchill in Marrakech over

Crew-cut on the beach for United States General Infantrymen before crossing the Channel in 1944.

127

the year-end holiday in 1943. 'But,' he continued, you have made thousands of friends as well.'

He found them in Bridport on 18 January 1944. They lined the streets for his mid-month tour of the 21st Army Group, brought together as the British invasion forces for the opening of the Second Front. 'Drive slowly,' General Montgomery ordered his driver, as he realised that East Street was crowded with cheering civilians. One lady pushed forward and succeeded in reaching his car. She thanked him for the 'wonderful job' he had done in North Africa and Italy. Then she reprimanded the policeman who had tried to restrain her: 'Constable, you cannot stop me from thanking the man who had saved his country!' Montgomery grinned broadly. Having seen the sidings being laid at West Bay for the provision of marshalling yards for the invasion stores, and met American officers from the extensive camp of the United States First Infantry Division based at the holiday camp at Freshwater, between Bridport and Burton Bradstock, he later returned to his old school, St Paul's at Hammersmith, which was where he had based his headquarters. There he

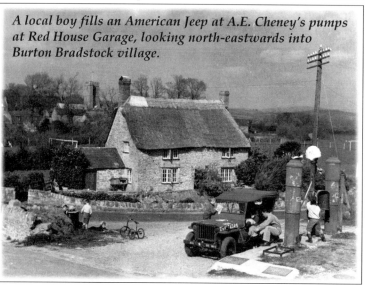

A local boy fills an American Jeep at A.E. Cheney's pumps at Red House Garage, looking north-eastwards into Burton Bradstock village.

revised the top-secret 'Cossack' plans for the invasion of Normandy. He first saw the details of Operation Overlord, of which he had been appointed overall land forces commander, whilst sitting beside Churchill's bed in Morocco on New Year's Day.

These plans were re-jigged on 16 April 1944. Although expected to gather in Portland and Weymouth for Operation Overlord, British invasion Force G was relocated eastwards to the harbours and inlets of the Solent and Southampton Water. Instead the Dorset ports were allocated to United States Force O. They were destined for what was designated as Omaha Beach, with the British troops poised to land in the next sector to the east, codenamed Gold Beach.

Captain J.J. McGlynn of the United States Navy took up his post as Commanding Officer United States Navy Advanced Amphibious Base Portland and Weymouth. This included the three hards at Portland and HMS *Grasshopper*, the Royal Navy shore-base at Weymouth, plus ancillary facilities. Captain McGlynn was responsible for the embarkation of V Corps of the First United States Army which comprised the 1st US Infantry division, 2nd US Infantry Division, 2nd US Armored Division, and

two Ranger battalions. The 'Fighting Firsts', or 'Big Red One' as America's famous First Infantry Division was known, had its Divisional Headquarters at Langton House, Langton Long Blandford. The Commanding General, Major-General Clarence R. Huebner, had at his command 34,142 men and 3,306 vehicles. It was estimated that there were a total of 80,000 American soldiers who were billeted in Dorset, from the chalets of Freshwater holiday camp on the coast at Burton Bradstock to Nissen huts in hazel coppices on Cranborne Chase.

Everything was being done, however, to persuade both Britons and Germans that this was a huge diversion, so that the enemy would prepare instead to receive the main thrust from Sussex and Kent, across the Pas de Calais. Hitler realised that the great beaches of Normandy were ideal for assault troops but had no facilities for landing supplies. These, in the form of concrete caissons comprising two purpose-built Mulberry Harbours, were to be towed across the Channel.

Meanwhile, an 'Exercise Tiger' took place in Lyme Bay, and at around 02.50 hours on Friday 28 April a convoy of eight American tank landing ships (LSTs), sailing as Convoy T-4 in a circuit eastwards from Slapton Sands, were intercepted by German E-boats. Motor torpedo boats of the 5th and 9th Schnellboot Flotillas ran amok amongst the Americans south-west of Portland Bill. A total of 441 United States soldiers were killed or drowned, together with 197 seamen, with the sinking of *LST501* and *LST531*. Twelve tanks were also lost and a third ship, *LST289*, was damaged by a torpedo and limped westwards towards Dartmouth. *LST511* was raked by gunfire and escaped the other way, around Portland Bill into Weymouth Bay.

The coastal gun batteries at Blacknor Fort, Portland, prepared to open fire but were ordered not to do so by the American commander, in view of the number of his men who were in the water. After the dead were recovered the bodies were stacked in piles on Castletown Pier in Portland Naval Dockyard. Offshore, visible on the horizon south of West Bay, teams of Navy divers worked for days to recover the identity discs from the other bodies, to account for all the missing and give Allied Naval Headquarters the welcome news that none had been fished out alive from the sea by the Germans and taken prisoner.

Confirmation of their demise was accompanied by immense feelings of relief. A secret memorandum put it bluntly: 'This cloud's silver lining is that the invasion plans remain safe and secure.'

The D-Day secret could have been compromised as 20 United States officers with the security classification 'Bigot' had to be accounted for, because they knew when and where the invasion of Europe was going to take place, and its American code-name sector beaches, Utah and Omaha. General Dwight D. Eisenhower, the Supreme Commander Allied Expeditionary Forces, had given strict instructions that under no circumstances should any Bigot-classified personnel take part in any operations before D-Day, in case they were captured by the Germans.

The result was the cover-up that created the folk-lore of Slapton Sands. E-boats were credited with an audacious attack on massed Allied invasion craft, plus 30 Allied warships up to the size of a cruiser, off the mid-Devon coast. That did not break the Eisenhower edict. Had the true location been admitted, 70 kilometres to the east in the open water of Lyme Bay – in reality the English Channel – 25 kilometres off Portland, then not only would Eisenhower have been defied but the question would have been asked as to why such a risky exercise had been mounted. Not only was there a lack of sufficient escort vessels but the manoeuvring of the LSTs was a simulation that could have revealed the route that was going to be taken on D Minus One for the landings on D-Day.

A disaster was nearly a calamity. As for the horrendous details, Leading Telegraphist Nigel Cresswell, wireless operator in *MTB701* based at Portland, was haunted by the memory:

On a bright, sunny late spring morning I saw us approaching what looked like an indoor swimming pool, but there were hundreds of bodies in the water and they were all dead. I was not quite 21 and had seen the odd dead body, but nothing to what we saw before us. It had a profound effect on us young men, and I will never forget it, ever. I remember examining two or three bodies that had been brought on board. Their Army denim uniforms had the button crimped to the material so that the buttons could not be removed. I remember two of the dog-tags had 'Rome City, New York'.

Their life-jackets were different from ours, with two circular rings sewn together with a small cylinder of gas at one end. When depressed the life-jacket would inflate. We were ordered by another MTB to the water, and in a letter to me, Able Seaman Torpedoman Wood said that we were supposed to puncture the life-jackets, as we had seen too much. I do distinctly remember a very few bodies in the water wearing British Army khaki battledress with the square red badges of Royal Artillerymen.

Returning to Portland on the morning of 29 April, Nigel Cresswell walked through the dockyard to see his current girlfriend, Wren Torpedo Mechanic Doreen Smedley. He was told that the Wrens were not about: 'Looking into the Torpedo Workshop from a distance of a few yards I saw lots of shrouded bodies. I was quickly ushered away.'

Immediately after the disaster, the Allied High Command initiated a total blackout of the event, and dispersed the survivors to various military hospitals along the South Coast. Medical staff were briefed not to inquire into the circumstances of their injuries. The failure for breaking this instruction would be courts martial. As for the bodies, they are said to have been buried in underground galleries below Verne Prison, the entrance to which was blown up and blocked when the naval dockyard closed in the 1990s. Relatives were later told that the men had died on D-Day.

Delayed for a day because of rough seas, on Tuesday 6 June 1944, Dorset's Americans became the heroes of 'Bloody Omaha', the scene of the worst Allied casualties of the D-Day invasion where the lives of 3,000 men were lost before they eventually secured beach-head objectives as dusk dropped 'on this longest day'. Total losses in the Battle of Normandy were 37,000 Allied dead, and 58,000 German fatalities.

The war was leaving Dorset and heading for the Baltic where Field-Marshal Montgomery took 'the surrender of all German armed forces in Holland, in north-west Germany including all islands, and in Denmark' at 18.30 hours on 4 May 1945. It took effect 'at 08.00 hours British Double Summer Time on Saturday 5 May 1945.' The nation and the town celebrated with Victory Europe Day on 8 May. The conflict continued in the Far East until the dropping of two atom bombs, followed by Victory Japan Day, in August 1945.

American GIs meet locals in the Dove Inn at Burton Bradstock in the winter of 1943, with the Reading poster (top right) brought to disguise the location.

Above: *Whitemore's Stores* (right) *and a bustling South Street, southwards to St Mary's Church* (centre) *in 1955.*

Left: *Proud moment for Bridport Mayor H.R.C. Palmer as his granddaughter, Anne Palmer, presents a bouquet to Princess Margaret in June 1953.*

Below: *East Street, downhill from the Royal Oak and the butchers Dewhurst* (right), *westwards to Colmer's Hill* (centre), *in 1957.*

Chapter 15

POSTWAR AUSTERITY & RECOVERY

Demobilisation and decommissioning wartime defences 'seemed to take forever'. That was partly because their complexity and scale was far greater than had been realised at the time. On 3 August 1947, Major A.B. Hartley of Southern Command announced that the 16th and 17th Bomb Disposal squads of the Royal Engineers had so far disposed of 9,000 anti-invasion mines along the coast eastwards from Weymouth. This included a total of some 3,200 from a mile of shingle beach and clayey cliffs at Ringstead Bay. The operations had cost the lives of three officers and 22 other ranks. One officer was blinded.

Fred Welch of Bridport won the National Town Criers Championship for the second time, in 1947. He also became the first town crier to appear on television, in the 'Picture Page' programme with Phyllis Robins and Gillie Potter. West Dorset was becoming a film set with *The Cruel Sea*, re-creating the Battle of the Atlantic, being filmed in the Royal Navy's sea danger area in Lyme Bay and featuring sloops and corvettes from Portland Harbour. The film *All Over the Town*, recorded at Lyme Regis – under the guise of Tormouth – was completed in 1948.

Founded in 1844, during the distressed decade known as 'the Hungry Forties', Litton Cheney Friendly Society members held their last club walk and church service on Whit Tuesday in 1948. For a century it provided for the sick and destitute of the village. 'Walking', as this annual club fête was known, was the major community occasion of the year. Everyone appeared in their best attire and marched behind a band and an embroidered banner seven feet high and eight feet wide. The new National Insurance scheme, which came into operation on 5 July 1948, had put an end to the last of the village benevolent societies.

The directors of Bridport Gas Company showed their appreciation to their staff in 1949:

... for devotion to duty over these long years of war and austerity, and keeping the town's ovens burning through the terrible cold in the winter of 1947 and the chronic fuel shortages last year.

Their reward was a May Day dinner in the Bridport Arms Hotel.

Bridport experienced a railway mishap at lunchtime on Sunday 23 July 1950. A brake van and wagon became detached from their ballast train during shunting at Bridport Station and ran away, down the gradient, crashing through newly painted level-crossing gates to the other side of the road at East Street Station. No one was passing on what had become a busy main road. Someone recorded the moment in verse and attached it to the remains of the gates:

> *We have a goods train once a day,*
> *From Saturday to Monday,*
> *But see the stately carriages,*
> *A battering-ram on Sunday.*

Dorset pet shops in 1950 were catering for the craze for golden hamsters, which spread from London and threatened to displace rabbits from their cages:

After all we now live in an age when we no longer have to eat our pets. These are not only tiny but scrupulously clean and wash with their paws like a cat. Great bulges around their necks are nothing to cause alarm, merely being surplus food which is stored in a pouch. This helped them survive in the Syrian desert and all are said to descend from a single pregnant female.

Charlie Ford of Clayhanger Farm, south-east of Abbotsbury, who was known as the 'Dorset Singing Minstrel' because of his repertoire of countless traditional folk songs, was killed in a road accident in 1950. He was 54. They said he was going to compose the ballad of Abbotsbury fisherman Jack Keech, a former gamekeeper and wartime commando, who

Esplanade and groynes at West Bay, looking eastwards from West Cliff, with plenty of cars in 1950 but no one on the beach.

Above: *Riverside Café and the Post Office, beside the backwater at West Bay.*

Right: *Brick-built shop and three-storey flats opposite the Town Hall where East Street joins West Street, with New Look, Steptoes and Cards & Things in 1997.*

The view westwards along East Street from a room in the Bull Hotel, across to Elmes, Woolworth, estate agents Allen and Whitfield and Emile, with a new Mini passing (centre) in 1961.

Right: *Bridport Sports and the Rax dairy along to Venues, on the north side of East Street, in 1997.*

Below: *West Pier and the west beach at West Bay, looking westwards to West Cliff.*

Below: *Cheers Video Store (right) opposite the sign for Crumbs Café (left) at the south end of Barrack Street, looking into East Street, in 1997.*

Right: *Barrack Street, formerly Stake Lane, in a view northwards in 1997.*

Below: *The A35 east of Bridport on 25 January 1963 – a month into 'the great freeze'.*

Below: *Preparing slates for roofing at West Bay in 1965.*

Princess Margaret, the Queen's sister, visited Bridport on 24 June 1953 in what was described as 'the first official royal visit in all Bridport's long history.'

The final fire in the retorts at Bridport Gas Works in South Street was lit by stoker Frank Thomas in 1958. Henceforth coal gas was to come by pipe from a quayside works at Poole and holding tanks in Bourne Valley, until the national conversion to natural North Sea gas in the 1970s. In 1978 W.G. Scott recorded his memories of working for Bridport Gas Company from 1958, as the last survivor of a staff of 26, apart from director C.W. Edwards of the Gables who joined the company in 1937:

I remember going into the retort house a month after the last retort was drawn and seeing the machinery already damp and rusting. It was a most eerie feeling; one could imagine there were ghosts of departed stokers watching. I never went in there again.

During my fifty years in the industry there were many incidents which in retrospect seem humorous but were not so funny at the time. One in the home of one of our directors was caused by a rook which had fallen down the chimney in the drawing room and was trapped behind a large and recently supplied gas fire. Removing a bird from a chimney is a tricky operation at any time but here there was an added complication. The room had just been decorated. In fact the decorators were just leaving the house as I arrived.

A dust-sheet was spread on the carpet and I carefully removed the fire. I shone a torch through the closure plate and beheld a pair of unwinking eyes staring at me. I lost no time in replacing the fire and cycling to the Bowling Club to tell the owner.

I suggested going home for my air-gun but this idea was turned down. There must be no loss of life. He would don gardening gloves and as I removed the fire he would grasp the bird and return it to its mate. Accordingly his hand closed over the bird – or rather the space it had occupied a few seconds before. There was a rushing noise as the bird tore past us and crashed into the window we had forgotten to open. From there it flew up to the ceiling and made a circuit of the room between the picture rail and ceiling. After much waving of arms the culprit moved off. The room had to be stripped and redecorated. To my surprise, the following day, I received a large tip for my efforts.

W.G. Scott was also lucky in his choice of customer for a major mishap at Haddon House, West Bay. Having given assurances there was no risk of dust reaching the billiards table – and having turned down the chance of having it covered – he proceeded to remove floorboards in the room above. Then he put his foot through the ceiling and returned to the billiards room. His apprentice uttered two words 'associated with strong men in times of great mental stress' as bells rang and maids appeared with dustpans and brushes. The elderly owner, entering the

Sea fishing from the end of West Pier, beside the channel into Bridport Harbour, in 1997.

caught and killed a basking shark nicknamed Moby Dick. The shark had broken numerous nets along this stretch of coast. The 15-foot carcass lay rotting on the shingle, perforated by the knife cuts inflicted by Keech and his crew. They netted the shark in shallow water and dragged it ashore.

Sometimes, in winter gales, the tide breaks over the 'winter ridge' of the Chesil Beach at Burton Freshwater, as it did in 1951. Water came pouring across farmer Bunny Lenthall's water-meadows into Burton Bradstock village, flooding the road, halting all traffic and swirling into the old low-lying cottages.

On 14 September 1952, after an 18-month fight between the railway executive and the local authorities, the railway line from Upwey to Abbotsbury closed to all traffic because of 'the economic circumstances'. Around the same time a film had been shot in Somerset, under somewhat similar circumstances – *The Titfield Thunderbolt* – and in the story the closed line was purchased, reopened, and privately operated. It brought about the suggestion: 'There's an idea for someone in Weymouth!'

A memorial to the war dead of the 43rd (Wessex) Division was unveiled on a wooded ridge above Winyard's Gap, Chedington, on 20 September 1952. It is a replica of the memorial on Hill 112 near Caen, Normandy, which the infantrymen stormed, and was unveiled by General Sir Ivor Thomas. Memorials of a similar style were erected on Castle Hill, Mere, and at Rough Tor, Cornwall, to give views spreading to all the counties from which this territorial division recruited. Its members included battalions of the Dorsetshire Regiment.

On Coronation Day in 1953 the Abbotsbury fishermen caught another shark. This time it was a thresher shark, smaller and more dangerous than a basker. They put the animal on a lorry and entered it into the carnival procession with the notice, 'You should have seen the one that got away'; and received the second prize for their efforts.

Restored station and carriages at West Bay, looking southwards, in 1997.

disaster zone in a wheelchair, was a model of calmness and composure. Having glanced at the chimney breast he looked up into the hole and observed: 'Your measurements were incorrect. You have come through much too far from the wall!'

The veteran gas-fitter also recalled a long-held belief that fumes from coal tar alleviated asthma and respiratory difficulties. Mothers used to tell children to breathe deeply when fresh tarmac was being laid in the street. Doctors sometimes advised a visit to the gas retorts for those with chest complaints. As a result, two boys appeared with their mother in the office:

Permission was given but on leaving the office, instead of turning right, they turned left and spent a dusty hour or so in the local refuse destructor yard before I spotted them and brought them into the works.

Another familiar smell – along with its sight and sound – departed from Bridport on 15 June 1959. The last two 45XX class 2-6-2 pannier tank engines to work the Bridport branch railway, Numbers 4507 and 4562, were withdrawn and replaced by diesel units.

Coupled together, the two steam engines were driven by Peter Miller to Weymouth motive-power depot. No. 4507, built in April 1907 at Stafford Road Works, Wolverhampton, had been No. 2168 until December 1912. She was scrapped at Swansea in the mid-1960s. The other engine, 4562, was built at Swindon in March 1924 and returned to the railway town in March 1960 on her way to the breaker's yard.

The strange thing was that at the same time a Bridport businessman found himself in a Birmingham scrapyard and stepped in front of a steam engine with the wording 'Bridport Fire Brigade' painted on the side. He bought the relic in 1960 and restored it to the town, where a glass-panelled building was found for it in front of the George Hotel on the green at West Bay. It was a time when everything was on the cusp of change.

Adela Curtis, who was born in 1864, died on 17 September 1960. Her memorial in the chapel which she built at the Christian Contemplatives' Charity, St Bride's Farm, Burton Bradstock, reads: 'I have loved thee with an everlasting love.' She had wished to be buried in the garden there but was cremated at Weymouth; which went against her beliefs in two ways as she disapproved of the use of gas and advocated that all natural wastes should be returned to the soil.

An echo of the past, in a modern format, was the imaginative bequest to the town in 1962 by Mabel Gale from one of Bridport's oldest rope-making families. She financed the building of 'a set of modern-day almshouses'. Four one-storey flats are in Victoria Grove – the Mabel Gale Bungalows – and six are in Parry's Hayes. They also continue an old tradition with an informative date stone: 'The gift of Mabel Gale, 1962.'

Track-side view, northwards to the town, from West Bay Station in 1997.

WEST BAY
BRIDPORT

Left: *Bridport's other station, at West Bay, was given back its sign in 1997.*

That year, in December, all operational use ceased on the southern end of the Bridport railway from the town to West Bay, with its closure to goods traffic. The final Sunday of the year, 30 December 1962, saw a blizzard which deposited a foot of snow all across Dorset. Much more was lying in drifts, reported Chief Constable Arthur Hambleton who requested the BBC to broadcast a message advising motorists not to travel into Dorset because main roads were blocked. Over 100 cars were caught in a slithering queue on one of the many hills on the A35 between Bridport and Dorchester, at Askerswell, with Bridport police finding accommodation for 50 stranded travellers. A total of 92 people were also being put up at the Bull Hotel in East Street, where every available space was in use, including bathrooms and the former Bridport Borough Council Social Club. 'Wherever we can put up a bed, we have someone,' said hotel director Mrs Elizabeth Forbes. To the north-east there were further problems with the A37 being entirely blocked all the way from Stratton to Warden Hill, above Evershot.

The valiant service provided by the Bridport branch railway in breaching the drifts would be recounted for years in efforts to preserve it for future winters in the debate that followed Dr Richard Beeching's infamous report on the future of Britain's railways.

On 25 August 1963, two steam pannier-tank locomotives of the old Great Western Railway, Nos 7782 and 4689, hauled a special train from Bridport to West Bay to give the town's coastal railway its last rites. The excursion was chartered by the Southern Counties Touring Society. The track would be lifted in 1965. Two decades later West Bay Station was restored and a short section of rails re-laid as a tourist attraction at the end of the line.

The Christian Contemplatives' Community at Burton Bradstock handed over their chapel, house, and land to the Othona Community in 1965. The latter was founded by ex-RAF padre Canon Norman Motley at Bradwell in Essex in 1946.

Playwright Robert Cedric Sherriff (1896–1975) lived at Downhouse Farm on the coastal slope of Eype Down. He loved the spot so much that when it came time to leave he gave his 176 acres, including the 508ft-high Thorncombe Beacon, to the National Trust, in 1966. His first performance, in aid of a school chapel restoration fund, was in 1921 and led to a professional career that started with *Journey's End* which was produced in London at the Savoy Theatre (1929). The works that followed included *Badger's Green* (1930), *Windfall* (1933), *St Helena* (1934), *Miss Mabel* (1948), *Home at Seven* (1950), *The White Carnation* (1953), *The Long Sunset* (1955), *The Telescope* (1957) and *A Shred of Evidence* (1960).

He went into television with *The Ogburn Story* (1963) but had long before established his reputation as a scriptwriter for the big screen, with *The Invisible Man* (1933), *Goodbye Mr Chips* (1936), *The Four Feathers* (1938), *Lady Quartet* (1948), *No Highway* (1950) and *The Dam Busters* (1955). R.C. Sherriff never reached the same peaks with his novels, but here too the output was substantial, with *The Fortnight in September* (1931), *Greengates* (1936), *The Hopkins Manuscript* (1939), *Chedworth* (1944), *Another Year* (1946), *King John's Treasure* (1954) and *The Bells of St Mary's* (1961). His autobiography was *No Leading Lady* (1968).

On 5 July 1968 a Hunter jet fighter crashed off West Bay. The pilot ejected and was rescued by a fishing boat. On being transferred to the inflatable shore rescue vessel from Lyme Regis he was given first aid and wrapped in a thermal blanket. On his arrival at hospital it was found that he had broken his spine.

An RAF Canberra bomber crashed into the sea at Lyme Bay during target-towing trials on 1 May 1970. Two of the crew were killed and one rescued. Six trawlers and four shellfish potting boats were operating from West Bay at that time.

A feature in the *Sunday Times* celebrated the 'Bridport Knot' on 7 November 1971 and pointed out that more knots are made in Bridport in a day than a troop of Boy Scouts ties in a year:

One hundred million of them between the time the knotmakers clock on in the morning and off in the evening. It is really one basic knot made over and over again. The Boy Scouts – and other students of the oldest of all man's methods of fastening – would recognise it as a sheet bend. Whether you call it that, or the Bridport Knot, a world-wide business is based upon it. For perhaps a thousand years or more the inhabitants of this Dorset town have employed their cunning of hand to make it, and throughout all that time the town's fortunes and their livings have largely depended upon it. Having a sheet bend like that is as good as money in the bank.

The slippery surface of a tarred section of Roman road near Compton Valence was blamed at an inquest in Dorchester in December 1971 for the death of a rider who fell from her horse. It slipped whilst Mrs Margaret Birley of Hyde Crook, Frampton, was hunting with the Cattistock hounds. She suffered a fractured skull and died the following morning. Other riders had warned her that the road was 'like glass'.

Bridport Arts Centre has its Allsop Room in commemoration of Dorset's best-known naturalist and broadcaster from the new television era. Charismatic outside, depressive within, Kenneth Allsop (1920–73) found inspiration and solace at Milton Mill in the hills between Powerstock and Bridport. Seeing the worst in everything and extrapolating further inevitable decline, he was convinced that he had no future and, much worse, that the planet had nowhere to go except backwards. What motivated him was a commitment

Ducks Bottom in Lower Eype with tiled Vine Cottage (right) and thatched Journey's End (left) which took its name from the first play by local landowner and author R.C. Sherriff.

Right: *The last traditional reed-thatched haystack in these parts, between Swyre and Puncknowle, in 1975.*

Left: *High seas battering the Esplanade at West Bay (centre background) in the prelude to the floods of February 1974, seen from East Cliff.*

Left: Kenneth Allsop at Milton Mill, near Bridport, where he died in 1973.

Right: Author and broadcaster Kenneth Allsop with daughter Amanda.

Below: Bird-watcher Kenneth Allsop beside the mill leat and lane at West Milton.

Right: Conservation speech by Kenneth Allsop, in Dorset at Tyneham, in 1972.

to wildlife and ecology, for which he had the vision and the passion that other such unhappy souls reserve for their religion.

That was my friend Kenneth Allsop who came into my life long before I met him. As I lay on the floor doing my homework, on the carpet in front of the fire, his was one of the most familiar voices from above, on the television. With deceptive dulcet tones and looks he did intense and incisive interviews for the BBC's flagship 'Tonight' news magazine. He was still engagingly youthful, as instantly recognisable by both sight and sound to just about every person in the country, when he came down from Hertfordshire to Dorset in 1970. I knew who it was on the telephone before he gave the magic name. It was an instant buzz and a little dance of excitement in the heart. That was a call about oilmen exploring in the deep-cut valleys north of Bridport. I was then the editor of *Dorset County Magazine* and the nearest thing that Dorset then had, or has since found, to an investigative environmental journalist.

Ken's enthusiasm and application to this and other countryside conflicts was constant and complete. His behaviour knew no bounds. No conventions held him in check. He would drive his E-type Jaguar on to the pavement in the middle of Belgravia and storm unannounced into the office of the chairman of the Nature Conservancy Council and berate him for some new offence of which he probably knew nothing. Articles followed in the *Daily Mail* and the *Sunday Times*, broadcasts would be set in motion, and acolytes like me would be mobilised on the ground to produce grassroots pressure.

Emerging from the soft features and apparent charm of perpetual boyish looks was an underlying anger that was brutal. It was excruciating to be part of the Ken Allsop circus. I saw him corner a Forestry Commission official from Bristol over a lunch-time fact-finding drink in the Three Horseshoes at Powerstock and proceed to reduce the inoffensive man to tears. 'You hate me, don't you!' he protested. Ken had won. He didn't even deny it, to the embarrassment of the rest of us who struggled to maintain social conventions. Kenneth Allsop used the power that was his, not through any position, or as a national newspaper columnist, broadcaster and author of many books, but that existed through sheer force of intellect and personality.

He was workaholic. As the ultimate professional he proved it daily. Often he would come through on the phone in the early evening from London and continue talking incessantly for a couple of hours. Then, suddenly, he said: 'I must go, they're waving for me to come through. I'm on.' The phone went dead as I reached across to touch the button on the telly. It was '24 Hours' or some such variation on the late-night theme and the music fell away as Ken said 'Good evening'. He sailed on into the programme as the ultimate pro he was, as if he had been rehearsing all evening instead of talking to me. Sometimes he would be back on the phone after returning to Dorset, in the middle of the night; naked and shivering I gripped the handset for another bout. That was Ken's time of day.

I hesitate writing of him as if I was were his friend. I did not so much know the man as share his obsessions. We had skipped the opportunity for friendship and moved on to something that was shared. Night-time meetings in 1972 floated on scotch 'when the words were flowing', which was his apt metaphor for typing in a house with an integral mill-race. They were the stuff of intensive ecology at a time when shallow ecology was a concept chasing its time. Books were everywhere. 'I need books like a hole in the head,' were words of his friend John Fowles that applied to the three of us.

Books for Allsop were not only wallpaper and upstairs insulation but they were also open and read. Evidence for this was annotations down the columns and underscoring for potential quotes. Many had come free and earned their place with newspaper and magazine reviews. They made for an eclectic and unsettling spread of shelves.

'Not a comfortable collection,' Bournemouth bookseller John Ruston told me after we conspired in the ultimate act of removal. Dispersing a library is a particular treachery that lays bare the mind of the owner. Ken had given me the manuscript of *In the Country*, after asking me to 'up-date Hardy' for him on changes to Bridport's countryside. Ruston handed it back to me and tersely summed up the themes of the stacks as he sorted and priced the titles. 'Very unpleasant,' he declaimed. 'Indicative of a troubled mind.' The covers reminded me that we discussed Wayland Drew's *Killing Wilderness* of 1972; to a backdrop of Aldous Huxley, Richard Jefferies, Henry David Thoreau, Henry Williamson and Eugene Zamiatin. We sought romantic reassurance in a fascist wilderness surrounded by the combined forces of totalitarian technology and socialist society. Something of this sacred place from the past had to be handed down to the future. 'In wilderness is the preservation of the world,' Thoreau wrote in 1851. He also said that 'all good things are wild and free'.

Ken longed to be both. His personality was as wild and uncontrolled as any I have ever encountered. He also demanded freedom – of the airwaves and his gas-guzzling sports car – and in defiance of the constraints of his crippled body. It was as dangerous and destructive as a holy war. His handsome appearance and mental agility belied the physical reality of the body below the television mask. This had been mangled in an assault training course in 1943; falling over hurdles whilst in the Royal Air Force. His hospitalisation continued until the end of the war when he finally ended it himself by insisting they amputated his tortured leg. Its stump continued to trouble him and taking painkillers was a matter of

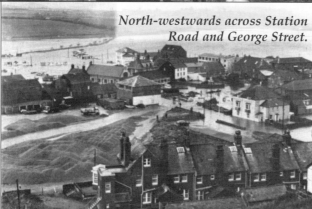

North-westwards across Station Road and George Street.

Above: *Overall scene at West Bay, looking westwards from East Cliff to Thorncombe Beacon and Doghouse Hill* (top left) *in the most remarkable of this series of photographs taken by Peter and Mary Payne on 11 February 1974.*

West Bay Station (centre) *and fields flooded either side of the line in February 1974.*

Left: 'Meals all day' probably off the menu at Riverside Café, West Bay, on 11 February 1974.

Right: *The Bingo Hall and First Aid Post beside the camping ground at West Bay.*

Left: *Watery view inland, northwards from the Wishing Well, towards Bridport.*

Right: *North-eastwards from the west side of the harbour and backwater, to the George Hotel* (top left).

routine, but he never showed this agony, even when he forced himself to keep up with us as we went on a site visit through the impenetrable boglands of Powerstock Common. Neither, on principle, would he accept a helping hand.

Eventually it was a cocktail of alcohol and drugs that would liberate his mind. Even that event was orchestrated. It was the cruellest date to choose to reject one's family, as daughter Mandy was celebrating her birthday that wet morning of 23 May 1973 and was up in London with her mother, Betty, leaving the house conveniently empty beneath a cloud of perpetual old-style West Country drizzle.

The previous morning he had phoned me at length. Chirpy and the epitome of charm he was, however, uncharacteristically concerned about various acts of past and present misunderstanding and omission. I had just sent him a photograph I had taken of him addressing an open-air environmental meeting in Dorset, at Tyneham, and I was directed to bring that issue up to date by having a critical letter sent to the *Sunday Times*. Material written by Ken had been edited out of the printed version of an article on the Lulworth Ranges and he wanted to put the record straight. Other layers of trivia were in the category of unfinished business.

'No, that wasn't taken badly, I'm sure she understood,' I said on behalf of countryside campaigner Margaret Kraft. He went on for an hour and a quarter spelling out just what he felt about this issue and that, and was probably ticking off his list as he went, interspersing superfluous apologies for things that had not been done or might have been taken wrongly.

In retrospect it all made sense and I am sure he must have made other calls to tidy the various loose ends of his life. 'I've a deadline to keep,' he wrote in a final flourish of the purple prose to which he was addicted. Otherwise his goodbye letter was a moving and tragic justification of the punishment he was about to inflict on his body, his family, and his friends; the ultimate rejection done thinkingly and in cool control of his faculties. Those of us who have been on that brink in fear and because of a loss of our grasp can only be amazed at his composure and logic.

His protest centred on the abuse by man and toxic chemicals that were causing the Peregrine falcons to fail to lay fertile eggs in the last Pembrokeshire stronghold. Ironically he could not have been proved more wrong. Not only had dioxin been withdrawn and their demise averted but within a few years these finest and fastest of predators would be expanding their range back into their old haunts, including the rocky eyrie on Steep Holm island which we bought in 1976 as Ken's nature-reserve memorial off the Somerset coast.

Much of the money for this came in small donations from a multitude of admirers who were devastated by his death. His demise came as a particular shock because it was not expected of any of the nation's

best-loved television personalities in what was still new as a mass medium. Previous to that only Gilbert Harding had dropped down dead. People on the telly were regarded as immortal (in a way they really are, with perpetual repeats of programmes and films).

Kenneth Allsop's lasting legacy in Bridport's hinterland is that Powerstock Common, which fellow conservationist Miss Helen Brotherton once regarded as 'too wild to be of any interest', is now the pride and joy of Dorset Wildlife Trust. Without Kenneth Allsop and his *cause célèbre*, it would have been clear-felled and replanted with conifers. There might have been many more victories if he had felt able to stay with us for his natural term. I am sure he would have been the first member of the Green Party to be elected from Britain to the European Parliament.

Two days of coastal flooding on 9–10 February 1974 were followed on Monday 11 February by 'a tidal wave' which combined to bring about the worst inundation at West Bay for half a century. Bridport Borough Council reported:

At approximately 9 am the sea started to breach the east beach and within a few minutes Station Road was impassable, and West Bay was, thereby, effectively cut off from both directions. By high tide excessive flooding had occurred and a number of shops and homes were seriously affected. Serious damage was done by the sea to the two shelters on the promenade and a section of the frontage wall at the turntable on the shipyard development was demolished. The road surface on the western side of the harbour was badly damaged and in some places various utility services were exposed.

The adjoining footpath was torn up for part of its length and the concrete capping forming the high path on the West Pier was partly demolished. The boat park in George Street was affected by the flooding. An enormous quantity of flotsam, including lump oil and timber and other rubbish, was scattered over a large area of West Bay and the adjoining fields.

As the ground floors of the Bridport Arms Hotel, George Hotel and West Bay Hotel were awash, the small boats in the backwater beyond the sluices were swept a mile up the River Brit to the Saxon location of the town's port. Riverside Café and the Post Office 'became an island'. The Pavilion and Letchworth Motel were on the high-tide line. The sea 'opened the door to the Harbour Master's office' and also flooded the yards and offices of Woolaway Constructions Limited in West Bay Road to a depth of five feet. A couple of caravans in the Municipal Camp Field stood alone in the sea after the others had been hauled to safety in the western corner.

Institutions, past and present, were also undergoing change. The village school at Thorncombe in West Dorset was burnt to the ground in 1974. Stokewater House, the large Victorian workhouse to

Left: *Essendon chalet and well-watered trees on the Municipal Camping Ground at West Bay in February 1974.*

A caravan left in splendid isolation after others had been moved to higher ground.

Left: *The Melplash showground between West Bay and Bridport.*

Right: *Bridport Harbour and boats left parked beside cars at low tide.*

Left: *Surviving railway crossing-gate and track in the tarmac at Bradpole.*

Below: *Single-line working, with the driver opening and closing the gates, at Bradpole in 1974.*

Below: *Inter-City ticket from Yeovil Pen Mill to Bridport issued on 28 May 1974.*

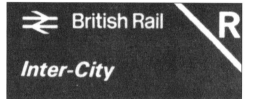

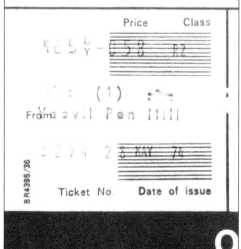

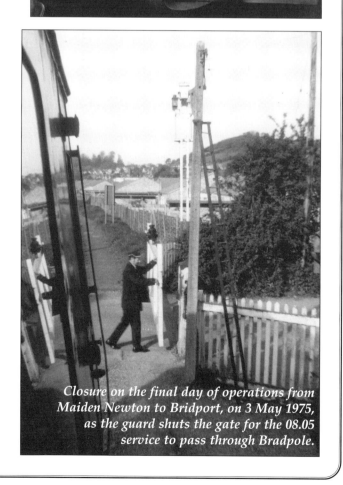

Closure on the final day of operations from Maiden Newton to Bridport, on 3 May 1975, as the guard shuts the gate for the 08.05 service to pass through Bradpole.

the west of Beaminster, which stands just inside the Stoke Abbott parish boundary, was being converted into flats. The building was bought from Dorset County Council in April 1972 by Spicer (Electrical) Limited for £15,000.

Time was running out for the Bridport railway. Aware of that fact I preserved my last ticket, 'Inter-City To Bridport' from Yeovil Pen Mill, on 28 May 1974. The closure of what had become Dorset's last branch railway took place on 3 May 1975 with the departure of the 20.40 hours passenger train from Bridport. It was driven by Reg Chappell from Westbury Depot and left to the sounds of alarm-warning detonators placed on the line. Arrival at Maiden Newton, the junction station nine and a quarter miles up the line, was logged at 21.02 hours. The track was lifted in 1977.

Novelist and playwright Thomas Ridley Sharpe (born 1928) moved to 170 St Andrew's Road, Bridport, from Cambridge in 1978. His first farce, *Riotous Assembly* (1971), was followed by some of the most successful books of the decade – *Indecent Exposure* (1973), *Porterhouse Blues* (1974), *Blott on the Landscape* (1975), *Wilt* (1976), *The Great Pursuit* (1977), followed by *The Throwback* and *The Wilt Alternative* in production when he moved into the town. Here he completed *Ancestral Vices*, to the distractions of a plot that was ironically turning into reality as the Bridport Bypass gouged its Blott in a close encounter to his 1.5-acre garden. He left the town.

Despite the onslaught of the roads programme more protected coastline was created east of Bridport in 1979 when the 225-acre farm at Labour-in-Vain, west of Abbotsbury, was accepted by the Treasury in lieu of capital transfer tax from the executors of the late J.R. Bridgman. It was transferred to the National Trust through the National Land Fund, which was established in memory of those who died in the Second World War. Bindbarrow, a Bronze-Age burial mound at Burton Bradstock – and its surrounding 18 acres of coastal grassland – was bought by the Trust in 1990. Further Trust acquisitions between Burton Bradstock and West Bexington followed in 1994 with 258 acres including Cogden Beach and the slopes beside the coast road.

Eric Hamblet, the Harbour Master at West Bay, reported in 1981 that only three ships had used the port in the past year. Each carried fertilisers. Commercial operations from the harbour were the lowest on record, there being only one trawler and a single pot-boat fishing for lobsters and crabs.

A £7 million Royal Navy Sea Harrier of 899 Naval Air Squadron, on a training flight from RNAS Yeovilton, went out of control above Cattistock at 09.34 hours on Friday 21 January 1983. It narrowly missed homes in West End and Beech Tree Close and crashed into a hedge one field away from the bungalows. No one was hurt. The pilot, 28-year-old Flight Lieutenant Kevin Fox, had ejected safely. Asked about the villagers' reactions, a huntsman told television reporters:

There may be some complaints from old women of both sexes but there are many military families in the area and most of us know that these things are bound to happen from time to time.

On 4 February 1985 the *The Times* diary column reported that a young West Dorset lad had no worries for the rest of the millennium. He had booked a table for eight at the Ritz for New Year's Eve – on 31 December 1999.

In September 1986, West Bay fisherman Jack Woolmington recovered the anchor of the 30-gun Dutch treasure-ship *Hope* which was plundered on the Chesil Beach, opposite Fleet, on 16–17 January 1784. It was found 75 yards offshore and was 14 feet long, rusty and pebble-encrusted. It now lies outside the appropriately named Anchor Inn at Seatown.

Roadworks gouging out the hills, creating causeways, and turning a part of the old railway into road, finally came to an end on 19 July 1987. Opening the 130-metre long River Brit Viaduct, the centrepiece of the £5 million Bridport Bypass, and aware that the Bridport Brewery was in sight from above Seaview Cottages, Roads and Traffic Minister Peter Bottomley came up with an appropriate metaphor: 'We have uncorked a bottleneck.' The new 7.3-metre single carriageway, 1.8 miles in length and landscaped with 27,000 trees and shrubs, carries the A35 trunk road down from the hills at Miles Cross to the B3157 at Sea Road South roundabout.

In 1989 old media hands mourned crime reporter Percy Hoskins (1904–89) who was born in Bridport. For half a century he was Fleet Street's ace sleuth. He was first with the news, for the *Daily Express*, of the defection to Russia of spies Guy Burgess and Donald Maclean in 1951. Hoskins was alone in championing the defence of Dr John Bodkin Adams, the fashionable Eastbourne doctor who was the victim of press whispers that he had been poisoning wealthy women. The jury agreed that the other hacks were wrong. Lord Beaverbrook celebrated success with his star reporter on 9 April 1957: 'Two men have been acquitted today – Adams and Hoskins.'

The body of Down's syndrome sufferer Jo Ramsden (1969–91), who disappeared from an adult training centre in Bridport on 9 April 1991, was discovered in woodland at Raymond's Hill, Wootton Fitzpaine, on the hill above Lyme Regis, by Forestry Commission workers on 11 March 1992. She had last been seen crossing the road in Bridport with 'a young man in a bright patterned jumper' and her decomposed remains were found accompanied by a Liverpool football bag and multi-coloured tracksuit of the type she had been wearing at the time of her disappearance.

Above: *Exit point for the Bridport Railway, at the town's station, in 1975.*

Left: *Final passenger Jamie Farquharson at Bridport Station in 1975.*

Below left: *End of the line, with Bridport Station reduced to one platform, looking southwards in 1974.*

Right: *Midway station, at Powerstock on the branch line from Maiden Newton, in 1974.*

Tragedy unfolded across the cold waters of Lyme Bay on the afternoon of Monday 20 March 1993. Two instructors with eight sixth-formers from Plymouth and their teacher had set off in canoes from a Lyme Regis activity centre shortly after 10.00 hours. They paddled eastwards and were then intending to turn inshore to land at Charmouth, with 13.00 being given as the estimated time of arrival. Nothing was done about their failure to reach land and Portland Coastguards were unaware of any canoeists out at sea until they received a radio call from the West Bay fishing boat *Spanish Eyes* at 14.43: 'Portland, we've picked up an empty canoe.' At 14.58 the Coastguards established that a party had left Lyme five hours earlier. A Land Rover was sent to coastal viewpoints to try to make visual contact. They could see nothing. Almost an hour later, at 15.51, the Coastguards scrambled the first of two Royal Navy Sea-King air-sea rescue helicopters from RNAS Portland. They arrived on the scene, about 17 miles north-west from their base, at 16.08. Coastguards then launched Lyme's Atlantic 21 inshore lifeboat at 16.11 and a rescue team from All Hallows public school also headed towards the search area. Meanwhile, at 16.29, the St Alban's Adventure Centre in Lyme identified the canoe recovered by the Bridport fishing boat and confirmed that it belonged to the group from Southway Comprehensive School.

A yellow Royal Air Force Wessex rescue helicopter was scrambled from RAF Chivenor in North Devon. At 17.17 HMS *Beaver* sent her Lynx helicopter to join the aerial search. By 17.38 the Lyme lifeboat had found survivors and was hauling two adults aboard, alive but suffering from hypothermia, and they were taken to West Bay, from where a helicopter took them to hospital. At 17.43 a Sea King picked up another canoeist, a mile east of Lyme Regis, followed by three others, by 17.55.

They were delivered to Weymouth General Hospital at 18.00. Minutes later, at 18.04, the RAF Wessex helicopter reported that it had picked up four more. Finally, at 18.44, the second Sea King picked up the last canoeist, who was still breathing, nearly nine hours after they set off and eight hours after they got into difficulties. Questions were are asked about why they went to sea without notifying the Coastguards or carrying a marine-band radio for just such an emergency. Had they undertaken capsize drill? Why was non-arrival at Charmouth not reported when they failed to come into sight at 13.00? Had the helicopters been scrambled at the earliest opportunity?

On the credit side, wetsuits and lifejackets were being worn and distress flares carried, although none appeared to have been fired. The prolonged nature of the search had taken its toll. Four teenagers pulled from the sea were either dead or dying and were named as Simon Dunne (16), Claire Langley (16), Dean Sayer (17) and Rachel Walker (16).

On 29 October 1993, golfing legend Group Captain George Houghton (1905–93), author of the *Golf Addict* books and 50 other titles, died at Bridport. He was reputed to have introduced the game into Russia and China during his travels in search of material. He lived at Coneygar House and the flag at Bridport Golf Club was flown at half-mast in tribute. Comedian Bob Hope wrote of him: 'In the game of golf, George Houghton has discovered laughs. I can't. Only tears.'

Back in 1976, playing the character of Reggie Perrin, actor Leonard Rossiter attempted vanishing into the sea at West Bay in the style of Thomas Hardy villain Sergeant Francis Troy (at Lulworth) and runaway politician John Stonehouse (in Miami). More concerted filming started in 1998 when 'Harbour Lights', starring Nick Berry of 'Heartbeat' fame, was filmed at West Bay. The programme did for the West Dorset coast what ITV's heart-throb achieved for the picturesque North Yorkshire village of Goathland. Berry, as the Harbour Master, co-starred with Tina Hobley from 'Coronation Street' and 'Holby City'. There were Nick Berry fridge magnets and similar offerings in souvenir shops as coachloads of fans abandoned 'Hollywood-on-the-Moors' for the delights of the Dorset seaside.

'Heritage wars' was how *The Times* described a real-life drama from Bridport which reached the House of Lords at the end of the millennium. The backlash against the building in the grounds of Downe Hall was started and spearheaded by philosophy writer Catherine Searle. It was 1995 and she was 47 years old when battle commenced to save the 14-acre grounds that formed the delightful setting to the mansion. Eventually, in 2000 at the highest court in the land, she failed to win her specific case, but succeeded in the wider cause of changing national planning guidance on the redevelopment of listed properties. Recriminations were aimed at council officers as well as the developers, as Catherine Searle told Gill Martin as she looked back on how her campaign turned into a crusade:

Downe Hall was a secret, its grounds like an island in the middle of Bridport. We could all see the park from the distance. It was beautiful. It touched me and made we want to fight to keep it. I couldn't sit by and watch it destroyed. The prospect of losing such a lovely, tranquil place also aroused great passion in the area. People didn't want to see huge original laurels and rhododendrons replaced by the back gardens of pretentious new houses with wallpaper-effect bricks. There was also strong feeling about the wildlife that would be lost.

Town members of Dorset Wildlife Trust – worried about the future of the badgers and woodpeckers – made common cause with the Countess of

Earth-moving vehicle, at Stoney Head, in the summer of 1972.

Right: *Road improvements beginning at Stoney Head in August 1972 with the removal of 16 tons of earth at a time.*

Left: *Two highways, with the new A35 vaulting a public path, in a view westwards towards Eype Down in 1986.*

Right: *Bridport town, amid the fields of a pre-bypass landscape, looking westwards from above Bothenhampton in 1967.*

Labour-in-Vain Farm, above Bexington, was given to the National Trust by the Treasury.

Left: *Traditional Bridport shop front of Smith & Smith ladies' and gents' tailors, outfitters, and habit and breeches makers at 8 West Street.*

Right: *Timber-framed seventeenth-century house, refurbished in brick and rendered, beside the Book Shop in South Street, in 1997.*

Left: *Pedestrian reclamation of the pavement, with Dorset Works narrowing the carriageway in South Street, in 1997.*

Left: *Janna and Connor Crabb, from one of the oldest of Bridport families, beside the new sea defences at West Bay in 2002.*

Below: *Seawards and south-eastwards, the view across Lyme Bay, as sea defences are constructed in 2002.*

Right: *Cranes frame the entrance to Bridport Harbour as boulders are laid to reinforce sea defences, looking eastwards to Burton Cliff in 2002.*

Below: *West Cliff, protected by traffic restrictions in a view north-westwards from the Esplanade in 2002.*

Sandwich of Mapperton Manor and her influential friends in the Garden History Society. Downe Hall's owner, Violet Snook, had gone into a nursing home and English Heritage put the building on its risk list. Developer Eddie Fry, through son and builder Philip Fry, came up with a solution that district architect David Oliver decided he had to accept:

The reason planning permission was granted was that it would pay for restoration. It was either that or the house would have disappeared. At a site meeting it was raining. There was six inches of water on the ground floor and a waterfall coming down the staircase. The roof was completely non-functional and water was pouring in everywhere. The owners put it up for sale and the owners wanted Mr Fry to have it.

The campaigner, Miss Searle, continued the battle for its setting until the House of Lords turned it into a lost cause and remitted the case to the High Court for adjudication of costs. By then she was nostalgic for her earlier reclusive lifestyle without a car, television or computer. Bridport remains one of those rare places where one can exist in a past time, although for how long is another matter.

The great new sea defences taking shape at West Bay are out of all proportion to what lies behind them. Fishermen predict it will all lead to 'the next great West Country marina project'. Countrymen are also fearful that the takeover of the villages 'by media personalities and the chattering classes' is undermining their historic traditions.

There are honourable exceptions. Where broadcaster Kenneth Allsop made his last stand to save Bridport's countryside, entertaining eccentric Hugh Fearnley-Whittingstall now celebrates its distinctive flavours, literally, with a novel series of home-cooking programmes on Channel Four that has developed into a book of *The River Cottage Year*. Moving on from traditional mainstays such as curing his own ham and fishing from the Chesil Beach – as well as shooting manorial pigeons – he has put the case for country produce and done as much as anyone to reinstate steer's testicles as a Dorset delicacy. In doing so, River Cottage enterprises show how much we have lost, in a scenic skirmish against insurmountable pressures for change.

The sign still hangs at the Star Inn, Netherbury, but inside it is de-licensed. On the nearby flagstones at Copper Beech Farm, Hubert Warren's cider press and barrels are the last of their kind in Dorset. When their turn comes to go into a museum then a line will have been drawn under a millennium of country life.

Granite groyne of boulders newly delivered by sea, looking southwards, at West Bay in 2002.

Right: *The cider press at Copper Beech Farm, Netherbury.*

Left: *Harry and Hubert Warren's barrels of cider at Copper Beech Farm, Netherbury, in 1975.*

Right: *West Bay reflections, south-westwards into the summer sun, in 1997.*

SUBSCRIBERS

SUBSCRIBERS

Howard D.S. Abbott, Ilford, Essex
Dr and Mrs Kenneth Abel, Walditch, Bridport, Dorset
Mr and Mrs S.A. Ackerman, Bridport, Dorset
Shayne Almond, Bridport, Dorset
Suzanne Abbott Angland, Hadleigh, Suffolk
Tony Anthony, Bridport, Dorset
John Backhurst, Bridport, Dorset
Dr Peter Balson
Ken Beak
Alun E. Beaven, Bridport, Dorset
Gerry, Ann, Maria, Cheryl Benbow, Bridport, Dorset
Kathleen Irene Berry, Bridport
AnneMarie Bishop-Spangenberg, Melplash, Dorset
Mrs Patricia Board (née Gall)
Stan Bourroughs, Peacehaven, Sussex
Terence W. Bown, Axminster, Devon
Grace Brake, Dottery
Bridport and West Dorset Golf Club
Jean L.E. Brownhill, West Bay, Dorset
Peter Brownlow, Bridport, Dorset
Richard Burleigh, Charmouth, Dorset
Mr F.J. Butt, Bridport, Dorset
Christine M. and John E. Case, Bridport, Dorset
Roland and Wendy Chalu, Bridport, Dorset
Ian Chantler, Huddersfield, West Yorkshire
Janet and Peter Chantler, Bridport, Dorset
Jillian Chick
Albert E.G. Clapp, North Allington, Bridport
Margaret J. Clapp, Bridport, Dorset
Richard E.G. Clapp, North Allington, Bridport
Lilian J. Clark, Bridport, Dorset
Adrian and Lynne Clarke, Bridport, Dorset
Mr J. Clarke, West Bay, Bridport
David A. Cole, Bridport, Dorset
Mr Robert V.R. Collins
Mr and Mrs David Cowburn, Bridport, Dorset
Tim Crabtree, Bridport
Leslie Crutchley, Shipton Gorge, Bridport
Philip Daubney, Bothenhampton, Bridport
Betty Denning, Bridport, Dorset
Mrs Ruby E. Dew, Bridport, Dorset
Mrs Helen Doble, Blackdown, Beaminster
Ian R. Draper, Loders, Bridport, Dorset
Ian Robert Draper, Loders, Bridport, Dorset
Edmund George Draper, Loders, Bridport, Dorset
Mrs S. Dunford, Dover, Kent
Sam Dunn, Bridport, Dorset

Sheila Edwards, Bridport, Dorset
Marjorie E. Elgood, Bridport, Dorset
Mrs E. Enbom, Bridport, Dorset
Michael and Ann Evans, Chetnole, Dorset
G.R. Eveleigh, Bridport, Dorset
Mrs Sylvia Eveleigh, Bridport
Alexander Farnes, Canterbury
John Fenton, Bothenhampton, Bridport, Dorset
Diana K. Fenton (née Beer), Bridport, Dorset
Mr and Mrs D.J. Ferns, Loders, Dorset
John and Dianne Ffoulkes, Kingston Russell, Dorset
Christopher G. Finch, Redbourn, Hertfordshire
Peter E. Foote, Bridport, Dorset
Roy Fursey, Netherbury, Dorset
Roy Fursman, Bridport
Peter C. Fuszard, Bridport, Dorset
M.J. Gale, Bridport, Dorset
Carole R. Garrett, Bridport, Dorset
Mr A.J. Gerrard, Bridport
Russell F. Granger, West Road, Bridport
Derek G. Green, Crewkerne, Somerset
Clive W. Groves
Anthony S. Gumbrill, Bridport, Dorset
Sarah L. Gumbrill, Bridport, Dorset
Miss C. Haddrell, West Bay, Dorset
Geoffrey S. Hall, Bridport, Dorset
Jim and Jan Hancock
Harbour House, West Bay, Bridport, Dorset
Tony Harrison, Bothenhampton, Bridport
Mr A.L.G. Harrison, Bridport
Andrew P. Harvey, Bridport, Dorset
Mrs Harwood (née Gurd), Maiden Newton
The Hawkins Family, formerly of Asker Terrace for 78 years
David and Lynne Hedworth, Burton Bradstock
Freda and Ross Hendry, The Book Shop, Bridport
Simon J. Hill, Bridport, Dorset
Robert and Alevtina Hird, Bridport, Dorset
W.G. Hobbs, Bridport, Dorset
Frederick A.R. Hodder, Bridport
Benjamin C. Holland, Bridport, Dorset
Richard and Elaine Hoskins, Newport, Gwent
Richard J. Hoskins, Newport, Gwent
David G. Hoskins, Wimbledon, London
Beryl M. Hounsell, Bridport, Dorset
Mr D.B. Hounsell, Bridport, Dorset
Jed K. Hughes, Walditch, Dorset
Andrew C. Hussey, Bridport, Dorset
Mrs Betty Hutchinson, Perth, Australia
Martin C. Hyde, Bridport, Dorset
Miss D.L. Ingram, Texas, USA

Daisy Jeans (née Burden), Bridport
Derek Charles Jones, Bridport, Dorset
Terrence Eric Joy
John J. Kelly, Bridport
William E. Kelly, Bridport
S. and J. Kiley, West Bay, Bridport
Mr Graham H.J. Knight, Bridport
Edward R. Kopecky, Bridport, Dorset
Roy Lidington, Symondsbury, Dorset
Jonny, Claire, Jennifer, and Simeon Long,
    Bridport
Paul and Valerie Loudon, Bridport, Dorset
A. Gordon Mackenzie
Richard N. Major, Exeter
G.E. Marsh, Bridport
Trevor and Angela Marshall, Bridport, Dorset
Rosemary Meakins (née Abbott), Hornchurch,
    Essex
Peter T. Minchell, Bridport, Dorset
Julian Moore, Mangerton, Bridport
Richard Morse, Runham, Norfolk
Tracie Newman, Symonsbury, Bridport,
    Dorset
Mrs H. Northover, Bridport, Dorset
Michael Nunn, Bridport, Dorset
The Pammenters, West Bay
Jennifer M. Parker, Bridport, Dorset
Mrs Patten, Bridport, Dorset
R. and E. Peck, Yeovil, Somerset
William T.G. Perrott, Bridport
Julia Peterson, Beaminster, Dorset
Gordon Pitcher, Bridport, Dorset
Stephen V. Poole, Bournemouth, Dorset
John and Sylvia Pound, Bridport, Dorset
Norman E. Purchase, Netherbury, Bridport,
    Dorset
Brian Pursey, Bridport, Dorset
Michael Pursey, Bridport, Dorset
Janet and John Quick, Bridport, Dorset
Kathleen M. Ramsden
Diana P. Read, Powerstock, Bridport
Mr Read and Mrs K.M. Masters
Doris and Ken Reyland, Harrow Weald,
    Middlesex
Mr M.S. and Mrs T.M. Richards, Bradpole,
    Bridport
W.B. and M.E. Richardson, Bridport, Dorset
Peter Ridler, Bridport, Dorset
Diana and Peter Riglar, Bridport
Mary Anne Rimer, Bridport, Dorset
Jennifer Roberts (née Symes), Caister on Sea
Ann and Mike Rogers, Bridport, Dorset
Paul Roper, High Wycombe,
    Buckinghamshire
Stephen and Ann Salter, Bradpole, Bridport
Geoffrey Sargent, Bothenhampton

Adrian Scadding, Bridport
Canon Gordon Sealy and Marilyn Sealy (née
    Chubb), West Bay, Dorset
Christopher Selman, Bridport, Dorset
George D. Skevington, Bridport, Dorset
Claire Louise Smith, Madrid, Spain
Mervyn A. Smith, Bridport, Dorset
Don Smith, Burton Bradstock
Leslie F. Sorrell, Shipton Gorge, Bridport
John Stickland, Bridport
Nick, Steph, Emma and Holly Sutton,
    Bridport, Dorset
Claire and Paul Symes, Heathfield, East Sussex
Alan W. Symon
David Tattershall, Bridport, Dorset
Steve and Anita Tattershall, Bridport, Dorset
Pete and Mary Toms, Burton Bradstock
Gerald Norman Tucker
Eustace Tunnicliff, Bridport
Gilbert R. Welch
Peter and Gwen Whiting, Uploders
Mr and Mrs J. Wilkinson
R. Alec Williams, West Bay, Bridport
Jill M. Wills (née Crabb), Bridport
Carol A. Windsor, Salway Ash, Dorset
Dr Keith Wood, St Albans
Shaun Wooldridge, Bridport, Dorset
S.C. and M.A. Wrighton, Allington, Dorset

Community Histories

The Book of Addiscombe • Canning & Clyde Road Residents Association & Friends
The Book of Addiscombe, Vol. II • Canning & Clyde Road Residents Association & Friends
The Book of Axminster with Kilmington • Les Berry
and Gerald Gosling
The Book of Bampton • Caroline Seward
The Book of Barnstaple • Avril Stone
The Book of Barnstaple, Vol. II • Avril Stone
The Book of The Bedwyns • The Bedwyn History Society
The Book of Bickington • Stuart Hands
Blandford Forum: A Millennium Portrait • Blandford Town Council
The Book of Bramford • Bramford Local History Group
The Book of Breage & Germoe • Stephen Polglase
The Book of Bridestowe • R. Cann
The Book of Bridport • Rodney Legg
The Book of Brixham • Frank Pearce
The Book of Buckfastleigh • Sandra Coleman
The Book of Buckland Monachorum & Yelverton • Hemery
The Book of Carharrack • Carharrack Old Cornwall Society
The Book of Carshalton • Stella Wilks and Gordon Rookledge
The Parish Book of Cerne Abbas • Vale and Vale
The Book of Chagford • Ian Rice
The Book of Chapel-en-le-Frith • Mike Smith
The Book of Chittlehamholt with
Warkleigh & Satterleigh • Richard Lethbridge
The Book of Chittlehampton • Various
The Book of Colney Heath • Bryan Lilley
The Book of Constantine • Moore and Trethowan
The Book of Cornwood & Lutton • Compiled by the People of the Parish
The Book of Creech St Michael • June Small
The Book of Cullompton • Compiled by the People of the Parish
The Book of Dawlish • Frank Pearce
The Book of Dulverton, Brushford,
Bury & Exebridge • Dulverton & District Civic Society
The Book of Dunster • Hilary Binding
The Book of Edale • Gordon Miller
The Ellacombe Book • Sydney R. Langmead
The Book of Exmouth • W.H. Pascoe
The Book of Grampound with Creed • Bane and Oliver
The Book of Hayling Island & Langstone • Rogers
The Book of Helston • Jenkin with Carter
The Book of Hemyock • Clist and Dracott
The Book of Herne Hill • Patricia Jenkyns
The Book of Hethersett • Hethersett Society Research Group
The Book of High Bickington • Avril Stone
The Book of Ilsington • Dick Wills
The Book of Kingskerswell • Carsewella Local History Group
The Book of Lamerton • Ann Cole & Friends
Lanner, A Cornish Mining Parish • Sharron
Schwartz and Roger Parker
The Book of Leigh & Bransford • Malcolm Scott
The Book of Litcham with Lexham & Mileham • Litcham Historical & Amenity Society
The Book of Loddiswell • Reg and Betty Sampson
The New Book of Lostwithiel • Barbara Fraser
The Book of Lulworth • Rodney Legg
The Book of Lustleigh • Joe Crowdy
The Book of Lyme Regis • Rodney Legg
The Book of Manaton • Compiled by the People of the Parish
The Book of Markyate • Markyate Local History Society
The Book of Mawnan • Mawnan Local History Group
The Book of Meavy • Pauline Hemery
The Book of Minehead with Alcombe • Binding and Stevens
The Book of Morchard Bishop • Jeff Kingaby

For details of any of the above titles or if you are
interested in writing your own history, please contact: Commissioning Editor Community Histories, Halsgrove House,
Lower Moor Way, Tiverton Business Park, Tiverton, Devon EX16 6SS, England; tel: 01884 259636;
email: katyc@halsgrove.com